How and When to Tell Your Kids About Sex

How and When to
Tell Your Kids About Sex

A Lifelong Approach to Shaping Your Child's Sexual Character

STAN AND BRENNA JONES

NAVPRESS

Discipleship Inside Out™

Discipleship Inside Out™

NavPress is the publishing ministry of The Navigators, an international Christian organization and leader in personal spiritual development. NavPress is committed to helping people grow spiritually and enjoy lives of meaning and hope through personal and group resources that are biblically rooted, culturally relevant, and highly practical.

For a free catalog go to www.NavPress.com
or call 1.800.366.7788 in the United States or 1.800.839.4769 in Canada.

ISBN 13: 978-1-60006-017-5

Cover design by Charles Brock | www.thedesignworksgroup.com
Cover photo by IndexStock
Creative Team: Terry Behimer, Susan Martins Miller, Amy Spencer, Kathy Mosier, Arvid Wallen, Pat Reinheimer

Some of the anecdotal illustrations in this book are true to life and are included with the permission of the persons involved. All other illustrations are composites of real situations, and any resemblance to people living or dead is coincidental.

Unless otherwise identified, all Scripture quotations in this publication are taken from the HOLY BIBLE: NEW INTERNATIONAL VERSION® (NIV®). Copyright © 1973, 1978, 1984 by International Bible Society. Used by permission of Zondervan Publishing House. All rights reserved. Other version used: the *Revised Standard Version Bible* (RSV), copyright 1946, 1952, 1971, by the Division of Christian Education of the National Council of the Churches of Christ in the USA, used by permission, all rights reserved.

Library of Congress Catalog Card Number: 93-22640

Printed in the United States of America

4 5 6 7 8 9 10 / 14 13 12 11 10

To our parents:

*In loving memory of Jerry Barber;
in continuing love and appreciation for
Wilma Barber
Marion and Edith Jones*

Contents

Acknowledgments

We would like to thank our friends with whom we have shared the joys and travails of the journey of parenting and with whom we have shared enriching dialogue about the ideas in this book. In the first edition, we thanked (and continue to thank) Miriam and Fred Antonini, Rich and Debbie Butman, Charley and Cindy Carlson, Steve and Jan Evans, Lori and Jim Hock, Lisa and Mark McMinn, Cindy and Marion Neal, Elizabeth and Bob Roberts, Linda Roberts and Lance Wilcox, Joni Carroll, and Jay and Janice Wood. To this list we add Bruce and Mitzie Barton, Steve and Linda Smith, Vince and Ellen Morris, and Trudy and John Zimmerman.

We continue to thank thirteen successive classes of graduate students in Stan's Human Sexuality summer course whose insightfulness, openness, and inquisitiveness so enriched our understanding of sexuality. Stan expresses particular thanks to the administration and faculty of Wheaton College for being a community where dedication to Christian faith and to intellectual excellence can come together seamlessly.

We express heartfelt thanks to the many parents who have shared their stories and perspectives, praise and disagreements, about the content of the GOD'S DESIGN FOR SEX series as we have spoken and taught about this subject around the world. Some of your stories have made it into the revised versions of these books! We have benefited from many spontaneous and thoughtful suggestions from readers of our first editions, but none more thorough and constructive than the many comments from Ted Witzig Jr. and his professional colleagues at their counseling center.

Special appreciation goes out to Mark and Lori Yarhouse for their extraordinarily thorough and helpful review of the GOD'S DESIGN FOR SEX series in preparation for revisions for this new edition, to Elaine Roberts for a remarkably thorough and wise review of all of the children's books, and to Steve Gerali for his careful review of *Facing the Facts*. We have appreciated and benefited from the careful editorial skills of Susan Martins Miller — many thanks.

Finally, we want to express our deep appreciation and love to our three children, Jennifer, Brandon, and Lindsay. You have, together and individually, enriched our lives far beyond what we could have ever imagined. Thank you for being our living laboratory for working out these ideas, for being so thoughtful and strong, and for loving us all these years.

PART 1

Foundations

CHAPTER I

The Big Picture

Preparing Healthy, Godly Adults

Sex is a gift from God. It is a frequently misunderstood, misused, and squandered gift, but a gift nonetheless. Our sexuality and the rules God has given us to direct our use of that gift are a tremendous blessing.

Many parents focus too narrowly and negatively when they think about goals for sex education. Worried by what they hear about sexual promiscuity, sexually transmitted diseases, and the like among young people, parents attempt to convince their kids not to have sex in an effort to protect them from the ravages that illicit and irresponsible sex can cause. Rightly so. But this goal is too small, too limited, too narrow. If we stop there, we seek to protect them only by stopping them from doing anything negative.

Don't we want to give them something profoundly positive? Protecting our children from the physical, emotional, and spiritual damage that can result from irresponsible and inappropriate sexual choices is important. But *our most important goal is to equip and empower our children to enter adulthood capable of living godly, wholesome, and fulfilled lives as Christian men and women, Christian husbands and wives.*

Our goal, then, is not just to protect our children from death or disease and not just to protect them from sin. Our goal is to prepare them to become adults who can have deep and meaningful marriages filled with spiritual, sexual, and emotional intimacy, and who can have loving and deep family relationships and friendships. Sex as God intended it is the giving over of the astonishing gift of our very selves to another in marital union. Sex education is about preparing our children for giving this gift rightly, preparing them to be able to love and trust and believe enough to commit their whole selves and their whole futures to their spouses. When we do this, we also protect them.

Parenting as God Intended

Christian parents have a wonderful opportunity to prepare their children to experience God's best in the area of sexuality. Parents are capable of being effective sex educators; they just need some advice, encouragement, information, and help to get there. That's what this book provides, along with the four children's books that go with it in the GOD'S DESIGN FOR SEX series.

How do we achieve this goal of godly sex education? Parents rightly want help from our churches and schools, but we cannot abdicate such an important task to these organizations. The primary responsibility belongs to us. How do we do it? What are we to do? Here again many Christian parents think too small. We think of sex education in terms of The Talk, the single, dramatic sex talk with the early teen. Clearly, one or even several focused sex talks with a twelve- or fourteen-year-old cannot turn the tide. Wherever they turn, our children are inundated with messages and "programming" about sexuality, all pointing them in the wrong direction. Can one talk counteract all of the destructive messages they receive? No.

Here is our vision: that children grow up with godly, age-appropriate discussion and teaching about sexuality as a regular part of their relationships with their parents. Why? Because parents are God's agents for shaping the sexual characters of their children. And we believe that both parents and children can trust God's wisdom about sexuality throughout their lives, because that wisdom is given for their good. Listen to two of the most important passages in the Bible about parenting and about the beauty of God's commandments:

These are the commands, decrees and laws the LORD your God directed me to teach you to observe in the land that you are crossing the Jordan to possess, *so that you, your children and their children after them* may fear the LORD your God as long as you live by keeping all his decrees and commands that I give you, and so that you may enjoy long life. Hear, O Israel, and be careful to obey *so that it may go well with you* and that you may increase greatly in a land flowing with milk and honey, just as the LORD, the God of your fathers, promised you.

Hear, O Israel: The LORD our God, the LORD is one. Love the LORD your God with all your heart and with all your soul and with all your strength. These commandments that I give you today are to be upon your hearts. *Impress them on your children. Talk about them when you sit at home* and when you walk along the road, when you lie down and when you get up. Tie them as symbols on your hands and bind them on your foreheads. Write them on the doorframes of your houses and on your gates. (Deuteronomy 6:1-9, emphasis added)

And now, O Israel, what does the LORD your God ask of you but to fear the LORD your God, to walk in all his ways, to love him, to serve the LORD your God with all your heart and with all your soul, and to observe the LORD's commands and decrees that I am giving you today *for your own good*? (Deuteronomy 10:12-13, emphasis added)

Parents are to shape children to become followers of the true God, to worship God in love and obedience. We are to do so trusting that God's commands are for their and our own good and are a source of blessing. Sex education is about making this great vision a reality in the area of sexuality.

Parenting is an extremely complex activity. Psychologists have been trying for quite some time to classify types of parents according to the most vital dimensions of parenting. The best research in this area should prove very encouraging to Christian parents.[1] Researchers have divided parents into four basic types on the basis of two major factors: (1) what the parents expect of their children and (2) how they respond to their children emotionally. The four types of parents are neglecting, permissive, authoritarian, and authoritative; and the authoritative style is clearly superior.

Neglecting parents expect little of their children and offer little emotional support. Permissive or indulgent parents are big on emotional support but expect little from their children and do not challenge their children to "be all they can be." Authoritarian parents overemphasize discipline, expectations, and control of their children; they push their children hard but are cold and disconnected emotionally, leaving their children feeling unloved, valued only for their accomplishments.

Authoritative parents are strong in both areas, offering both high expectations and lavish love and support to their children. These parents have things they want to teach their children, but they combine an emphasis on discipline with warmth, communication, respect, and affection. *The consensus today is that this is the most effective parenting style and produces the healthiest kids.* Research suggests that children with this type of parent tend to have the highest levels of self-esteem, self-reliance, and social competence as compared to all of the other groups. They tend to perform better in school, having a strong motivation to achieve.

This research reinforces our belief that parents are representatives of God in the lives of their children.[2] Righteousness and love are two fundamental facets of God's character. God is perfect love and perfect righteousness. A Christian understanding of God balances these two realities. Overemphasize God's love to the exclusion of His righteousness, and God becomes the cosmic Santa Claus. Overemphasize God's righteousness to the exclusion of His love, and God becomes a terrifying Cosmic Tyrant toward whom we can feel only fear. God's perfect balance of these two characteristics is at the heart of the gospel.

Authoritative parenting reflects God's character to our children by manifesting both expectations and love. In having demands and expectations for their children, parents embody God's character of justice and righteousness, in which He reveals His will for His people and desires us to live up to it for our own good. In being accepting and loving parents, we embody God's loving and merciful character, in which time and again He pursues His wayward people out of love until He brings them home. Your child's future sexual choices will be affected by the overall quality of your relationship with him or her. We have the opportunity, as we function as the shapers of our children's sexual characters, to embody these two qualities as God would intend, indeed as God does Himself, by being authoritative parents as we do lifelong sex education in the family.

The Benefits of Following God

At the deepest level, we approach the task of sex education convinced that God's people will prosper as they handle the gift of their sexuality the way

God, the Gift-Giver, intended. They will prosper in three ways.

Prosper in Pleasing God

First, they prosper in pleasing God. The greatest benefit of conducting our sexual lives in the manner in which God urges us to, and teaching our children to do the same, is that we can know that we are doing what our Father wants us to do and that we are pleasing Him. Scripture promises that, in obedience — in living as God wishes — our faith can be completed or perfected:

> [Jesus said,] "If you love me, you will obey what I command. . . . Whoever has my commands and obeys them, he is the one who loves me. He who loves me will be loved by my Father, and I too will love him and show myself to him. . . . If anyone loves me, he will obey my teaching. My Father will love him, and we will come to him and make our home with him. He who does not love me will not obey my teaching. These words you hear are not my own; they belong to the Father who sent me." (John 14:15,21,23-24)

> We know that we have come to know him if we obey his commands. The man who says, "I know him," but does not do what he commands is a liar, and the truth is not in him. But if anyone obeys his word, God's love is truly made complete in him. This is how we know we are in him: Whoever claims to live in him must walk as Jesus did. (1 John 2:3-6)

Prosper in Safety

Second, we prosper in safety. In living according to God's law, we experience the joy and blessing of sex as God meant it, free from fear. Obedience creates safety; we can live without fear of the devastation that can come from illicit sex. As you will soon see, sexual activity rates remain high among teens, with approximately 75 percent having had sexual intercourse by age 19 or 20.[3] Sexually transmitted disease rates continue to climb, and teen pregnancy in the United States, though down from ten years ago, is the highest in the developed world.[4] Premarital chastity and marital monogamy are safeguards against unwanted pregnancy and the transmission of sexually transmitted diseases. More broadly, obedient Christians are also safer from the relational confusion and emotional traumas that premature and inappropriate sexual intimacy can foster. We are not only safe from bad things, we also have the blessing of experiencing the good that God intended in giving us the gift of sexuality.

Prosper in Marriage

Third, we prosper in marriage. Sexual chastity contributes to a successful marriage. While chastity before marriage is no guarantee of having a good marriage, the evidence that it helps is indisputable. An important sociological study of marriage found results that Christians will appreciate:[5]

- *The single most powerful predictor of a good marriage was whether couples pray together regularly.*
- *Couples able to pray together and enjoy good sex together were the least likely to divorce.*
- *Cohabitation before marriage approximately doubled the degree to which couples themselves believed they were likely to get a divorce; this reinforces numerous other studies that show cohabitation is bad for marriage rather than good preparation for it, as so many claim.*
- *The higher the incidence of premarital sex, the less the likelihood of the couple reporting high sexual satisfaction and the greater the likelihood of infidelity in marriage.*

The Twelve Principles of Christian Sex Education

This book is built around twelve core principles of Christian sex education. We want to explain our vision of Christian sex education in the family as we introduce these principles.

Principle 1:
Sex education is the shaping of character.

We have been discussing this principle already. If we are going to get this right, we must understand what we are doing. Many parents mistakenly think that sex education primarily is about providing information—biological information. No wonder we shy away from the task! Most of us don't have college degrees in sexuality and biology, so how can we even get started?

But above all else, sex education is about shaping a child's character. Giving the child information is part of that, but only a part. We must also shape the values and attitudes of our kids, shape their worldviews, provide them with the emotional strength they will need to make godly decisions, and instill in them the skills to implement the good decisions they make. Most important, their behavior will spring from their hearts, which will be formed by their personal relationships with and devotion to God. Therefore, influencing their spiritual growth must be a top priority.

In chapter 3 we give you a way of thinking about your child's character that will help you understand how to shape his or her character; we build on this throughout this book. How your child responds to pressure to experiment with sex at age fifteen or to view pornography at age thirteen will have less to do with the biology he knows and more to do with his moral character and strength. The job of building his character belongs first and foremost with you as the parent.

Principle 2:
Parents are the principal sex educators.

No one will have an influence on your children like you do. If you avoid dealing with this topic, your influence will be confusing, frustrating, unsure, and unclear. If you take it on directly, you have the opportunity to have a powerful, clear, healthy, and positive influence on your child. Sex education is about much more than "sex-proofing" children through the teenage years. It is about preparing them to handle God's gift of sexuality rightly throughout life, preparing them to experience the fullness of God's blessing as they date, get engaged, marry, and have children themselves.

Children start learning about sexuality from their earliest moments. They learn about sexuality from watching how their mom and dad treat each other. They soak in the messages of the media, of their peers, of our culture in general. We urge you to start sex education early in the life of your children.

Principle 3:
First messages are the most potent.

Think of it this way: You wouldn't want your child to learn the wrong teachings about God for years and years, and *then* try to correct those erroneous lessons after the fact. So why do we let our kids learn about sexuality from everyone except us for years and years, and then try to correct all the wrong they have learned with an in-depth conversation when they are thirteen? It will be much more powerful, much more effective, to provide your children with a solid and age-appropriate foundation from the start.

Remember also that if you do not talk to your kids about sex, your silence is not just an absence of information. Your silence in fact teaches your kids that Dad and Mom do not want to talk about sex, are uncomfortable talking about sex, and probably are not good sources of information about sex. By seizing the opportunity to teach them about sex, you communicate the opposite: that you, the parents, are trustworthy resources for learning the truth about this most private and potent aspect of life. The children's books in the GOD'S DESIGN FOR SEX series are meant to provide starter conversations between you and your child. Reading them with your child opens up the topic, gets the words and ideas out on the table, and gives you a base from which to start.

Principle 4:
We should seize those teachable moments and become askable parents.

Many of the most precious opportunities to shape your children's characters come at unexpected moments. The pregnant mom at church, the foul word or leer in a movie preview, the news item about sexual abuse, the sexual affair of a celebrity, the mating animals in the zoo — these and hundreds of other events provide rich opportunities to discuss sexuality with your kids and thus to shape their characters.

Principle 5:
Stories are powerful teaching tools.

As you have these conversations, don't forget the teaching tool Jesus used so effectively — the story. You can teach your children a dry concept like "immoral sex can have bad consequences," or you can have a powerful impact on your children by sharing with them real stories of the difficulties faced by a real person who had a child out of wedlock. Why is the media so powerful? In large part because it teaches by telling stories. Help your kids to learn the truth from real stories. Of course, we start with Bible stories, but we add to these the stories around us about real life.

Principle 6:
Accurate and explicit messages are best.

There is an old joke about the child who is looking around the parents' bedroom with a curious but doubtful look on his face. The puzzled father asks, "What are you looking for?"

"The shovel," replies the son.

"What shovel?" asks the father.

"The shovel you use when you have sex."

"Come again?" says the father.

"You told me that having sex is when you plant the sperm inside Mom's body, and you plant things with a shovel, so where's the shovel?" replied the boy.

Accurate messages are always best. They tell children that you care about them, that you respect their questions, and that you are a trustworthy source of truth. Explicit does not mean graphic or crude. It means that you give direct, truthful answers in an age-appropriate way. As we move through the developmental stages in this book, we will give numerous examples of how to give such appropriate messages.

Principle 7:
Positive messages are more powerful than negative messages.

We rob Christian faith of its power when we shrink the Christian teaching about sexuality to a list of don'ts. The first messages in the Bible about sexuality in Genesis 1 and 2 are wildly positive. God the Father and Creator made humanity — the first man and woman — as physical and sexual beings, male and female created equally in God's image. He made them (and us) so that the one man and the one woman could be blessed to form an exclusive and lifelong marital union, unite sexually and become "one flesh," and experience the joy of sexual and personal union. They could also conceive and raise children. We even learn in the New Testament that Christian marriage serves as an earthly model of Christ's love for His bride, the church (see Ephesians 5:25-33). Yes, the Bible has to warn us that God hates sexual immorality, but this negative message is grounded in a profoundly positive reality.

Principle 8:
We must inoculate our children against destructive moral messages.

Try as we might to teach our kids the truth and nothing but the truth, the distorted beliefs of a world that has lost its balance will seep into the hearts and minds of our children. Will they be prepared? All parents know that a mild exposure to germs, whether in the form of a medical immunization or an exposure to real-world germs, can help to activate a child's immune system to fight off infection. In contrast, providing an environment that is too antiseptic (too much antibacterial hand soap, antibiotics, air purifiers, and so forth) can actually result in a child being more vulnerable, not less, to infection. In direct parallel, parents who expose their children to the destructive moral messages they will eventually encounter anyway help to strengthen their children by taking the surprise out of the destructive messages and teaching their children how to counteract them.

Principle 9:
Repetition is critical; repetition is really, really important.

Sex education is never done. You will think that you have already covered something, but if your child was not ready to hear it, it is as if you never said it. Kids need to hear the most important lessons over and over again.

Principle 10:
Close, positive parent-child relationships are crucial.

Research has shown that teenagers will be less likely to experiment with sex if they are close to at least one of their parents. It is not all about the information that is in their heads; it is also about what is in their hearts. Diet experts tell those trying to lose weight to never go to the grocery store hungry. Why would we let our kids go out on dates or out into the confusing world of teen relationships starving for affection and affirmation? A close relationship with a parent sends them to the relational grocery store full and strong. Such a close relationship also helps them remember that what they do sexually is ultimately about whom they love—do they love you and show that love by honoring what you have taught them? Do they love Jesus and honor Him with obedience?

The final two principles are about balance.

Principle 11:
Sexuality is not the most important thing in life.

Principle 12:
Our God can forgive, heal, and redeem anything.

You should not make the mistake of focusing so much on sexuality that it gets out of proportion with life. Yes, the stakes are enormous; a bad decision can have life-altering consequences. But God does not focus only on sexuality, and neither should you as a parent. And you should not make the mistake of thinking that bad decisions on your child's part will be the end of life as you know it. We worship a God who brings good out of evil, life out of death, sweetness out of bitterness. Live as a parent in the confidence and freedom of knowing that God is in control, and He is a loving and merciful Father.

So the big picture is of parents and children in ever-expanding and deepening conversations about our sexuality. These conversations help to draw you together and help to deepen your children's faith in the goodness and love of God.

Here again are the principles in this book:

- *Principle 1: Sex education is the shaping of character.*
- *Principle 2: Parents are the principal sex educators.*
- *Principle 3: First messages are the most potent.*
- *Principle 4: We should seize those teachable moments and become askable parents.*
- *Principle 5: Stories are powerful teaching tools.*
- *Principle 6: Accurate and explicit messages are best.*
- *Principle 7: Positive messages are more powerful than negative messages.*
- *Principle 8: We must inoculate our children against destructive moral messages.*
- *Principle 9: Repetition is critical; repetition is really, really important.*
- *Principle 10: Close, positive parent-child relationships are crucial.*
- *Principle 11: Sexuality is not the most important thing in life.*
- *Principle 12: Our God can forgive, heal, and redeem anything.*

The objectives of this book revolve around giving you, the parent, the tools you need to instill in your child a distinctively Christian sexual character. We hope, in this way, that you will be able to equip your children to make godly and wise decisions about their sexuality in their teenage years. We also hope, just as importantly, that you will lay the foundations for them to experience the blessings of God's gift of sexuality as mature and responsible adults, whether married or single.

CHAPTER 2

The Challenge

Good news! Sexual intercourse among teenagers has decreased slightly in the last decade, as have teen pregnancy and abortion. Many more young people are committed to abstinence from sex until they are married than anyone dreamed possible twenty years ago. Thousands and thousands of young people are making good decisions. The church is much more prepared to deal properly with sexuality than in decades past.

But the challenges are considerable. You know this already, but we want to underscore a few of the most disconcerting facts to motivate you to get started now, to start early, in shaping your child's sexual character.

The Realities

Sexual Intercourse

We begin with a graph showing the percentage of young people from ages fifteen to twenty-four who have had sexual intercourse.[1]

The statistics for the high school years are sobering. At fifteen, about one-fourth of both young men and women have already had intercourse. By age eighteen, about two-thirds have had sex. At the age when many

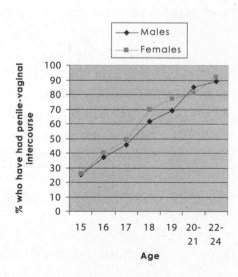

kids are completing their first year in college, three-fourths have had sex. The percentages continue to climb through the college years.

The greatest changes in sexual behavior over recent decades have occurred among young women. While the percentage of men who have had sexual intercourse has edged up only a few percentage points over the last five decades, the rates for women have increased dramatically. Estimates in the 1950s were that less than 20 percent of young women were nonvirgins when graduating from high school. Estimates from the early 1990s showed radically increased sexual activity levels among women but had young women still trailing men of the same age by a few percentage points. Now you can see in the graph above that women are slightly *more* likely than their male peers to have had sex at almost every teenage year. The sexual revolution for teens has been that young women have adopted the same sexually active patterns that young men have followed for some time.

Many of those who have sex do so with multiple partners. For eighteen- to nineteen-year-olds, 16 percent of men and 14 percent of women reported two partners in the last year, and an additional 15 percent of men and 17 percent of women reported three or more partners in the last year.

Oral Sex

Researchers have begun asking more questions about a wider range of sexual behaviors that can spread disease just as intercourse does. Years ago, few teenagers knew of or had engaged in oral sex. That has changed. Most of those who have had intercourse have also engaged in oral sex. And a considerable number who have not had intercourse *have* engaged in oral sex instead. For young men, an additional 10 to 14 percent of ages fifteen to nineteen have had oral sex even if they have not had vaginal sex (so for example, 62 percent of men at age eighteen report having had vaginal sex, and an additional 10 percent have had oral sex without having vaginal sex). For young women, an additional 8 to 15 percent of ages fifteen to nineteen have had oral sex even if they have not had vaginal sex (so for example, 70 percent of women at age eighteen report having had vaginal sex and an additional 8 percent have had oral sex without having vaginal sex).

Part of the reason for the increase in oral sex is that many teens think that it "is not sex" and therefore that there is no risk of pregnancy (which is correct) or of passing STDs (which is incorrect; many STDs are passed this way).

Anal Sex

Parents may be surprised to learn that teenagers are also engaging in anal sex. Eleven percent of men ages fifteen to nineteen report having engaged in anal sex; the figure climbs to 15 percent when you look just at eighteen- to nineteen-year-olds, and to 32 percent of twenty- to twenty-four-year-olds. The figures are not too different for females; 11 percent of females fifteen to nineteen have received anal sex, and almost 19 percent of eighteen- to nine-teen-year-olds and 30 percent of twenty- to twenty-four-year-old females have received anal sex.

Same-Sex Activity

In the fifteen to nineteen age group, 2.4 percent of young men have had sex with another male in the last year, and 4.5 percent have had sex with another male sometime in their lives. Same-sex activity is more common among young women: 7.7 percent report some kind of same-sex experience in the last year and 10.6 percent with another female sometime in their lives. We suspect, based on conversations with young people and on anecdotes, that much of the same-sex activity reported for young women is of the kissing and caressing type, compared to the stimulation-to-orgasm type for males. Even so, these statistics indicate how radically things have changed from when most parents were teens.

Teen Pregnancy

Here is a smattering of the sobering facts about teen pregnancy in the United States:

- *Almost one million pregnancies occur each year among American teenage females.*
- *The teenage pregnancy rate is at its lowest in decades. Through the 1980s and early 1990s, the pregnancy rate hovered between 100 and 116 pregnancies each year for every 1,000 teenage women, but it began to decline in 1996 and in the early 2000s stands in the range of around 83 per 1,000. This decline is due in part to women delaying*

intercourse, but mostly (it is thought) to couples using condoms and other birth control when they have sex.[2]

- *About one out of five girls who have sex each year gets pregnant.*
- *Over 250,000 teenage pregnancies end in abortions each year.*
- *About a half million babies are brought to live birth by teenage mothers each year; the vast majority of these are outside marriage.*

Abortion

And here are the parallel facts about abortion in the United States:[3]

- *Over 250,000 abortions are performed annually on teenage women.*
- *Fifty-two percent of U.S. women having abortions are younger than twenty-five years old.*
- *It is estimated that just under one million abortions take place annually for all women at all ages; this is down from almost 1.5 million annually in 1990.*
- *More than 45 million abortions have been performed in the United States since 1973, as of 2006.*
- *About 13,000 abortions each year are attributed to rape and incest — representing only 1 percent of all abortions.*

Sexually Transmitted Diseases (STDs)

The best estimates are that almost 19 million new cases of STDs are contracted every year, and about half of these new cases occur in the fifteen to twenty-four age range. According to a Centers for Disease Control report, "The direct medical cost of these diseases to 15- to 24-year-olds alone was estimated at 6.5 billion dollars in the year 2000."[4] Sexually active teenagers have a higher rate of contracting STDs than any other age group for two basic reasons. First, teenagers are more likely to have multiple sex partners. Second, they are more likely not to use contraception, and if they do attempt contraception, they tend to use methods that are ineffective at preventing the spread of disease (such as withdrawal) or to use improperly a potentially effective method. Once they get an STD, teens are less likely than adults to get effective treatment and are more likely to have complications from it. Many parents know of and fear HIV/AIDS, but we (and our children) ought to fear other rapidly spreading STDs. Following are the three most common, in descending order of their prevalence:[5]

- **HPV (human papillomavirus)** *is a viral infection estimated currently to infect 9.2 million Americans ages fifteen to twenty-four. Condoms do not completely stop its transmission, because it infests the skin of the genital region, not just semen and vaginal secretions. Estimates from university health centers are that about 33 percent of female university students are infected with HPV. At this time, there are no known cures for HPV.[6] It has no noticeable symptoms (except those varieties that cause warts on the genitals and elsewhere). Women who get HPV are at greatly elevated risk of developing cancer of the cervix later in life.*
- **Chlamydia** *is a bacterial infection. It is estimated that 1.5 million new cases are transmitted each year among fifteen- to twenty-four-year-olds. It can be effectively treated if detected early, but chlamydia has no noticeable symptoms for men or women, so infected teens rarely are diagnosed and treated. The chlamydia infection may spread through a woman's body and produce scarring and scar tissue in the uterus and fallopian tubes. If untreated, it can leave the infected woman unable to ever have children.*
- **Trichomoniasis** *is an infection from a type of protozoa, a single-celled parasite that flourishes in the urinary tract of a man and in the vagina and urinary tract of a woman. It is more common in the developing world than in America but is growing here. It is estimated that between 1 and 2 million new cases occur annually for fifteen- to twenty-four-year-olds. Men rarely have any symptoms of infection, and some women have no symptoms. People who have trichomoniasis are more vulnerable to getting infected with HIV, and women who have it are more likely to deliver premature babies.*

We could go on, citing statistics about rape, date rape, drug and alcohol use, and so forth, but we suspect you get the point: Your child is going to have to be well prepared and extremely strong to remain sexually chaste in the society in which he or she is growing up. Where will our help come from in this daunting task?

Where Are Our Allies?

Who is assisting us in shaping our children in the kind of sexual purity and wholeness that is honoring to God?

The Media? No.

The media? Are you kidding? From the grotesque headlines of grocery store tabloids to the sexual humor of sitcoms to sexual exploits on display in television dramas (exploits that rarely have real-life consequences like pregnancy, abortion, or STDs), and from the sexually graphic lyrics of much of contemporary music to the titillation of contemporary movies, the media is a parent's worst enemy in trying to teach kids a godly understanding of the gift of sexuality.

The Internet? No.

What about that great spigot of information into our home, the Internet? This is one of the most frightening developments of the past fifteen years. There is no more aggressive distribution outlet for sexual depravity than the Internet, no better current example of the apostle Peter's description that "your enemy the devil prowls around like a roaring lion looking for someone to devour. Resist him, standing firm in the faith" (1 Peter 5:8-9). Predators, both purveyors of pornography and actual sexual predators, are seeking our children through Internet chat rooms, e-mail solicitations, lewd pop-up ads, free offers of pornography, and other means. A recent news investigation concluded that "last year, one in five kids aged ten to seventeen received an Internet sexual solicitation"[7]

Secular Sex Education? Sometimes, but Often No.

Are secular sex-education programs in schools and in the community allies of Christian parents? While they provide some accurate information about sexuality to young people, we are very concerned about the place of morality in such programs. Many such programs position themselves as "value-neutral," but in fact value neutrality is impossible in the arena of human sexuality. Anthropologists agree from cross-cultural study that human sexual union means something unique and distinct in every culture, and what it means is almost always connected to the culture's religious understandings of the world and of their lives. To treat human sexuality as pure biology is to strip it of its moral and religious meaning and thus to present a distorted and limited understanding of sex.

Secular sex education is not value-neutral. Any illusion that sex education is value-neutral is shattered by reading the professional literature of sexuality educators. For example, even as the AIDS crisis was brewing, two leading sex educators spoke of their goals for sex education in a widely read journal. They expressed their hope that sex education would knock down "the negative barriers that have been used to limit the number of sexual contacts"; that teenagers could all be "rendered temporarily infertile through skin implants" of contraceptives so that they would be "free to engage in sexual activity without those fears that so inhibited their parents and grandparents"; that sex education programs could someday probe sexual expression "in infancy, childhood, . . . with same-sex and other-sex partners and even cross racial and generational lines"; and that our children could be taught to see activities that had once been called "perversions" or "abnormality" as "life-enhancing activity."[8]

Other obvious examples of ideas contrary to Christian values arise in supposedly value-neutral sex education. In college-level human sexuality textbooks, traditional Christian views of sexuality and sexual morality are often presented as oppressive and destructive. Cohabitation is often lauded as an effective way to prepare for marriage and to ensure sexual compatibility, in spite of the fact that every major scientific study ever performed comparing relational outcomes for cohabiting and married persons has shown that people who cohabit have worse outcomes (less relational stability or satisfaction, more abuse, less sexual satisfaction) than those of married people. These textbooks are now consistently also mainstreaming homosexual practice by presenting it alongside heterosexual practice as just another variation in the way humans legitimately express their sexual natures.

We have seen in the past fifteen years a dramatic shift toward an emphasis on abstinence-based sex education in the public schools. This shift coincides almost exactly with the modest decrease in the sex rates among teenagers. Even so, there is still great resistance to true promotion of sexual abstinence among teenagers, and often these abstinence curricula are being taught by teachers who do not share the values of so many Christian parents. Secular sex education is often an uncertain ally of the Christian parent.

The Church? Yes, but Much Remains to Be Done.

We begin to actually find real allies in our churches. Conservative, biblically sound churches slowly are rising up and offering more support to parents in the sex-education task. Often they are supplementing the work of Christian parents by offering sexuality education, but all too often this is coming too late, after our children have already been negatively influenced by their culture. A new partnership is needed between parents and the church to provide for young people a comprehensive and supportive understanding of their sexuality.

Parents and Churches Together

Two of the most powerful predictors of whether teenagers will engage in sexual experimentation are (1) whether they feel close to at least one parent and (2) whether they are seriously committed to their religious faith.[9] Christian faith is vitally important to many teens, and with help they can be strengthened in seeing sexual purity as an integral part of their calling to follow Christ. Teens who report being able to talk to a parent and who feel close to that parent appear to have a solid foundation in that relationship that allows them to make better decisions and to better resist peer pressure toward sexual activity.

What If I Get Started Late?

There is no such thing as too late. Earlier is better. Any sex education we give to our kids is a gift, an improvement over no communication whatsoever. And you are reading this book because you love your child enough to want to give him or her that gift.

If you're starting late, at least you're starting. Remember, our God is a God who wants to start a good work in us and keep at it until it's done (see Philippians 1:6). God is willing to start His good work anytime we are ready; it's never too late with God. Earlier would have been better, but don't be discouraged; now is a wonderful time to start in God's view. Here are our concrete suggestions.

Start Now!

First, however old your child is, start sex education now. Give yourself a crash course with this or other books, and dive in. Don't put it off for more preparation or out of a defeatist sense of having already waited too long. Any discussion you can have with your child that follows the guidelines we discuss in this book will bear fruit. Start now. If you are starting late, it is probably due in part to uncomfortable feelings about this topic. We hope this book will make you more comfortable.

Share honestly with your children your hesitancies in communicating about sex, and confess to them your embarrassment for getting this late start. Parents should not always try to be strong and perfect before their children. A parent who is uncomfortable communicating about sex but goes ahead anyway despite obvious distress is moving ahead in the task of sex education and is communicating to the child that the parent cares so deeply about the child that he or she is willing to endure embarrassment and discomfort for the child's sake. That is a sacrifice of love that can bear fruit.

Assess Your Relationship Honestly

Second, we urge you to make an honest assessment of the kind of relationship you have with your child. In addition to working on sex education, work diligently on the quality of your relationship. Build on its strengths. Use those strengths as a launchpad to build a better relationship. Pour energy into making your relationship with your child stronger.

Assess Your Child's Faith

Third, honestly assess your child's faith in Christ. Have you done everything you can to encourage your child's faith? Remember that doing everything you can do doesn't mean smothering your child with Bible lessons, Scripture memorization, Christian music, and church every evening of the week. Faith is best caught, not taught. Your child can catch faith from you if your faith is alive enough to be a "communicable disease." Your child can also catch faith from a community of faith, whether Christian friends at school, the church youth group, the church in general, or the quiet witness of one neighbor. Pray that your child might grow into a sincere and deep faith in Christ.

Pray for Your Children

Finally, we urge you to pray for your children. You can pray for their general welfare and for their particular concerns on a day-to-day basis. But it may also be helpful to pray in disciplined ways for specific developments in their lives. For instance, pray through the Ephesians 6:13-17 list of the armor of God, beseeching God to equip your kids. Pray through Galatians 5:22-23, the fruit of the Spirit, and Matthew 5:1-12, the beatitudes of our Lord. Pray through Christ's parables or through the letters from John's revelation that Christ dictated to the seven churches (Revelation 2–3), and so forth.

Such prayer can have a profound impact. God works through prayer, both to impact our children and to impact us. We don't know why or how, but God has chosen to work through the prayers of His people. Your prayers may be a critical element in God's direct intervention with your kids. God may stir you up as you pray for them. If you actually pray with your children out loud, you share powerfully with them your hopes and values for their lives. That itself may have a compelling effect. Pray with your child for his or her future spouse. Pray for the future spouse's growth, protection, and sexual integrity. This may help your child to understand at yet a deeper level how enormous the decisions are that he or she is making during adolescence.

Wherever your starting point is, start now! God will honor your efforts. He is a God of new beginnings, a God who puts the past behind us and moves us forward into new adventures.

Join the Revolution

Tim Stafford, an effective and wise Christian author in the area of sexuality, has argued that we need nothing less now than to create a Christian sexual counterculture, to sponsor a Christian "sexual revolution."[10] That is what raising a generation of pure kids will amount to. Will such a generation of kids have anything to offer to a sex-obsessed world? Yes. They will form a community that will experience, for all the world to see, the benefits of handling sexuality God's way.

Our ultimate goal in sex education is to shape a child's character so that the child will glorify God in all areas of life, including sexuality. He or she will please God in choices and actions and by the very nature of the character the child manifests. As a part of this, we must look at the child's choices in the teenage years as absolutely essential, but we must also look past the teenage years. We must have a vision for what kind of adult we want the child to be.

We must think of the whole person while we teach sex education. We are preparing our children not just to resist sexual temptation in the teenage years, but also to be godly people who understand and accept their sexuality. With this foundation, they can make good decisions about sexuality in the teenage years. This will help them to enjoy the full fruits of God's gifts when they marry. Any approach to sex education that ignores the dangers of sexual expressions beyond the bounds of God's revealed will is in serious error. But so is any approach that emphasizes the dangers to the extent that it cripples the child's ability to obtain the fruits God hopes to develop in his or her life as a married adult.

Do we really want the best for our children? Are we willing to sacrifice and work hard to provide the best for them? If you said yes, this book series is for you.

CHAPTER 3

Understanding Character Formation

"Okay, look — I'm not pushing you to go all the way, but at least let me touch you! You say you like me, and I really care about you. It's natural for guys and girls to express their caring with their bodies, not just with words. People who care, share! And I'm not just being selfish — I want you to touch me too. That way, we can enjoy each other. Come on!"

Lindy is returning from a poorly chaperoned eighth-grade field trip. She looks around with a sense of desperation. The cold bus is dark, and the exhausted teacher is sitting, head down, apparently asleep, in the far front of the bus. A lot of the guys and girls are paired up and are making out. They are in their seats with coats piled up all over them so that it's not at all clear what is going on between their necks and their knees.

Lindy and Derek have been a couple for three weeks, and she really does like him. He hasn't been aggressive up until now; they have exchanged only a few brief kisses. She has a sick feeling that she should never have paired off with Derek for the trip home. She is feeling scared, excited, guilty, curious, and confused all at the same time. What will she do? She feels the pressure from Derek; he seems to really care, and shouldn't love be expressed? And what might he say about her if she says, "Hands off!"? And her parents! She remembers what her mom said about petting. But then, her mom had been very unclear as to why it wasn't right. And what about God — would Jesus want her to do what Derek wants her to do? But does Jesus care about just touching? What will she do?

Is what Lindy does in that seat on the bus determined by the biology facts stuffed into her head in sex-ed classes? No. Her behavior will be a function of her character. What she does will be the product of who she is as a person at that moment in her life.

Principle 1:
Sex education is the shaping of character.

Sex education is not primarily a matter of providing information. That's certainly part of the process, but only part. And shaping our children's sexual characters is just one dimension of our broad task as parents of shaping the overall characters of our children. Sadly, it is an often-neglected part of our task as parents.

Think again on the Deuteronomy 6 passage quoted in chapter 1. In godly families, reflection on the law of God should be a preoccupation, and teaching our children about the love and instruction of God a constant theme. We should impress these things on our children; we should "talk about them when [we] sit at home and when [we] walk along the road, when [we] lie down and when [we] get up" (verse 7).

Our obedience to God's commands influences not only our own faith but the faith of our children as well. The living obedience of parents is the foundation for any purposeful teaching that we do with our children. Teaching must flow from living. Our lives, our obedience as parents, are a living witness of God's work, for good or for ill. Truth about our God is meant to consume the totality of our lives. The truths of the faith are to be so important that they shape every aspect, especially in our families. In this way, our lives will shape the characters of our children, helping them to learn how to give their lives to following God in joyful obedience to the commandments God gave for their good.

This kind of character formation will shape how Lindy responds in the back of that bus on that eighth-grade field trip. You, the parent, are the most important influence on your child's character. Either you will be a haphazard and thoughtless teacher who gives little thought to what you are doing in your parenting, or you will be a prepared, thoughtful, responsible teacher. You get to choose, with God's help, which you will be.

Principle 2:
Parents are the principal sex educators.

Remember:

- *We teach by what we say to our kids.*
- *We teach by what we do to our kids. Consequences, punishment, and praise all teach richly.*
- *We teach by who we are before our kids. This is the most powerful teaching method. Kids soak in the material of our lives like sponges. Our lives are a story we are telling our kids.*

In our love for and discipline of our kids, we live out and show forth what our children will understand to be God's personality. We will also exhibit God's personality in our marriages by how we treat each other as spouses. That is the primary message in Ephesians 5, is it not? Christian marriage is meant to be an object lesson to the world, including and especially to our children, about the character of Christ's relationship to His bride, the church.

Thinking About Your Child's Character

How can we understand the process of shaping character? The core ideas we want to focus on in understanding a child's character are the child's *needs, values, beliefs, skills,* and *supports.*[1] The diagram on page 40 portrays our needs as our guts — our "bowels," to use a biblical metaphor. Our values form our hearts. Our core beliefs constitute the minds of our characters. Our skills are our bones and muscles by which we act. Our supports help us to push back against the challenges that come at us.

Think of a long-distance runner in training. What are the major factors that go into her success in competition? First, her basic *needs* as an athlete must be met — proper sleep, good nutrition, time for practice, and so forth. Second, she must have *values* that support her efforts. She might desire to win a parent's approval, impress a boyfriend, win a college scholarship, or distinguish herself to enhance her ability to witness for Christ; any number of motivations are possible. She must have core *beliefs* that support her endeavors, including such beliefs as "running is important," "I can excel at this sport," "I can trust the guidance I get from my coach," and so

forth. She needs *skills*, for both thinking and acting. Thinking skills might include knowing how to pace herself, how to develop a strategy for a race, and how much and when to practice. Acting skills might include the raw physical ability it takes to run a race and the ability to catch herself when she stumbles. Finally, who she is as a runner is powerfully influenced by her *supports* — a roommate who keeps her up all night before the big race, a distracted coach, and so forth can detract from her performance, while good coaching before the race and cheering family and friends can make all the difference as she approaches the finish line.

Needs, values, beliefs, skills, supports. These are the building blocks of character in general and of sexual character in particular. Your children will stand the greatest chance of living a chaste life, a life conforming to God's will about sexuality, if

- *their needs for relatedness and significance are met in the family and in healthy friendships, and if they themselves understand these needs for what they truly are;*
- *they value the right things, the things God values;*

- *they believe God's view of their own sexual nature and have accurate knowledge;*
- *they have the skills to make good decisions and to act on those good decisions with strength and confidence;*
- *they have more positive supports for their making right decisions than negative challenges that pull them away from the right path.*

Needs

Every human being shares certain needs. Beyond our obvious physical needs, we believe there are two basic psychological needs: *relatedness* and *significance* (or love and work). These needs are never utterly fulfilled. Like the need for food, we have to address them again and again. But like the physical need for calcium to make bones grow strong at critical periods, the period of childhood dramatically shapes how your child will experience his or her needs throughout the rest of life. When these needs are met adequately in childhood, your child will face adolescence and adulthood with a foundation of vital strength for facing the challenges of life.

We see these needs described in the Creation account. God made Adam and Eve to rule (see Genesis 1:26), which was their work in the created order. In Genesis 2, God placed the first man, Adam, in the Garden of Eden "to work it and take care of it" (verse 15). God made us for significant work, for a purpose that transcends our own individual pleasure and sustenance.

After commanding Adam not to eat of the tree of the knowledge of good and evil, the Lord God said, "It is not good for the man to be alone. I will make a helper suitable for him" (verse 18). When Eve was brought before Adam, Adam said, "This is now bone of my bones and flesh of my flesh; she shall be called 'woman,' for she was taken out of man." The passage continues, "For this reason a man will leave his father and mother and be united to his wife, and they will become one flesh" (verses 23-24). God commanded the first man and woman to be fruitful and multiply, something we cannot do without relating. As fruit of our relating, new life is created.

Relatedness

Our need for relatedness means we need to love and be loved, to affirm and be affirmed. Being loved forms a foundation for life and gives us a stability we cannot have without that bond. Truly, "what a man desires is unfailing love" (Proverbs 19:22). Many problems, especially sexual problems, begin when this fundamental need goes unmet in childhood, leaving a child feeling unloved or rejected. Books about sexual addictions talk about people who go into adolescence and adulthood with an unresolved hunger for any personal connection that will begin to satisfy this raging need that parents were meant to fill.

There is no one way, no quick and easy formula, to meet this need for loving relatedness. Families differ in how they express genuine love and acceptance. Children will differ in their individual needs: one child's needs might be met by one hug a day, while another might be in constant need of reassurance and affection. The needs of children also change over time. Truly responsive parents will respect and adjust to the changing needs of their children. You meet the need for loving relatedness by having your relationships with your children be a foundation for their lives. Strive to fill your children with an indisputable sense of being loved, of being accepted by the most important people in their lives. We need to do so from their earliest days, when they do not understand words at all, but can understand that the parent looking into their eyes exudes a sense of joy and warmth and love, that a loving embrace expresses the deepest acceptance imaginable that the parent feels for the child.

Significance

The need for significance is equally profound. God means for you to have a vocation, a calling to meaningful work in your life from which you derive a sense of significance. God has meaningful work for you to do. Your vocation may or may not overlap with your employment. The meaningfulness of your work is not defined by its grandeur or its earthly success, and it makes no difference if the work is "sacred" or "secular." We need to recapture the biblical sense of the apostle Paul's instructions to slaves, who in their day did work that was utterly despised by free men:

> Slaves, obey your earthly masters in everything; and do it, not only when their eye is on you and to win their favor, but with sincerity of heart and reverence for the Lord. Whatever you do, work at it with all your heart, as working for the Lord, not for men, since you know that you will receive an inheritance from the Lord as a reward. It is the Lord Christ you are serving. (Colossians 3:22-24)

Any work done for the Lord is significant work. We can change dirty diapers for the Lord, empty garbage cans for the Lord, program computers for the Lord, install appliances for the Lord, and pastor churches for the Lord.

Meeting your children's need for significance is both present-oriented and future-oriented. In the present, you can give them a sense of significance by assigning them meaningful places in the overall functioning of the family and by esteeming the work they do. It matters to you whether they do their homework and clean their rooms. See their play and friendships as some of their most important work, for out of these will emerge patterns for their entire lives. See them as having a calling here and now to be about the Father's business (see Luke 2:49). You also give your children a sense of significance for the future through your expectations for their lives. Affirm their growing gifts and abilities as shown in school, in sports, in friendships. Express confidence in the future God has in store for them and in their ability to contribute meaningfully to God's work in His kingdom.

Two strong predictors of sexual experimentation emerge from research time and again: emotional closeness to a parent and academic confidence.[2] Children who feel close to a parent and children who do well in school tend to delay or avoid sexual experimentation and pregnancy. Children who are close to a parent have that relationship as a foundation in meeting their needs for loving relatedness. Children who do well in school probably have a sense of significance and hope for their work of the future. (And your child does not have to be an academic whiz to feel significant; we can teach our children how to be significant in God's eyes regardless of GPA.)

Understanding and acting to meet your children's needs for relatedness and significance are the foundations for shaping their characters. You can never meet all of their needs, and you should not try to do so. But you can provide a foundation for meeting their needs for relatedness and significance. This foundation can be the basis on which they face the world in strength, able to make decisions that God will bless. Imagine the difference between a sixteen-year-old girl out on a date who is confident of her significance and filled with her parents' love for her and a disillusioned and hopeless girl who is thirsty for anyone to accept and love her. Which girl is going to make the right decision when pressured to have sex?

Values

Our children's characters are founded also on what they value, and parents are the most important influences in forming those values. The needs for relatedness and significance exist whether we feel them or not. But we all embrace unique sets of values as we grow up. If the needs for relatedness and significance are the final destination, our values are the compass that tells us how to get there. Values tell each of us what helps us in our life quest for relatedness and significance on a moment-to-moment basis. We do not typically try to be loved and significant directly, but we generate values, purposes, or goals as ways to get what we really need.

We Communicate Values in Choices

What you say about goals or values is important, but you probably express your goals and values most honestly and directly in the choices you make. The father who says he values time with his children but never makes the choices necessary to spend that time with them is speaking clearly about his real values through his actions. People often seem blind to their own values. We know what we ought to value much more intimately than what we truly value.

Parents teach their values to their children most powerfully by the values they as parents live by. Children read parents like a book; our lives tell our children what we deem important and unimportant. It behooves all of us to do an honest assessment of where our time is going and what this says about our values. Then we have to go the additional step and ask, "Is this what I want to teach my child to value; is this what really matters?"

We Communicate Values in Praise

We also communicate our values in our praise. Do you praise your children for grades they get, or for the skills that they are developing? Do you praise your children for fitting in, for being popular, for going with the flow, or for showing strength, independence, and character even when they are not as accepted by others as they might otherwise have been?

We need to think deliberately as Christians about the values we want our children to manifest.

Vibrant faith. A vibrant faith is a child's most fundamental need for the future. Parents shape children to value such a faith by modeling that faith themselves, by talking openly about how important that faith is, and by praising any manifestation of such a faith in their children. As parents we often reminded our own three children, "We really are proud that you are doing well in school (or piano, baseball, friendships, Bible school, and so on), but never forget (and help me never to forget) that the only thing that matters is whether you love God with your whole heart and are following Him in obedience. If you do that, your life will have value. Without that, nothing really matters. God is calling you right now to be a student (pianist, second baseman, and so on), and I think God is happy that you are doing well at that for Him."

Christian virtue. Next, it is critical to shape children to value Christian virtue. Beyond any particular outcome or achievement, children will be successful and blessed if they manifest the vital Christian virtues of faith, hope, and love (see 1 Corinthians 13:13) because they have a lively faith in Jesus Christ. The fruit of the Spirit listed in Galatians 5:22-23 is "love, joy, peace, patience, kindness, goodness, faithfulness, gentleness and self-control." While this fruit flows from the presence of the Holy Spirit in a person's life, it also is clearly built on preexisting human traits and characteristics. Parents can begin to develop these traits in their children. In an era of rampant cynicism and hurtfulness, do you cultivate the trait of gentleness in your children? In a time of impulsiveness and licentiousness, do you encourage self-control in your children? In an era that demands instant answers and instant success, are you able to teach your children to value patience?

Purity and chastity. Most directly relevant to this book, we must teach our children to value purity and chastity. Do we lead them to commit themselves to such chastity? Do we teach them to value faithfulness to their vows to God and to their future spouses? We should. It's good in the eyes of God for an unmarried person to be a virgin. It's good to handle oneself with self-control and to have pure motives in relationships. This doesn't mean it's bad to feel sexual feelings or to struggle with those feelings. In fact, God wants us to be the sexually alive people He made us to be. To be sexual and pure is God's intent. Our children's deep need for relatedness — to God, to a future spouse, and to loving friends — will be most deeply and fully met by living by God's standard of purity. Whereas the world says that immoral sex is a way to get your love need met, the best evidence suggests that living life by

God's rules is the best way. Chaste people are likely to have more satisfying and stable marriages and to have better sex lives in their marriages. God's way is the best way.

Beliefs

In addition to our basic needs and the values that direct us, human beings also are distinguished by our unique core beliefs. If needs are the destination and values our compass, then beliefs form the road map for how we will live our lives. We often absorb these beliefs as children from what we see modeled in the lives of our parents. Many of us never seriously question these beliefs; they become so second nature to us that they are as transparent as the air within which we move every day. For many, awareness of basic beliefs comes only at times of crisis, when we cry out because our ways of understanding the world are not working, when everything is chaos and nothing is happening the way we think it should. Our crises can be avenues through which God reveals our core beliefs and the ways in which they are failing us. At such times we may learn that we have accepted seriously distorted beliefs about life, such as the following:

- *I am acceptable to God only if I am good in every way.*
- *Life should be easy, fair, peaceful, and happy, even through the worst crises; if it is not, then I am being punished for my weak faith.*
- *God wants to meet my every need perfectly, so if life is tough it must be because of my sin and defective faith.*
- *Good Christians do not feel angry, fearful, or down.*
- *I should hide my imperfections so I do not disgrace God.*

Many of the most important core beliefs God would have our children embrace are so fundamental that parents often take them for granted. Hence we ignore them. This entire book is, in part, about the proper beliefs about relationships and sexuality that we want to pass on to our children, so a few examples here will suffice. We want our children to believe the following:

- *They are loved. We teach our children that they are loved by speaking of and by acting on our love.*
- *Their choices matter; they make a difference. We teach our children*

that they are responsible for their actions and for the consequences produced by their actions. We teach them that their choices matter by the way we respect them and discipline them. We respect our children when we let them make choices, honor their choices, and let them live with the consequences.

- *The goal of life is not necessarily to be happy, but to love God and to become good in the way God intended.*
- *They are children of God, made in His image, and their sexuality is His gift to them, meant to serve beautiful and wonderful purposes.*
- *God's law is a trustworthy guide for living, in the area of sexuality and in every area of life.*

Skills

Christians are used to thinking in terms of needs we must meet, purposes we must pursue, and beliefs we ought to embrace. We are not so used to thinking in terms of our skills, but many of the things we take to be permanent, inborn traits in people are actually learned skills. Think of the skill of throwing a baseball. The child watches parents and siblings throw, attempts to throw himself by trial and error, receives instruction from parents on how to do it better, and is praised (or criticized) by parents for his progress. Skills in listening or expressing care are developed in the same way.

Deliberately think about the kinds of skills that will help children to be effective, godly adults, and work hard to encourage those skills while they are young. As we said in our earlier example of the athlete in training, skills have both thinking and acting components; most skills are combinations of both.

In the example opening this chapter, Lindy must be able to think of possible things to do on the bus and decide among those options. She must then be able to act out the option she has chosen. If she can think of only two options — to let her boyfriend do anything he wants or, at the other extreme, to scream for help — her choices are impoverished. She really has many more options than those. If she has trouble choosing options, she will be paralyzed. Further, she must be able to act on her choices; if she has never before forcefully told another person, "You will not touch me and if you persist there will be consequences," then the very newness of such an action may make her unlikely to do it. Let's briefly examine a few key skills.

Empathy

We teach empathy through empathizing with our own children. We can help the young child to pay attention to what his friend is feeling when he has just taken that friend's favorite toy away from him. The capacity for empathy is critical in the area of sexual character because the child who is going to develop good friendships and have rewarding romantic relationships is one who can be sensitive and empathetic to others' feelings. Empathy also helps the child to better understand the consequences of sexual behavior. The consequences of adolescent sexual behavior are unlike anything else the child would ever have experienced. The child who can understand and empathize with the devastation of an unwanted pregnancy, with the guilt of a person who has had an abortion, or with the grief of a friend who finds out she is infertile because of an earlier sexually transmitted disease is going to be at less risk for sexual irresponsibility.

Interpersonal Strength or Assertiveness

Jesus had the strength to do what His Father called Him to do. He condemned hypocritical Pharisees, cleansed the temple, exhorted and rebuked His disciples, and fearlessly proclaimed the good news. Strength submitted to God's use and under God's control is a great virtue. We need to praise our children for speaking their minds, for asking questions, and for demonstrating their strength, teaching them to exercise this strength as God desires, especially in preserving their purity.

Self-Control

Children need to become less and less dependent on external factors, rules, and guides, and more dependent on the rules they have taken within themselves.

Delay of Gratification

Children need to learn that greater joy often comes through sacrificing immediate gratification of a desire for the sake of obtaining something much better later. Parents can teach this in many ways, but a child's handling of money is an excellent way to teach delay of gratification.

Relationship Skills

We can help our children learn to be good conversationalists and good listeners. We can teach them how to praise others honestly, to be abundant in expressing the positive. We can teach them how to share their opinions in a way that respects others but communicates confidence in themselves. We can teach them to be kind.

Decision Making

We can help our children to understand accurately the nature of the problems they confront, to generate alternative views of the problems, to brainstorm all possible solutions, and to evaluate the feasibility and possible outcomes of different responses to the problems.

Supports

When we think about character, we usually think about things inside the person. But what people do, and indeed who people are, is strongly influenced by their environment. The scientific research on sexual behavior of adolescents finds that another powerful predictor of whether or not a teen will be sexually active is what that teen's peers are doing. Sexually active peers put strong pressure on a teen to follow suit.

The Bible is realistic in recognizing this factor. On the negative side, "bad company corrupts good character" (1 Corinthians 15:33). On the positive side, many of the exhortations in the New Testament Epistles are targeted at shaping the interpersonal environments in which we live as Christians with the expectation that good relationships will help us be good people.

Strengthen Family Support

Begin by carefully attending to the family environment. Have you created an environment of love, respect, listening, affirmation, humor, and support? Remember, a close relationship between parent and child is one of the best predictors for the child acting responsibly in adolescence. A close, supportive relationship with the parent becomes a support that determines who that child is. Additionally, the supportive family helps to meet critical needs of the child, reinforces proper values and beliefs, and reinforces important skills.

Strengthen Peer Support

Peers and friends powerfully shape a child's environment. Because you care for your children, you will try to respectfully influence their choices of friends and the ways they spend time with those friends. You can try to channel your children's peer groups into productive and rewarding recreational activities as opposed to destructive pursuits. By finding a church and youth-group environment that is rewarding, healthy, supportive, and fun, you help your child to form supports properly. We can encourage some friendships and discourage others. We need to be extremely cautious in doing this, lest we manipulate our children or interfere in an inappropriate way.

Train Them to Shape Their Environments

Teach children how to shape their own environments. Actively train them how to recognize high-risk situations, to avoid them or get out of them early, and to develop the skills needed to deal effectively with such situations.

Lindy could have benefited from knowing that bus rides after dark can be pressure situations, from knowing how to negotiate limits on relationships early, and from having thought through how to resist sexual pressure. For children to do this, they must develop an understanding of their own limits and how to compensate for areas where they lack strength.

Your child's needs, values, beliefs, skills, and supports are the main elements of his or her character. Taking steps at each point in the parenting journey to shape these facets of character as God would desire is among the greatest gifts you can give your child. All of what we propose in what follows is structured around shaping each of these facets of character. As a parent, you can have a powerful influence on your child in each of these areas.

PART 2

The Cornerstone Years:

Infancy Through Kindergarten

CHAPTER 4

Biblical Foundations for Understanding Sexuality

It's for a specific purpose that we're starting this section on the cornerstone years with a discussion of the biblical foundations of human sexuality. We want to show parents how biblical teachings about all of life, but particularly about sexuality, have immediate implications for our parenting and for what we teach our children. So this chapter has two parts: a discussion of biblical truths and the application of those biblical truths to sex education with very young children.

There are four major "acts" in the biblical drama of God's dealing with His people: Creation, Fall, redemption, and glorification. The curtain has not been raised on the final act as yet. In this drama, we never finish an earlier act before we move into the next; rather, the new chapter unfolds as the previous act continues.

God began with His good work of Creation. The Fall marred the creation, but the reality of God's marvelous creation continues on. The Fall modifies it but never destroys it. Then, through Jesus Christ's birth, life, death, and resurrection, God's work of redemption intrudes on the drama and changes the reality of both creation and the Fall. God's redemptive work changes everything, and yet creation is still an underlying reality, as is the Fall. The glorification at the end of all things here on earth is yet to come, but the reality that God will make all things new changes our understanding of our existence here and now. Creation-Fall-redemption-glorification is an important order through which to see all of life, but it is also an essential part of seeing our sexuality through God's eyes.

This is the proper order for parents as well. In teaching children about sex, start with the fundamental reality of Creation. Then move through the effect of the Fall on creation and then to the healing effect Christ's work of redemption has on our sexuality. All along the way, we teach in light of the coming glorification. We are out of order if we start, as so many Christians do, with the Fall in teaching our children about sex. It's too easy to let teaching focus only on the dangers and evils of sex when it is misused. Equally tragic is starting and ending with Creation, as if sin were not a reality for each of us and we can simply trust all our instincts and follow all our whims.

Creation

Based on their struggles, guilt, shame, and ignorance, many Christians have grave doubts about the basic goodness of their physical bodies and of their sexuality. But while struggles, guilt, shame, ignorance, and doubt are real problems, they do not reflect the most fundamental truth about our physical existence or our sexuality. The fundamental truth is found in Creation. In the Creation story in Genesis 1 and 2, we find a set of rich and deep truths about our sexuality.

Physical Beings

First, we are physical beings by God's perfect design. God could have made the first human pair in some other way or out of some other material, but He made physical bodies for us. Many Christians think that "the real me" is an immaterial soul planted within a mere physical shell, but this is not the Christian view. Genesis 2:7-8 says, "The LORD God formed the man from the dust of the ground and breathed into his nostrils the breath of life, and the man became a living being." *Living being* literally means "soul," so this verse means that when God breathed life into the earthly body of Adam, the whole person of Adam, including his body, became a soul. Adam's body was an indispensable and good part of who he was. We do not just have bodies; we *are* bodies.

Three great Christian doctrines support positive attitudes about our bodies. The first is the doctrine of Creation. The second is the doctrine of the Incarnation, which teaches that Christ, the perfect Son of God, became flesh. And "since the children have flesh and blood, he too shared in their humanity" (Hebrews 2:14; see also John 1:14). If having a physical body were inherently bad, how could perfect holiness have taken on a body? Third, the doctrine of our coming resurrection teaches that we will live as bodies, perfected bodies, forever (see 1 Corinthians 15:35-44,53-54; Philippians 3:20-21).

Many Christians have a vague sense that their bodies are somehow bad or deficient. This seems to be a leftover of older Bible translations that warn us about the "flesh" being the enemy of the Spirit (Romans 8:6, RSV) and warn us against the "works of the flesh" (Galatians 5:19-21, RSV). Biblical scholars now recognize that it is not the body that is the enemy, but rather our tendency to rebel against God. Thus they are increasingly translating this term as "sinful nature" rather than "flesh." The sinful self is the whole person or any part of the person — body, mind, soul, emotions, spirit, will, heart — that is in rebellion against God. The spiritual self is the whole person or any part of the person — body, mind, soul, emotions, spirit, will, heart — that is submitted to God for His cleansing, direction, and enabling. And thus the body really is a gift from God on a par with all other parts of the person.

Sexual Beings

Second, Creation teaches us that our existence as specifically sexual beings, male and female, is good. "Male and female he created them" (Genesis 1:27), and then God declared it "very good" (verse 31). Scripture mentions at least four basic purposes of our sexuality: procreation, union, pleasure and gratification, and instruction.

Procreation. In Genesis 1:28, God blesses His precious creations by urging them to beget children. This truth forms the foundation for the positive Christian view of family as a fundamental unit of God's blessing. God made families!

Union. Genesis 2:24 points to the uniting power of sexual intercourse. Jesus makes this teaching the foundation of His instruction on marriage and divorce in Matthew 19 and Mark 10. In 1 Corinthians 6:12-20, the apostle Paul teaches explicitly that even casual sexual union such as visiting a prostitute results in the uniting of two strangers in some mysterious way. What is the meaning of the uniting of two persons in marriage? What does it mean for two individuals to become one flesh? Sadly but happily, this is and will remain a great mystery.

Physical pleasure and gratification. In 1 Corinthians 7:1-9, the apostle Paul speaks in the most matter-of-fact way about sexual need and the obligation of spouses to meet each other's needs. He speaks of the problem of burning with passion and how the physical pleasures of sex in marriage take care of those needs. The Bible speaks poetically of the beauty of physical love: "May your fountain be blessed, and may you rejoice in the wife of your youth. A loving doe, a graceful deer — may her breasts satisfy you always, may you ever be captivated by her love" (Proverbs 5:18-19). And of course the Song of Songs (or of Solomon) speaks powerfully of the delights of romantic love and physical rapture. God does not shy away from acknowledging the basic truth that sex feels great because He made it that way.

Instruction. We believe that God means to instruct us about His truth through our sexuality. Romans 1:20 speaks of aspects of God's divine nature being clearly seen in what He has made. In being made men and women who inevitably feel the urge for union with another whom we love, we learn experientially that we are incomplete in ourselves and that we need union with the Other to be truly ourselves. No marriage, no matter how wonderful, ever fully satisfies our need for completion, but through our sexuality, we are directed out beyond ourselves for that completion. And good Christian marriages in turn teach the world about God's love for His people by serving as earthly models of this heavenly truth (see Ephesians 5:25-33).

Relational Beings

Because we are physical, sexual beings, we are necessarily relational beings. In Genesis we read, "It is not good for the man to be alone" (2:18). We are made to love. In some mysterious way, we mirror God's capacity to be one and at the same time three (the doctrine of the Trinity) in our capacity to be separate people and yet united in marriage. In fact, when we combine the creational declaration that "a man will leave his father and mother and be united to his wife, and they will become one flesh" (2:24) with the promise of Jesus that "where two or three come together in my name, there am I with them" (Matthew 18:20; see also the discussion of abiding in Christ in John 15), we find a wonderful parallel: in Christian marriage, three (husband, wife, Christ) become one. In some mysterious way, the glue for this blessed union is the husband and wife's sexual union. Sexuality in general (including our distinctions as male and female and our inclination to love and to feel sexual longing) and sexual intercourse in particular were made good by God for His purposes and our benefit.

Fall

While many conservative Christians need to be reminded of a Creation foundation for our view of sexuality, we do not typically need to be reminded about the effects of the Fall. Adam and Eve rebelled against God, and their shame over their nakedness was the first and most immediate effect of the Fall from grace. Even though there was nothing wrong with their physical nakedness, they could not bear the vulnerability of nakedness before God or each other. Shame remains part of our fallen human heritage. Beyond shame over what we have done, we feel shame at what we are.

Immediately after Adam and Eve sinned, God told them that power struggles between the two of them — and between women and men forever — would be one of the legacies of their choices (see Genesis 3). The Fall brought the distortions of selfishness and pride into our sexual lives. Disease, increased pain in childbirth, and death also entered the world and our sexual relationships. We became people who could worship sex as an idol. We became capable of treating people as objects to be used for our selfish gratification. The motives of rebellion against God — greed, insecurity, anger, possessiveness, and more — became part of our experience, including our sexual experience. And we became capable of becoming enslaved to our lusts.

We are more than just physical, sexual, relational beings; we are also sinful beings. Truly our depravity is total. Our whole nature, including our sexual nature, is polluted by sin. Because we are broken, it was necessary that God reach down to save us, or we would be lost forever.

Redemption

God began His work of redemption by revealing to His people His will or rules for their lives. God gave these commands and decrees to us for our own good (see Deuteronomy 10:13). These rules accomplished two things. First, in our blindness, these commands showed us how we could honor God and live good lives. Without these rules for living, we would be blind slaves to our own sinful appetites, and human culture would be in chaos. Second, God's rules diagnose our sinfulness by offering objective measures that show us that our lives are off-kilter.

Then God offered His own dear Son to die for the forgiveness of our sins and thereby conquer death. Life in Christ through forgiveness of sins is the starting point for eradicating the effects of sin. This includes our sexuality. We are to sanctify our sexuality, to make it pure and clean, first by receiving forgiveness for what we have done wrong. We are to reclaim the good gift of our sexuality with thanksgiving (see 1 Timothy 4:1-5). And then, with the help of the Holy Spirit, we are to dedicate our lives to becoming more Christlike, to becoming more of the person God means each of us to be. And that includes the sexual dimension of each of us; we are to discover and shape our sexuality in the manner God intends for us. We are to accept and delight in the gift of our sexual nature. A major part of this book is dedicated to enabling us as parents to help our children be the sexual people God means them to be.

This work of redemption requires two-fold action on our part: turning away from sin and turning our lives over to God. We are to "flee from sexual immorality" but also to recognize that our bodies are the "temple of the Holy Spirit." Therefore, we are to "honor God with [our] bod[ies]" (1 Corinthians 6:18-20). God wants us to offer our sexuality to Him for His redemptive work.

Glorification

God will ultimately bring an end to life as we know it and move His dear children into the next and final stage of life. We will live in glorious and perfect fellowship with God, His angels, and all the saints who have ever lived. This life is a preparation for what is to come later. This makes an enormous difference in how we live our lives now.

First, the reality of our future glorification lets us know that we will never fully understand our lives here and now. Adults know what it is like to understand a broader context that our little children cannot. We have held them screaming while a doctor gave them the shot that made them well; we have held them tight to prevent them from chasing a ball into a busy street. They did not know why we did what we did, but we knew. Thankfully, much of God's will makes sense to us because He has revealed His truth in the Bible and placed the Holy Spirit in our hearts. Not all of it makes sense now, but it will. As the old song says, "We'll understand it all by and by." For now, we trust.

Second, our coming glorification teaches and encourages us to live in hope. Someday all our suffering and difficulties will be over. The apostle

Paul said, "I consider that our present sufferings are not worth comparing with the glory that will be revealed in us. . . . For in this hope we were saved. But hope that is seen is no hope at all. Who hopes for what he already has?" (Romans 8:18,24). Does obedience to God hurt sometimes? Does it cause us to deny ourselves what seems immediately gratifying? Of course. But this is small change in comparison to the treasure God offers us for eternity. And so in hope we live and teach our children to live.

Application of the Biblical Foundation

This biblical material has practical implications for shaping the sexual characters of our children in the early years. Earlier, we said that because the Bible starts with Creation, we should start there too. In these cornerstone years from infancy to kindergarten, we major on themes based on a creational understanding of our sexuality, namely,

- *We establish that our children are loved beyond measure by us, their parents, and by God, their heavenly Father.*
- *We teach them that God intended the family to be the primary arena for the experience of life-devotion, love, and unity.*
- *We develop their trust in God's law as reliable and good.*
- *We convince them that their physical bodies, their sexual natures, and their capacities for sexual pleasure are all good blessings from God.*

We will develop the first three in this chapter, and the last point in the next chapter.

"You Are Loved"

The foundation of all sex education is enabling your child to give and receive love. At the heart of Christian theology is the notion that our God is a relational God who loves and who imparted into His creation the capacity to love and be loved: "For God so loved the world" (John 3:16); "God is love" (1 John 4:16). Deuteronomy 6 suggests that the heart of parenting is to create a family environment where the truth of the faith will be incarnated, lived out, and made substantial and real in such a way that our children will find it natural to believe the gospel and live it.

The loving parent. Which is more convincing in teaching children that

God loves them: the distant, rigid, unemotional parent who forces a child to memorize "God is love" and other Bible verses while rarely embracing the child, or the loving parent who shares with a child the joys of God's love while holding and hugging that child, thus embodying God's love in a vivid way? A counselee of Stan's struggled with an obsessive preoccupation with sex but had a poor sexual relationship with his wife. He described his family like this: "It was a Christian home all right. We had Bible verses and 'God's rules' and hymns shoved down our throats at all hours. And through it all, I always knew that it wasn't me that mattered; it was the rules. I had to perform to meet up to the expectations, but no one cared about me. As long as I knew verses and was a 'good boy' I got approval. But neither my father nor my mother really cared about me; they never wanted to know what I thought after I spouted off a verse. If I expressed a doubt or asked a question, I was a 'bad boy' who had to get back in line. I never knew love. They wanted my performance, but not me."

Secure bonding. Many psychologists today emphasize the vital importance of the infant and toddler bonding with one or both parents, usually the mother. While the emotional availability of parents to their children is always important, probably there is no more crucial period than the first two years of life. Bonding or attachment seems to occur as a natural response to the parent's provision of loving affection, warmth, and gentleness. This bonding provides the basis of security from which the child can venture forth and explore the world. A child who is securely attached to the mother will frequently venture forth to explore his world and return after a short period for a time of "emotional refueling," followed by increasingly confident explorations. If this process is successful, the child emerges between eighteen and thirty-six months of age with a secure sense of identity.

Love shapes character. Is simply loving your child as an infant really a part of shaping your child's sexual character? Absolutely. Our sexuality is a part of our relational nature, our capacity to give and receive love. Learning to love and be loved in the family is the true bedrock of all sexual development. When you give children a secure base of trust from which to launch out into the world, you are preparing them for oneness in an eventual marriage.

Thankfully, parents do not have to meet their child's needs perfectly. One approach to psychology has coined the concept of being a "good enough" parent, a parent who is able to do a basically adequate job of meeting the child's needs. Parenting is like the weaving of a grand tapestry; there are no critical threads, but rather what matters is the overall shape the artwork takes. And in our original sketch of the character of the child, bonding forms the foundation for meeting your child's need for loving relatedness for the rest of life.

Our relationships with very young children bear a striking resemblance to the Creation and Fall stories, in which Adam and Eve lived in utter dependence on God and yet were given by God an existence and identity separate from Himself. They had the opportunity to choose. We live out in our families the same drama that occurred in the garden: We shower our children with love while allowing them, as they are able, to make choices that will shape their identities. We pray they will choose better than Adam and Eve. In this way they are separate in identity but connected and bonded to others through love and trust. In this loving family environment the child can grow to love God and others.

The Centrality of Family

A battle rages in our society to define *family*. For instance, proponents of gay rights are attempting to redefine a same-sex couple as a family that is just as legitimate as a heterosexual couple. Where should the line between family and nonfamily be drawn? This is a moral question of whether there is one ideal of what a family is meant to be or whether humans are free to define family as it suits their needs of the time.[1]

Scripture's picture of family. The thrust of Scripture is that God has an ideal for marriage and hence for families. That ideal is for one woman and one man to be united for life and for children to spring from that union. This is what God meant family to be. Other groupings of people do not fully represent the ideal. God designed marriage as an earthly model of the singular devotion of Christ and His church to each other (see Ephesians 5), a devotion that permanently unites two different but equal and complementary types of beings (Christ and His people; a man and a woman).

Family — the ideal type of family God means people to experience — is thus important to God as the primary place where He intends us to learn and experience love, devotion, and union. We need to teach this courageously, but not arrogantly, to our children. We need to teach them that if God should will to bless them with a family, it is His intent that it take place in the context of marriage. We should extol the benefits and goodness of this path of life.

At the same time, we should not in arrogance deny that some people experience much that is good in other family structures. Many people have no choice in living in other family forms. Many divorced parents never would have chosen that way of life had other options been possible. Few singles are unmarried by deliberate effort, and few childless couples are childless by choice. Others are in nontraditional families because of choices that in retrospect they recognize to have been wrong (for example, the teenage single mother). We should celebrate the good that God can work in those families. Even more, as believers we have the obligation to help those people experience as much of God's blessing as possible by supporting, helping, and loving them and teaching our children to do the same.

Teachable moments for the family. Perhaps the best way to teach these lessons is to seize upon teachable moments at weddings, confirmations, or baptisms; upon hearing of a divorce in the neighborhood; upon seeing a gay couple holding hands in public; or when interacting with children from single-parent homes. We can use these times to talk about God's ideal. We can teach our children that their heart desire, which they will increasingly recognize as they grow, is to have one special other person with whom they can share life permanently, and that this is a good desire. We can teach them that the desire for oneness and union will not be met the way God meant it to be in cohabitation, a homosexual "marriage," or any other arrangement that is outside God's ideal will. We can also use these times to talk about how we should think about arrangements that do not meet that ideal. In doing so, we should have the humility to admit that our own traditional families always fall short of God's ideal as well, so no one is in a position to boast.

God's Law Is a Trustworthy Guide

In disciplining our young children, we want to teach them to trust God and God's law. We want to teach them the value of obedience to that law. We do this by trusting God ourselves, by teaching God's rules, and by explaining, defending, and praising those rules. Even more broadly, we want to reenact in our families God's redemptive dealings with us, His children. The heart of Christian faith is rooted in our responsiveness to God's love for us — our realization of our sin, confession of that sin to God, and receiving from God forgiveness and restoration of our relationship with Him. Even when we extend forgiveness to each other and from God, the consequences of sin still follow. Asking for forgiveness for having gossiped does not erase the broken relationships and hurt feelings our actions created.

This is the drama we should reenact in our discipline. Make every act of discipline with your child an opportunity to understand how God loves, forgives, and disciplines us. If you as a parent simply spank a child for doing something wrong and are done with the discipline, you miss a wonderful opportunity to teach your child about God's love for her or him.

We have tried in our own family never to let our children have a moment to doubt how deeply they are loved. When they did something wrong, our relationship was fractured, but not broken. We confronted the wrong and asked them to acknowledge (confess) it. We insisted that our children label what they did as wrong. We briefly explained why it was wrong, hopefully explaining how God's rules make sense. We might have said something like this:

"Jennifer, I want you to tell me what you did wrong."

"I took Brandon's toy."

"Yes, and what else?"

"I lied to you about doing it."

"Was that the right thing to do?"

"No, it was wrong and mean, and I'm really sorry."

When they said they were sorry, we then offered our forgiveness. "I'm glad you said that, Jennifer. It is right to confess when we have done a bad thing. That's how God wants us to be honest with Him when we do bad things, and He will always love us and forgive us just like I love and forgive you." The consequence then followed: a spanking, a time-out, a loss of privileges. After that, we sought to wholeheartedly return to a normal relationship without holding a grudge or punishing them by rejection. We tried to make this reconciliation a time of close affection, hugging and comforting our children to make the reconciliation feel real.

We hoped that by reenacting daily the biblical drama of confession-forgiveness-discipline-reconciliation in small ways in our family, we were laying the groundwork for our children to instinctively know the truth of the gospel as revealed in the Scriptures. Life in our family, hopefully, thus became a living lesson in God's truth.

CHAPTER 5

Teaching the Goodness of Our Sexuality

Jen was from a family that never talked about sex. Her parents treated the whole area of sexuality as a shameful and unfortunate aspect of life. She and her husband, Roger, were happy by and large, and she genuinely respected his integrity and commitment to the Lord. They hardly ever talked about their sexual relationship. Sex for her was not unpleasant, but it was not the rapturous experience she had expected. But she was ecstatic to be a new mother of a beautiful little baby boy. Little Luke, six weeks old, was the joy of her life.

But there was a dark cloud in her life. She had begun to notice that her little infant often had erections when he was nursing. She had first noticed it when he had done a BM in his diaper while nursing, and she had rushed to change him, interrupting the feeding. When she opened the diaper, her little one clearly had an erection. Since then, out of concern, she had touched his crotch briefly during nursing and found several times that he had one again.

What did this mean? Was this normal? She had thought that boys did not begin to get sexual until puberty. How should she feel about it? Was she doing something wrong to cause him to react this way?

The Beginnings of Sexual Development

Your child spent nine months developing in the womb before you ever got to hold him in your arms or see him with your own eyes. His gender was set at the moment of conception, depending on whether a Y-chromosome sperm (male) or an X-chromosome sperm (female) from the father fertilized the ovum contributed by the mother, which contained an X chromosome. Though the gender was set from conception, male and female fetuses are indistinguishable until approximately after the first trimester of fetal development.

Sexual Differences

From about the fifth to seventh week of fetal life, male and female children develop identical genital structures, which scientists call the genital mound. It is a bump, almost a wart, that at first looks identical for male and female fetuses. The first change that begins to distinguish boys and girls is the conversion of identical little internal buds of tissue into the ovaries in a girl and the testes in a boy. After these sex glands are formed, the genital organs begin to form. From about the seventh or eighth week through about the midpoint of life within the womb, an amazing transformation occurs. The exact same tissues in the genital mound (nerves, muscles, skin) are transformed into the head of the penis in a boy and the head of the clitoris in a girl, the shaft of the penis in a boy and the shaft of the clitoris in a girl, the scrotum in a boy and the labia in a girl. By the final stage of pregnancy, a normal child's external sexual anatomy matches the identity of its gonads (ovaries or testes) and its chromosomes.

Gendered Brains

The brains of boys and girls are different from early development on, though we are just beginning to understand the differences. Most likely the same hormones that influence the differentiation of the genitals also cause the brains of boys and girls to develop with slight but important differences. At the very minimum, these differences prepare the female's brain to regulate her periods of menstruation and fertility later in life, while a boy's brain lacks such cyclical regulating structures. Other more complicated gender-based behavior patterns may be influenced by brain development during the time in the womb.

Children Are Sexual Beings

Because of brain structures and their genitals, it is indisputable that our children are sexual beings, even in the womb. Ultrasound studies corroborate this by suggesting that male children may even experience erections of the penis inside the womb before birth. The infant is a sexual being after birth as well. It is not uncommon, for instance, for an infant boy to experience an erection within moments of birth and while breast-feeding. Similarly, scientific studies have suggested that it is not uncommon for infant girls to experience the feminine signs of sexual arousal (firming of the clitoris and vaginal lubrication) during nursing. Boys will experience periodic erections throughout their childhoods, frequently if they touch themselves for pleasure, but even if they do not. These will become more frequent during and after puberty. It appears that girls similarly experience regular vaginal lubrication, though they can be quite unaware of this, especially if they have never heard that this happens.

Because of this, Jen needn't worry about her infant Luke's erections. Even as a baby, he is a sexual creature. Young children probably respond with sexual reactions such as erection or vaginal lubrication because they respond as whole beings to any pleasure they experience. God made each of our children to be a sexual being. He made our bodies sexual in indisputable ways by His divine will, and He called our sexuality very good. Thus our vital task as parents is to pass on to our children the same blessing God gave to Adam and Eve — knowing that the goodness of God's work in them is deeper and more fundamental than the sin that afflicts them.

Be First to the Story

We should talk to our children about these realities. This brings us to our next principle of Christian sex education:

Principle 3:
First messages are the most potent.

By seizing opportunities to share with your children God's perspectives on their developing sexuality, you build their beliefs around God's truth rather than the world's distortions. This also establishes you, the parent, as a trusted authority who tells them the truth.

The Story of Me, the first book in the GOD'S DESIGN FOR SEX series, is a resource for parents in starting the conversation about sexuality with their child during the ages of three to five. If you have a track record of dealing comfortably with sexuality, conversations on this topic may be commonplace. But your child may not be comfortable yet in talking with you, so reading *The Story of Me* with your child may well get this conversation going. This can then lead to wonderful casual conversations like the following.

While soaping himself during his bath, four-year-old Kevin gets an erection.

CHILD: Daddy, why does my penis get hard like this sometimes?

PARENT: Well, God made us men so that our penises are very sensitive. It feels good to touch them sometimes. When your penis starts to feel good, a little extra blood from other parts of your body goes into your penis, and that makes it get a bit bigger and harder.

CHILD: Is it a bad thing?

PARENT: No, not at all. God made you that way. It's just part of being a man.

Positive Response

Parents can't do anything to stop their children from being sexual. If Jen were to respond negatively to her child for being sexual (spanking him, rejecting him by withholding attention, or some other punishment), the trauma to her child would be significant. She would be punishing him for being how God made him — a sexual child. She would be teaching him to repress or reject an aspect of himself that God gave him as a gift. At these earliest ages, the child needs no verbal comment or particular response from the parent. Luke doesn't even know he has a penis! But he can sense whether Jen loves him or if she is hesitant, withdrawn, or rejecting. Early on is the time for you to work on your own responses to the child's sexuality. When you are changing diapers, look at your child's genitals and say a prayer of thanksgiving that God made that child sexual. Be honest with yourself and with God about any negative or ambivalent feelings you have. Resolve to do something about those feelings by reading, praying, or talking with someone who can help.

Not only children are sexual; parents are too. We as parents may need to receive for ourselves a grace and acceptance similar to what we want to give our kids. We are not always comfortable with our own sexual reactions. For example, a woman's breasts are richly endowed with pleasure sensors that are connected to the healthy woman's sexual responsiveness. Many women experience breast-feeding to be pleasurable (after getting over the initial uncomfortable adjustment period), and it is not at all uncommon for mothers to experience sexual arousal from the stimulation of nursing. This may be akin to the way a man may experience any stimulation of his penis as arousing even when he doesn't want to be aroused. A father holding a squirming child in his lap may begin to get an erection when he does not feel erotic feelings toward his child. In all such cases, it is vital that the mother or father be honest and realistic in admitting to himself or herself that sexual arousal is occurring. Be clear about what is causing those feelings and what they mean. Such responses are not sinful or depraved; they are one more manifestation of how we are all sexual beings.

Teaching Goodness by Teaching Words

Direct sex education of our children begins with naming body parts. We teach our kids that they have elbows, chins, eyes, fingers. Why do we then teach them that they have woo-woos and ding-dings? God made sexual organs with the same degree of deliberateness and perfect divine intent as He made all other parts of our kids' bodies. Teach your child basic proper names for sexual organs. Teach boys that they have a penis and scrotum (the skin/muscle bag under the penis) and that inside the scrotum they have two testes (or testicles; singular: testis or testicle).

Labeling female genitals is a bit harder, because the proper name for the entire external genital area, vulva, tends to be less commonly used than any other proper name. It does not help that most of the slang terms for female genitals are quite negative, unattractive, and even degrading to women. You can teach a girl that all the genitals she can see are the vulva, or you can teach just the significant parts for this age, which are the labia and the vagina. To see her own vagina, the girl will need to sit down and either use a mirror or be able to bend over. You can explain that while urine does come out of a boy's penis, it does not come out of her vagina; her urine comes out of a small and hard-to-see opening just up from her vagina. A girl may discover and ask about her clitoris, located just above her urinary opening. You can tell her, "That is your clitoris; God made that part of you to give you good feelings, especially when you are a grown and married woman." We will discuss touching and self-pleasuring in the next chapter.

Teaching Goodness by Sharing Our Praise to God

In teaching children about their own bodies, emphasize that their bodies are beautiful works of art that they can thank God for. Their own bodies should be "received with thanksgiving" (1 Timothy 4:3). When our own children were young, we tried to encourage them to an early sense of thankfulness by playing "What's that? Who made that?" It went like this: "What's that?" "That's my chin!" "Who made that?" "God did!" "That is a beautiful chin! I love that chin! What's that?" "That's my penis!" "Who made that penis? Did the doctor?" "No, God did!" "That's right, and God made your penis just right; it is beautiful! And what's that? . . ."

Bath times are also great opportunities to affirm the beautiful creation of our children's bodies. "I'm so glad that God made you a boy, Billy. God made you wonderfully." As parents, we can show our children our honest wonder as we consider the complex miracle that is the human body. We can help them to be full of thanksgiving because we are filled with deep gratitude and appreciation of who God made them to be. We can say, "What a beautiful body God has given you!" We can touch them in appreciation and wonder, but also teach them the privacy of their genitals by not touching them there except to wash or care for them when injured.

Goodness and Touch

Some women grow up never touching themselves on the genitals. These women tend to grow up unaware of themselves sexually and to have difficulty in their sexual relationships in marriage. Many a young girl has been taught that her vagina is dirty; after all, she bleeds from there. Some women have been taught to wipe themselves with tissue, wash themselves with a washrag, and never touch their labia, vaginas, or clitorises directly at all. By comparison, boys have to handle their genitals in the process of urinating and in bathing and often seem to be much more comfortable with and accepting of their genitals.

Teaching young girls never to touch themselves is destructive. The woman's genitals are not dirty. Medical studies have suggested that in terms of germs, the healthy vagina is about as clean as or cleaner than the mouth. Through its secretions, the vagina cleans itself. Teaching a girl not to touch herself alienates her emotionally and experientially from her own sexuality and promotes ignorance and a sense of dirtiness that will have destructive effects in the long run. We should teach girls that their genitals are a beautiful creation by the Master Artist and are one of God's gifts to them.

Explaining Reproduction, Pregnancy, and Childbirth

Explain basic reproduction to children at an early age. Even before age three, most children can understand that babies grow inside the mommy's belly until they are too big for the mommy to carry anymore, and then the mommy goes to the hospital so that the doctors there can help the baby come out of the mommy's belly through her vagina. The following dialogue might be typical for a young child of four:

> **PARENT:** That's right. Sue went into the hospital today to have her baby; she might even be having it right now.
>
> **CHILD:** Mommy, is the baby really in her belly?
>
> **PARENT:** Yes, though the baby is not in her stomach where the food goes. Right below her stomach, every woman has a uterus or womb. You have a womb too, Caitlin. It is right down inside here [touches Caitlin between her navel and her genitals], and do you know how big it is? Make a fist with your hand; good — it's about that big and it's inside of you. Every baby — Sue's baby and you when you were a baby — starts out very tiny, as tiny as a speck like this [points to a tiny crumb on the kitchen counter] inside the mommy's womb and then grows over nine months into a baby who stretches the womb and the mommy's whole tummy to be as big as Sue's tummy was!
>
> **CHILD:** Doesn't it hurt to grow that big?
>
> **PARENT:** Well, sometimes it doesn't feel great, but it happens very slowly, and that helps, and mommies love their babies a lot and that helps. And God made women like me and like you in the most amazing way so our bodies can stretch out and hold a baby. It is even more amazing to me that the babies can come out through our vaginas.
>
> **CHILD:** My vagina is too small for that!
>
> **PARENT:** Well, it certainly is now. But God made you so that when you are

bigger, and pregnant, you will be able to have a baby come out there because those muscles can stretch really big to let a baby through. It hurts quite a bit, but you love the baby so much you are glad to do it, and you are so happy to have the baby that the pain is well worth it. When I held you, I didn't think much about any hurt that I had.

CHILD: I hope Sue doesn't hurt too much from having the baby.

PARENT: Me too. Maybe when Sue gets back from the hospital she will show you how the baby drinks milk from her breasts. Another wonderful thing that God made women like you and me able to do is to feed our babies right from our own bodies. Your breasts are little right now, but later they will get bigger, and when you have a baby, they are ready to make milk for your baby. Sue is planning to feed her baby by letting him nurse from her breasts. That's what I did with you and with your brother.

Positive Anticipation of Sexual Growth

Help your children to view positively the development of what doctors call "secondary sex characteristics." These are the various changes other than genital structure that distinguish men from women after puberty. Young women experience growth of the breasts and pubic hair (as well as leg and armpit hair) and develop an adult female body form, including wider hips. Young men experience growth of the penis, scrotum, and pubic, facial, and body hair; a general growth spurt; and deepening of the voice. You can anticipate these positively for the child.

CHILD: Dad, why do you have hair on your chest and everywhere while I only have hair on my head?

PARENT: Well, if you look closely, you have hair on your arms, legs, and all over your body. When the time is right, though, your hair will start to grow in many places, and it will get darker and thicker. This will happen some on your arms and legs, but especially on your face, where you will someday be able to grow a beard, and especially right over your penis. In fact, growing hair right over your penis is one of the first signs that you are beginning to change from being a boy to being a man.

CHILD: But what if I'm not ready to become a man?

PARENT: [Laughs] Well, God knows when you're ready, even if it seems a little scary now. He made your body so that it just starts to change whether you think you're ready or not. And don't worry; I want to help you during the time you are becoming a man. I'll gladly tell you anything you want to know, and I'll talk with you about what it feels like. This is exactly what God wants for you; it's an exciting and wonderful thing.

Many a parent has grown up in a family that treats sexual development negatively. Whether it is a talk about "the curse" (menstruation) or derogatory talk about men as sexual animals or women as sexual objects, these sorts of ideas can be very confusing and disheartening to children. We must strive as Christians to have the attitudes toward our wondrous bodies that God Himself has.

Teaching at a Teachable Moment

The best sex education parents can give their children may not occur during premeditated lessons. Rather it happens during special moments when children are naturally interested in finding out about sex — optimally, when they themselves initiate the conversation by asking a question. At such moments, discussion and instruction mesh naturally with the events and needs of daily life. When you respond well, your child comes to see you as an askable parent whom he or she can come to with questions. Thus our next principle is this:

Principle 4:
We should seize those teachable moments and become askable parents.

A well-rounded ability to instruct kids about sex has three major components: initiating instruction, taking advantage of teachable moments, and responding to questions.

Initiating Instruction

The first component is the parent-initiated instruction session; you have something you want your child to understand, and so you tell the child.

These do not have to be dour discussions in front of a chalkboard, but can be lively and interesting. The key is that you initiate them because it is time for the child to know about some subject. The four books in our GOD'S DESIGN FOR SEX series provide parents with the tools to get such conversations started and to cover the essential, age-appropriate material with their child.

Taking Advantage of Teachable Moments

The second component is the use of the teachable moment. When you seize a teachable moment, you move spontaneously from an event into a related teaching opportunity. The event may be a beer commercial during a ball game, bath time, toilet training, a neighbor who is obviously pregnant, baby-sitting lessons that lead an older child to watch while you are changing a diaper, seeing a woman breast-feeding her baby, unusual genitals on a zoo animal ("Mommy, what is that?! Is it sick?"), a neighborhood dog mounting and thrusting on a child's leg, or an innocent report of a dirty joke going around that the child does not understand. In a teachable moment, you seize the moment to teach your child.

A father rounds the corner in his home to find his four-year-old girl sitting in the middle of her room naked and bent over looking at her vaginal opening. She has her fingers pulling apart her labia. As she hears him, she suddenly sits upright and looks guilty. This is a situation that would be very easy to pass over, to ignore, or to let his wife deal with. But how could this be a teaching opportunity?

PARENT: Hi! What were you looking at?

CHILD: Nothing . . . [a look of guilt and embarrassment]

PARENT: Were you looking at your vagina? That is a fine thing to look at, you know.

CHILD: No . . . yeah.

PARENT: It really is a wonderful part of you to look at and to understand. Do you know why? Because God made that part of you just like He made the rest of you. Who made that vagina?

CHILD: God did!

PARENT: And do you know what your vagina is for? It is so amazing that God made you so that some day, if you marry and God blesses you with children, a baby will live and grow in your tummy for nine months and then come out through your vagina so that you can hold it and nurse it and love it like we love you.

CHILD: Does Tammy [a neighbor who had just given birth] have a vagina? Is that where her baby came out?

PARENT: Yes, that's right. And do you know if boys have vaginas?

CHILD: No, they don't. They have penises.

PARENT: That is exactly right. Boys are blessed by God to have penises, but girls are blessed by God with vaginas. Boys will never know what it means to have a baby grow inside and then to let it out through a vagina. Do you ever want to have a baby?

CHILD: Yes, I do!

Responding to Questions

When the parent has proved himself or herself as being capable of talking about sex with some degree of comfort, children will begin asking questions. Responding to and encouraging questions is the third vital part of a well-rounded capacity to do sex education in the home. It is vital to encourage questions, to praise kids lavishly for asking questions. This should be easy to do, because there are few greater gifts than having a child who will bring his or her questions to you. But typically you must earn this gift by establishing a track record.

Your child happens to find a used sanitary pad in the trash with a little blood leaked through. The mother simply takes the opportunity to explain menstruation.

CHILD: Mom, what is that? Is someone bleeding? Did someone cut themselves?

PARENT: No, honey. That blood came out of my vagina. But I'm not sick or cut. Do you know why that happened? It is because I'm having what women call "my period" right now.

CHILD: Your period? What's that?

PARENT: You know how God made all women so that they can carry a baby in their tummy, in their womb? Well, the baby needs some way to get food and air for the nine months it is in there, and the baby gets both from the mommy's blood. But I don't have a baby in my tummy right now. God made women so that when they're old enough to get a baby in their tummy, every month they get a little extra blood in their womb just in case a little baby starts to grow in there. That way the baby will have food and air. But if there is no baby, the extra blood just comes out so that new fresh blood can be ready the next month if a baby comes then. So I bleed just a little every month, and that's what a period is.

CHILD: Does it hurt? It always hurts when you bleed!

PARENT: Well, it doesn't hurt like a cut hurts. But it doesn't always feel great either. It might hurt a bit for a couple of days, but it's not too bad. I'm just so glad that God made my body in such a special way that I can carry a baby inside of me and take care of it, like I did for you. That's a real miracle! And my period every month reminds me of what a miracle my body is. Yours too!

But What If I Don't Know the Answer?

Parents are often daunted by the prospect of being asked questions they can't answer. To deal with this concern, we suggest first you be prepared to say, "Well, I don't know the answer to that, but how about if I try to find out and tell you in the next few days?" Then it's vital that you follow through with that commitment. Second, we suggest you be listening for the opportunity to instruct the child from God's perspective on sexuality. The questions most likely to stump you are the detailed questions about the functioning of the human body and the miracle of reproduction. Remember, this is the type of information least likely to really matter to your children in the long run. What really matters is the sexual character you are helping to build. When a child asks a question, never miss the opportunity to build character by sharing God's perspective, even if you don't know the factual answer to the question.

Five-year-old Billy raises a perplexing question after seeing his younger sister nurse:

CHILD: Dad, how do a mother's breasts make milk?

PARENT: You know, I really don't understand it myself. I know every woman has little things called milk glands or ducts in her breasts that make the milk. I guess they take water, protein, sugar, and other things the baby needs out of the mother's blood and mix them together in a new way to make the milk. What amazes me is that God made women so that the milk they make for their babies is the perfect food for them. It's one of God's ways to show His love for the baby by taking such good care of him or her.

CHILD: What do you mean, it's the perfect food?

PARENT: Well, did you know that during the first few days after a baby is born, the mother's breasts don't make milk at all? They make a liquid that is like medicine for the baby. This helps make it much harder for the baby to catch any sickness. That stuff protects the baby. After that, the mother's milk is better for the baby than anything else. Cow milk is perfect for cow babies, goat milk for goat babies, and human milk for human babies. Each kind of milk gives that kind of baby just what the baby needs. God knows so well how to take care of us perfectly; that's why it is so important that we trust what He tells us in the Bible. God loves us and wants to make our lives good.

Preserving Manners and Privacy

Occasionally, after a discussion of human reproduction, the curious child might ask the mother very pointedly, "Where did I come out of you? Show me!" Such a question presents a parent with a wonderful opportunity to teach the child basic sexual manners without discouraging curiosity. The best answer to this is for the mother to say, "No, my vagina is a private part of me that I share only with your father. Your vagina is a private part of you too. Mommy and Daddy only touch you there to wash you. But I will draw a picture [or show you a picture in a book] that can show you what that part of a woman looks like." This matter-of-fact way of dealing with this request can be quite beneficial for a child.

Parents often are concerned about the issue of nudity in the home. Family traditions in this area range from paranoia about anyone seeing anyone, resulting in locked doors and frantic screams for kids to get clothes on, to almost social nudity that seems founded in a naive disregard for any possible negative fallout from such practices. And the biblical virtues of modesty and concern for chastity are difficult to apply because standards of modesty vary from culture to culture. Our highly conservative, restrained, and modest friends here in Wheaton would have been branded as profligate exhibitionists had they worn discreet one-piece swimsuits publicly just fifty years ago.

We have no certain answer to this dilemma. But we do regard the concerns on each end of the spectrum as legitimate. On the one hand, overly restrictive attitudes about nudity are dangerous. They communicate that our sexuality is suspect at best and dangerous at worst and that people's responses to our bodies are not to be trusted even within our own families. On the other hand, overly casual attitudes about nudity fail to help the child to learn appropriate boundaries for his or her own sexuality and do not encourage a proper sense of privacy. Further, inappropriate nudity can prematurely sexualize a child. An overemphasis on or unconscious encouragement of the child's visual examination of other members of the family can lead to inappropriate curiosity or even fondling, excesses we should guard against. We would recommend that parents not obsessively guard against seeing family members naked, but also that nudity not be flaunted in the family. Within those broad parameters is room for freedom of choice based on personal comfort levels.

The Power of Stories

Have you ever stopped to ponder why the biblical revelation is given predominantly in the "story" mode rather than the "teaching of principle" mode? Have you ever wondered why Jesus Himself spent so much time on parables and stories when He could have been spinning out detailed systematic theology and ethics? Though the apostle Paul taught largely by principle, Christ and most of the Old Testament writers relied more on stories. This probably reflects the power that stories have in our lives. For example, we need principles such as "flee sexual immorality," but we probably need stories such as Joseph fleeing from Potiphar's wife just as much. Stories are a vital way we can surround our children with symbols and reminders of the faith. This is our fifth principle:

Principle 5:
Stories are powerful teaching tools.

Stories can get into our souls, whereas cold statistics and facts and principles never seem to have quite that effect. This helps to explain the powerful effect of the media, which almost always presents stories that communicate their message. And herein lies the greatest danger of the media: it often presents powerful stories that distort the truth.

Stories are an especially powerful way of teaching values, and we should use them lavishly in sex education in the home. We can be swept up into the power of a story, and in taking it into our hearts, we take in the values of that story as well. Stories teach both positively and negatively. Positively, stories have heroes children can identify with and present vivid pictures of positive values and virtues. Stories also have villains and teach about human vices and failings. Both positive and negative stories, and the positive and negative aspects of a single story, are vitally important. Use stories to foster discussion about character, values, beliefs, morals, integrity.

Stories come in many forms: books, movies, plays, songs. Our foundation, of course, is the stories of the Bible. We have tried to make the Bible stories of faith come alive to our children by reading, discussing, and even enacting them. Immerse your family in the lives of the saints of the Scriptures. Picture or story Bibles also help the stories of the Scriptures come alive for young children. Talk about these stories; make the characters come alive by imagining what they were thinking and feeling. Apply the lessons from the lives of the saints to our lives today by asking kids questions about the lessons of the stories. Besides the story of Joseph and Potiphar's wife (Genesis 39), important Bible stories that teach important lessons about sexuality include Adam and Eve (Genesis 1–4), Jacob and Rachel (Genesis 29), David and Bathsheba (2 Samuel 11), Solomon and his many wives (1 Kings 11), the noble woman of Proverbs 31, the Song of Songs (or of Solomon) love poem, and many others.

But we should not think only in terms of biblical stories. Our own children benefited from the great stories we find in literature. Reading with our children was a family ritual. Christian and nonreligious fiction that expresses the eternal values of our faith is a great resource. For example, we read through C. S. Lewis's *The Chronicles of Narnia* several times, as well as other works of fiction by Christians, such as *The Archives of Anthropos* book series by John White, J. R. R. Tolkien's *The Hobbit* and *The Lord of the Rings*, and others. Nonreligious fiction like the *Little House on the Prairie* series or Lloyd Alexander's *The Chronicles of Prydain* was wonderful in fostering discussions of virtue and honor. A number of helpful guides to children's literature can serve to inspire and guide you in your selection of literature; talk to your librarian or bookstore staff about books that can help build character.

Movies are useful story resources as well. We tried to select movies with some degree of care, searching for those with enduring values that we hoped to promote. The images of these and many more stories are imprinted on the hearts of our children.

Finally, do not forget your own stories and those of your families and friends. Some of the most powerful stories for our kids were from our own lives. You have had many experiences, some that you have not thought about in years but that could serve to instruct your kids about the roles of love and sexuality in their lives before God. Tell stories about the lives of your extended families: the faithful loves, divorces and affairs, triumphs and brokenness. Tell them about going through puberty, your first crush, first date, worst and best relationships, falling in love with your spouse, and about what it is like to love your children. Your own stories will have a powerful effect. Stories have a power to move the human spirit and to imprint values and truths, a power that mere logical lessons cannot approach. We must carefully choose the stories that are shaping our children's lives.

Deuteronomy 6 teaches us to strive to shape our children to accept the faith of Abraham and Moses, of Peter and Paul — a saving faith in the one Lord God and His Son, Jesus Christ. Three elements of family life are absolutely critical: our personal obedience to God as parents; our communication or teaching of His law, His truth, to our kids; and our immersing their lives in stories and reminders about the faith. Don't forget the stories!

CHAPTER 6

Handling Sexual Curiosity and Other Challenges

Curt has a bad back that sometimes makes him stoop over in pain. His physician recommended back rubs with a vibrator. One evening, he could hardly move. He kicked himself mentally for having helped that neighbor load his moving van. Dana, his wife, volunteered to rub his back with the vibrator to try to relieve the pain and allow him to be able to move tomorrow. Their three-year-old, Susie, watched with great interest, making frequent comments: "I love you, Daddy. Does it hurt bad? I'm sorry. Mommy, what is that thing you're rubbing on Daddy? Does that feel good, Daddy?"

After the back rub, Dana helped Curt get off the bed and go into the bathroom.

When they walked back into the bedroom, they stood paralyzed. Little Susie had turned on the television and was calmly watching a children's program, sitting with the vibrator between her legs, turned on, pressed against her genitals.

"Susie, does that feel good?" stammered Dana.

"Yes, Mommy, it really feels good. Daddy was right, it feels real good," Susie replied.

Sexual Pleasure — A Good Gift from God

Curt and Dana found out that even three-year-olds know their genitals can be a source of physical pleasure. Children learn the location of their genitals just as they learn about other parts of their bodies. Infants experience touching or rubbing of their genitals as pleasurable; some children even develop patterns of deliberate self-stimulation (what we call masturbation in adolescents and adults) during the first year of their lives.

The foundation for talking with our children about curiosity and sex play is an extension of our discussion in chapter 5 on the goodness of our physical bodies and our sexuality. If our bodies are the result of a divine act of creation by God, then our capacity for sexual pleasure is a divine gift. Our task is to help our children to see sexual pleasure as a gift. However, we have the potential to abuse that gift as a result of the Fall, so we also need to teach our kids to enjoy the gift in the way the Creator intended.

Why So Young?

Why talk to children about sexual pleasure at a relatively young age? Because your best chance of influencing their beliefs will come from being the one who forms the bedrock of their thinking about sexuality. We have already offered this as one of our major principles: First messages are the most potent. It is far more powerful to form a child's view of sexuality from scratch than it is to correct the distortions the child will pick up in the world. Why wait until your child learns some distorted view of sexual pleasure on the school playground or from a pornographic video at a neighbor's house? Why risk your child misunderstanding your views because all he or she hears from you is silence? Parents must lay the foundation. We should have the first say when our influence is greatest and our children's trust of us is highest.

Designed for Pleasure

Our sexual organs are made for pleasure by God's design. The clitoris of the woman is exquisitely sensitive and pleasurable, and it serves no known purpose other than to give the woman pleasure from her marriage relationship. By all indications, the pleasure afforded by our sexuality is a gift, pure and simple, from God! And this is how we should describe it to our children. But we should go further; we should describe it as a gift for which the Gift-Giver has a purpose in mind.

Cindy and Bill placed three-year-old Steve in the tub with the warm water running vigorously out of the tap. They were chatting quietly, focusing on each other, when they began to hear squeals and saw Steve holding his penis under the running water and grinning with delight. Oblivious to his parents, Steve stepped back from the water, looked down at his penis with wonder, and then stepped back to the tap so that the water ran over his penis again, resulting in more squeals. Bill drew a deep breath, and then turned off the water and used this teachable moment.

PARENT: You were running the water over your penis.

CHILD: [Steve nods, unsure of how his dad is going to react.]

PARENT: I heard you laughing. Were you laughing because it felt so good?

CHILD: Yeah, it felt funny!

PARENT: It really does feel funny and good. Did you know that God made your penis that way, so that it could make you feel really good?

CHILD: He did?

PARENT: Yes, it's true. And do you know why God did that? Because when you grow up and marry, God wants you to be able to share some wonderful fun with your wife and only your wife. God wanted to give you a way to love her and her a way to love you that is so special it will help to hold the two of you together like you are glued together! So every time you think about your penis feeling good, you can think of how God made it that way as a special gift to you to make you happy.

It's good for the child to discover that the genitals are made for pleasure. This gives the parent the opportunity to put that gift in its right perspective. God made and gave the gift, but He means for us to use it in a certain way. We agree with secular sex educators who warn parents that it can harm children to shame, criticize, or even punish them for discovering that their bodies are a source of pleasure. This can program doubts and negative reactions into the child's earliest understandings of himself or herself. It's one thing to teach manners; it's another to punish a positive experiencing of sexual pleasure. But many of these secular experts go too far in celebrating the discovery of sexual pleasure by not properly establishing boundaries on sexual play and self-stimulation.

Handling Sexual Curiosity and Play

How should we respond when we find our dear little one playing doctor in the basement or peeing together with four other little boys in a secluded spot in the backyard or negotiating "show me yours and I'll show you mine" in her bedroom with the child from next door?

The single most important principle is not to exaggerate the importance of the incident, but instead to use it as a teaching opportunity about the privacy of your child's body and what a blessed gift and miracle that body is. If you handle such an incident in a calm, positive, and reasonable fashion, it can be a constructive experience. If you overreact, you run the danger of instilling in your children a deep sense of guilt or the sense that sexual interests and feelings are bad, and of pushing them away from you when they have questions or concerns about sexuality. You also risk encouraging a misplaced curiosity about this aspect of life.

A healthy response to instances like those described above will incorporate the following elements:

- *God's gift is good. Reaffirm the goodness of the child's body as God's special creation and gift.*
- *God's gift is private. Use the opportunity to teach the child that because of the special nature of God's gift of sex, the body, especially his or her sexual organs, is meant to be private. God created sexual organs for a special purpose, and not as play toys with other kids! (See the discussion on privacy in chapter 5.)*
- *Curiosity is good. Affirm the goodness of your child's curiosity. We might say, "I understand exactly why you are interested in other people's bodies and why they're interested in yours. We all know inside that those parts are special, and we want to know about special things. It's like wanting to unwrap a Christmas present before Christmas! It's just natural to feel that way. And it's also natural to want to know more about private things; it makes us feel grown up to know about private things."*
- *Set boundaries. Set clear boundaries and expectations. To continue the hypothetical monologue above, "But even though it is a fine thing to be curious, I don't want you to show your penis [vagina, privates] to other kids. And I don't want you to ask to see theirs. If you keep*

those parts of you private and special, it will help you to always feel that God made you in an especially wonderful way."

Such a parental response should lay the groundwork for children to handle themselves properly. Should sex play reoccur, repeat the above admonitions but add a concrete punishment such as a time-out or loss of a privilege for disobeying your directions. Be careful in such times to punish for disobedience of the parent. Don't slip over into punishing the child for sexual curiosity or, worse yet, for some sort of "perversion."

Some sex play will be with children of the same sex. This is quite natural, and parents should not be inordinately concerned about this. Children naturally have as much curiosity about their own gender as about the other. Children wonder if other kids look like they do. Same-gender sex play should only be a concern if it becomes a recurrent pattern. We will discuss how to handle this in chapter 8.

One final word on this matter: When parents do overreact to kids in this area, it's because they assume that the kids have the same sexual motives as adults—lust, adult sexual desire, and so forth. Except for sexually abused or traumatized children, this is not likely to be the case. We must not attribute adult sexual motives to our kids' sexual curiosity and sex play or to their self-touching.

Self-Stimulation

As you may perceive already, we do not feel that occasional self-touching by children is a problem morally or psychologically. Morally, all of the typical concerns about adult masturbation simply seem not to apply to young kids. Children do not lust, as we understand it for adults, and they are not "programming their minds" with destructive fantasies. (We will deal with moral concerns about masturbation in chapter 13.) Children need to understand that their sexual organs are a marvelous creation and gift, that they are capable of giving pleasure by God's design, and that it is good for them to be aware of their own sexuality and comfortable with themselves.

Inappropriate Time and Place

Sometimes the child's self-touching can occur at an inappropriate time or place. This gives the parent the opportunity to teach the child manners and discretion. A gentle but firm instruction in manners — "Honey, please don't rub your penis through your pants when you are around other people. Your penis is a very private part of you and other people can feel very uncomfortable if you do that" — is probably all you need to say to most children in this situation.

But some children can move toward too much self-stimulation or inappropriate self-stimulation. For instance, one couple we know had an eighteen-month-old daughter whom they had always thought of as very active and a "wiggleworm." In one of Stan's classes on sexuality, the father began to realize that she was wiggling with a purpose. The parents were in the habit of carrying her on their hips, one arm supporting her bottom, with her legs on either side of the parent's body, so that her vulva was resting on their hips in such a way that a little wiggling produced pleasurable stimulation of her clitoris. When they held her in this way, she immediately began to wiggle. They began to notice that she was also now reaching her hand down into her diaper to stimulate herself. And of course, they asked with some embarrassment, "What do we do?" Other older children can display similar inappropriate behavior in touching themselves publicly or by announcing their touching to others.

Compensation for Neglect

Self-stimulation for children is unlikely to be a problem. But it can become a problem in certain circumstances: under conditions of prolonged boredom and absence of adequate intellectual or activity stimulation, under conditions of emotional neglect or deprivation, and perhaps as an attention-getting manipulation. Children in families where resources are low and boredom common might move in the direction of masturbating to relieve boredom.

One of the truly compulsive masturbators whom Stan has counseled masturbated on average four to six times per day well into his adulthood. He had begun this pattern in adolescence. Here the real problem was not his sexuality per se; rather he used the masturbation like a drug to cover up or compensate for the deep emotional anguish he felt because of the horrible abuse and neglect he had suffered as a child. A child who masturbates to compensate for neglect is a concern, but this problem does not occur that frequently and is definitely not likely to occur in the family of a parent concerned enough to be reading books on parenting in the area of sexuality.

Seeking Attention

Finally, a child can engage in self-stimulation because of the reaction it engenders in his or her parents. It may be a great way of getting attention or getting a highly emotional reaction from the parents. This is one more reason for parents not to overreact in this area. If the child's basic emotional needs for relatedness and significance are being met and if his or her world is sufficiently interesting and engaging, any interest in self-stimulation is most likely to simply be a passing one that needs no intervention from the parent other than making sure family standards of politeness and consideration for others are maintained. This is exactly what we told the parents of the eighteen-month-old who was self-stimulating. They simply changed the customary way they held the little girl; made sure she had other engaging things to do, including getting her into several play groups with other children; and gently instructed her in manners; after several months her self-stimulation diminished. She is now a healthy and well-adjusted adult.

Handling "Dirty" Language

We need to distinguish between technical or proper terms, acceptable slang, and unacceptable or "dirty" language. Not everyone grows up learning technical terms like penis or vulva. And what we regard as dirty language depends on what we have been exposed to. Some people grow up more comfortable using the terms *dick* or *peter* instead of *penis*; *boner* or *hard-on* instead of *erection*; *boobs* instead of *breasts*, and so forth. But a lot of slang is clearly crude or even predatory in its implications.

There is no divine blessing on certain words rather than others, but clearly we want our children to learn language that does not carry baggage that might deceive or mislead them. And not all of the polite slang is helpful to our Christian cause; we are particularly averse to using the slang term *making love* as a synonym for having sexual intercourse, because by our moral standards a couple is not really making love unless the intercourse occurs in marriage. So in response to a television program or movie that describes two single people "making love," we are likely to remark to our kids, "They did not make love; maybe they made lust when they had sex, maybe they expressed affection, but they did not make love, because real love unites people and is rooted in lifelong commitment." Our point here is that not all slang is unacceptable; parents must make their own decisions.

Children may bring home slang out of genuine confusion, wanting to know what a term means. They may also bring it home to test your ability as a parent to discuss hot issues, to be understanding and levelheaded. In either case, the best strategy is to treat the whole issue in a very matter-of-fact manner. Above all, the parent should never punish or scold the child for asking about the meaning of slang or for using inappropriate slang the first time.

CHILD: [finishing a story at the dinner table] So then Jimmy said, "And forget ever playing with my toys, ever!" What a prick he is!

PARENT: [recovering from shock] Why did you call him a prick? What do you mean?

CHILD: Well, that's what Jason calls everyone he's mad at. I don't know what it means.

PARENT: Well, prick is sort of an ugly word for a man's penis. I would rather you not call people by words like that, because God made your penis and all men's penises to be a wonderful gift. He didn't make them something nasty. So please don't call him a prick, or a penis for that matter. I would rather you not call Jimmy anything like "jerk" or "stupid" either. If he behaves poorly, tell the truth: he was rude or selfish or even acted like a bozo.

CHILD: [again at the dinner table] Mom, what is "f***"? Cathy said "f*** you" to me.

PARENT: I'm very glad you asked me. F*** means to have sex. Remember how we talked about sexual intercourse being when a man's penis goes in a woman's vagina, how God made this as a gift for married people, and how God wants you and me to do that only with the person we are married to? But most people use the word f*** as a dirty word. That's the way Cathy meant it. She probably meant "I'm mad at you so I'm going to say something dirty to you." And that is sad, because she took God's beautiful gift of sex and pretended it was something ugly. I don't think that makes God happy. So would you please not use that word?

You need to settle in your own mind what you believe to be the proper terms for sexual anatomy and what slang terms are acceptable. Then set standards for what kinds of language you will and will not allow in your home. Handle improper language in a calm, matter-of-fact way when it first occurs, with no punishment for bringing such terms into the home. Rather, welcome the opportunity to instruct your children and thank God that they can talk to you about these issues. Only when your child uses foul language after you have informed him or her of its unacceptability should you implement discipline for such behavior.

CHAPTER 7

Preventing and Overcoming Sexual Molestation

Andre and Carol were horrified by what their four-year-old, Tricia, was telling them. She was in tears as she reported that Lisa, the rude and spoiled five-year-old down the street, had been playing house with her in the play-house in Lisa's yard. Lisa had forced Tricia to pull down her pants and panties "or she said she wouldn't let me go home, Mommy!" Lisa had then rubbed Tricia's labia "really hard" and, as best the parents could gather, had tried to force her finger into Tricia's vagina but had stopped when Tricia burst out crying, saying that it hurt. Lisa had let her go only after forcing her to promise not to tell her parents. Tricia probably would not have told, either, but she hadn't been able to control her fear that night when she went to bed and her terror and hurt welled up, leading her parents to get her to tell the secret even though she was afraid.

Janet knew something was not right. Her son Brad had never been so clingy and reluctant to go outside and play with the neighborhood kids. She had sensed a change over the last two weeks, ever since the adult daughter of the older couple next door had moved back home after leaving her husband. The woman's three kids had joined the play in the neighborhood. Ever since then, Janet's own kids had seemed sneakier, more secretive. But this change in Brad had been sudden, just in the last two days.

She confronted Brad, saying she knew something had happened and that he had to tell her what it was. She was stunned by what he told her. Her son, her four-year-old, had been subjected to having oral sex! The seven-year-old from the new family had enticed the younger kids to act out the "movie he saw." He had wheedled and bullied and induced the younger kids to do what he directed them to. Brad and neighbor Melissa had acted out oral sex, with Melissa putting her mouth on Brad's penis while four other kids watched. Becky, the three-year-old from across the street, had acted out intercourse with the new five-year-old from the family in question, though she had kept her panties on. And all of this in Janet's garage!

These are true stories from average, "nice" neighborhoods. And sadly, much worse happens more commonly than we think. We write this chapter with personal pain, as one of our own children was a victim of sexual molestation, thankfully not extreme. This experience heightened our own awareness of how this can occur, and how hard it is to recover from such an experience.

The Facts

Abuse during childhood is not so common that you should be constantly watching for it. But as more and more children are exposed to sexual material of all kinds, including increasing video pornography from cable suppliers and on the Internet, it's likely that more and more sexual experimentation among young children will take place.

The Risks

Some estimate that between 10 and 20 percent of men today experienced some significant unwanted or premature sexual activity and that between 20 and 40 percent (or more) of women experienced some significant unwanted or premature sexual activity. These are very rough and uncertain estimates. A great deal of this unwanted experience comes in adolescence. We deal with these issues in talking about the dangers of Internet and cybersex victimization, date rape, and other troubling topics in part 5, our section on adolescence.

The vast majority of sexual abuse is perpetrated by males, but abuse by females is not unknown and may be increasing in frequency. Sexual abuse (we use the term to mean unwanted sexual contact or stimulation, not limited to intercourse) of children is most likely to be committed by someone familiar to the child. The nightmare of the anonymous stranger who commits an abuse crime is a real fear, but not the one most likely to occur. Most sexual abuse occurs within families. Surprisingly, the most frequent kind of abuse appears to be the least talked about — abuse perpetrated by an older brother on a younger sister. The best estimates are that this type of abuse is five times as common as the most publicized form of abuse: father-daughter abuse. Sibling abuse is less discussed and much less reported, probably because intense family shame keeps it covered up and because there is less likelihood that high levels of violence are used to force participation. This leads the parents and the girl herself to put more of the blame on her.

The likelihood of sexual abuse approximately doubles in blended families; stepbrothers and stepfathers appear to be among the most frequent perpetrators. Other factors that increase the risk of abuse occurring are a mother with extremely negative views about and reactions toward any discussions about sex, the child being isolated by having few friends and a poor relationship with the mother, and the family being poor and the parents poorly educated. In homes where neither parents nor siblings are likely to abuse, some risk still exists from friends and acquaintances in the neighborhood. As we said previously, as the distortions of pornography grow in influence, we are likely to see this risk increase.

The Effects

A strong majority of abuse most likely does not involve intercourse. But don't take this to mean that events short of intercourse (oral sex, fondling) are not serious. Like an attempted rape that ends without vaginal penetration, the results can nevertheless be devastating for the victim. Don't assume that only intercourse hurts a child and that anything less than that is minor. But we must be equally wary of the opposite exaggeration, which is the belief that any abuse experience always devastates your child and leaves the child scarred forever. The degree of damage in the life of the child is determined by many factors, including the nature of the sexual abuse itself, how often it happened, how the child was persuaded to participate, the age of the child when it happened, the degree of isolation of the child from one or both parents, how the parent or parents respond to the revelation of the abuse, the personality of the child, and the presence of other counterbalancing factors in the child's life (such as truly loving relationships with siblings or friends, successful performance in school, sustained safe periods of time spent with grandparents or other safe relatives).

Prevention of Abuse

Many "experts" today, in their rush to always make kids feel good about their sexuality and in their hesitancy to establish any moral norms whatsoever, recommend parental tolerance of even the most outrageous of childhood sexual experiences. This is unwise. Establishing clear norms for acceptable and unacceptable behavior for your children is part of protecting them. It's part of helping them enforce clear boundaries of protection for themselves. The best way to prevent abuse of your children is to build their characters (see chapter 3) by giving them the beliefs, skills, and supportive environment that will best protect them.

Beliefs

Critical core beliefs include "rules" that serve to protect kids. Most discussions of rules for children boil down to three crucial rules (in words for children):

1. Your body is private. "Your body, like the bodies of all other children, is yours alone. Your body is private, especially your genital area (your penis or vagina). God wants that part of you to be private. No one has the right to look at or touch you there except Mommy or Daddy when we bathe you or think you might be sick there, and the doctor when he or she examines you there."

2. Don't keep secrets. "You must never keep a secret about anyone who looks at or touches you there. Some people may try to touch you there or ask if they can and then may tell you that you have to keep it a secret. They may even tell you that we will be mad at you and that we want you to keep it secret. That is a lie. We will protect you, but we can protect you only if you tell us the truth. We will never be angry with you if you tell us something like that; we will be so happy you did the right thing in telling. Remember, if anyone ever asks you to keep a secret of touching from us, it is always wrong, even if that person is a police officer, your teacher, a minister, or a nurse or doctor."

3. Trust your feelings. "Your body belongs to you. We will trust you, and we want you to trust your own feelings if you feel bad about or don't like the way someone touches you or looks at you. You don't have to kiss or hug someone you don't like. When you don't like what other kids or grownups are doing, if it makes you feel uncomfortable, we want you to trust your feelings and leave."

Skills

But it is not enough to give children the right rules. We also need to empower them to be able to act by those rules. Part of this empowerment comes from encouraging the development of certain critical skills or strengths in your children.

Recognize danger. The first of these is the thinking skill of being able to recognize dangerous situations. It is not enough to tell your children the rule about trusting their feelings or about "good touch and bad touch." You need to encourage them to be aware of their feelings and to develop that awareness. Pay attention to how they report their interactions with other kids at school or in the neighborhood. And when they talk about a child or adult who acts in a shady or inappropriate way, ask what they felt and praise them for being aware of their reactions. Praise their good judgment. Try not to encourage paranoia, but teach them caution. Also, talk about abuse incidents that happened to other children and how your child can be wary of such situations.

Be assertive. The critical action skill is assertiveness. Unfortunately, parents and society tend to teach girls to be docile and passive, and this seems to be a particular problem in Christian homes. We must not confuse the Christian virtues of gentleness, kindness, meekness, and even submissiveness with weakness. But rather we should link assertiveness with the biblical concept of meekness.

Meekness is not weakness. Christians often mistakenly identify meekness with weakness. When they think of a meek individual, they think of a person so weak as to be a doormat for everyone else. Then, because Scripture identifies meekness as a positive virtue, Christians mistakenly sanctify weakness as a virtue.

But this is not the biblical way of thinking. Scripture explicitly identifies as meek only two persons: Jesus Christ and Moses. Neither of these men would qualify as weak. Jesus Christ was forceful when the situation called for action. Moses repeatedly strode into the throne room of the most powerful potentate on earth to demand the freedom of his people. He led his people at God's command, disciplining and judging them through the hardest of times.

There is no Christian virtue of weakness. We should seek to develop the assertiveness of our children and then teach them how to submit that inner personal strength to God's use. Praise your children for speaking their minds, for asking questions, for demonstrating strength. Mold them so that they make better and better judgments as to when to exercise this strength. For example, it's one thing for a Christian woman to deliberately allow a needy friend, to whom she feels called to minister, to break into her family time with phone calls and visits; it's another for a different woman to be chronically unable to say no to the people who steal her precious time with her children with their insensitive demands. We can all appreciate meaningful sacrifice, but none of us wants our young child to be the victim of sexual abuse or our teenage daughter to be sexually victimized by aggressive boys because of lack of strength to forcefully say, "No!"

No means no. How do we build such strength? Teach young children that their no is respected. We used to have a family tradition of tickle fights involving all of the family and of "Daddy-Monster Versus the Children" wrestling matches. In both, we encouraged our kids to forcefully say or yell, "Stop!" when they had enough tickling, headlocks, Vulcan death-grips, or whatever. We taught them to abide by this rule with each other as well. "Stop!" or "No more!" is to be respected, and respected instantly. We taught them that anger is justified when anyone — parents, siblings, or friends — does not honor this demand instantly. We used such playtime as an opportunity to practice saying no.

Don't expect your child to be able to say no in other situations if he or she has never been allowed or encouraged to say no even in safe situations at home. We praised our own kids when they said no with friends. When your kids discuss their neighborhood play, be aware of the importance of this skill and praise it when you see it or hear of it — provided, of course, they are within appropriate limits. "Christy, I heard you really telling Joshua that you were not going to do what he said in that game. I don't know what you were arguing about, but I'm so glad you were able to say with such strength what you would and would not do. That's great!"

Supportive Environment

Creating a supportive environment for your child means encouraging her to talk to you, trusting her feelings the way you want her to, and taking action to protect her so that she can definitely trust you, the parent.

Stand behind your children. This involves, in part, being willing to stand behind your children when they don't want to hug an older cousin or choose not to sit on Uncle Sam's lap. Praise the child for being polite but assertive: "Thank you, Uncle Sam, for having us to your house, but no, I do not want to sit on your lap right now." Support them to others who don't like their choices: "No, I'm not really concerned that Meghan might seem rude; I want her to be polite but also strong. She may not always make the perfect choices, but I won't always be there to help her make choices, so I'm glad to see her willing to make some on her own now." Tell your kids you are proud of the strength they show.

Reinforce the three critical rules. Creating a supportive environment also means reminding children occasionally of the three critical rules we described above. It means reminding them that there are to be no secrets where their bodies are concerned. Their bodies are private, a special gift from God.

Be aware of your child's world. Finally, creating a supportive environment means taking the time to be aware of your child's world. We need to have a sense of which kids in the neighborhood and school are trustworthy and which are not. We need to gently encourage our child to forge friendships that are likely to be safe and positive. We need to develop a sense of which parents are wise, supportive, and in agreement with our general goals for raising children. We may need to go to some lengths of sacrifice to make our own home a center for childhood play, a center where we can carefully supervise what goes on.

All of these steps will make it less likely that our children will be victims of sexual molestation. But even the best preparations cannot perfectly guard them.

Healing from Abuse

First, you need to know when to get help. Professional counsel need not be the first resort. Caring, skilled parents can deal with a lot. But if you have little track record of talking with your kids about sexual matters and if you suspect that significant hurt has occurred somehow, it may be useful to talk with someone accustomed to dealing with such problems.

Listening and Sharing

The first item on the parental agenda when a child has been abused is to listen and to talk.

Control anger. Beware of the tendency to react with anger that someone has hurt your child. The greatest danger is that you might convert that anger into criticism of your child for not protecting himself better. You must be extremely careful about showing that you are angry at all before the child, because children almost always believe you are angry *with them* regardless of your statements to the contrary. Don't criticize at all. Later, much later, you can gently suggest ways he can make better choices next time.

Also beware of the tendency to conduct the equivalent of an arraignment hearing to get the facts. Knowing the precise facts in your first discussion is not important compared to knowing your child's perceptions of and reactions to what happened. Responding well can also be made quite difficult by your own feelings of guilt for not having been there to protect your child and your sense of helplessness over not being able to fix what happened. Forget your personal remorse and guilt for the moment; you must make your child comfortable with the difficulty of talking about what happened.

Hear the pain. Your immediate task is to listen and really hear the pain of the child. She probably feels hurt, afraid, regretful, angry, helpless, and dirty. But she will have trouble talking about any feelings. Listen to her talk, and ask gentle questions to get her to talk more. Show that you understand the feelings she expresses. Share her hurt — "I feel so angry at him [the perpetrator] too; what he did to you was very wrong." Let her talk about her hurt for as long as it takes; don't rush or be impatient ("You ought to get over this"). Don't make empty promises, but do express resolve to help.

Share the burden of hurt. The best help for healing is to share the burden of the hurt, thus relieving your child from bearing it alone. This is a direct parallel to the role of the Holy Spirit that the apostle Paul discusses in 2 Corinthians 1:3-7. God does not promise to make our sufferings go away. Rather He promises to be with us in our sufferings and to share our burdens. This passage explicitly says that the comfort the Spirit gives us as individuals is meant to overflow in our capacity to comfort others, and this is precisely what we have the opportunity to do in being a companion to a child in pain. Pray for and with your child for Christ's presence in your child's pain and for His divine touch in healing.

Express confidence. Finally, we should express confidence that there will be an end to the pain; it will gradually recede to a dull ache and then slowly recede into the distance. The child will need to talk a lot about it at first, then gradually less, with periodic flare-ups when other events frighten or upset the child. These are to be expected.

In this way, recovering from an abuse experience is much like grieving. We can't rush people through grief or minimize their hurt by insensitive exhortations to "look on the bright side." But we should share the pain of the loss. We should be there to support and to talk. The parallel with grief is a good one; abused children have lost something forever. They have lost a certain aspect of their innocence and of their sense of security and certainty in the world. They have lost forever the degree of trust they previously had. These are significant wounds, and they should be properly mourned.

Creating Safety

Unless we help a child to feel safe and in fact to be safe, healing from abuse will not happen. It's our job as parents to provide that safety. When Andre and Carol learned what happened to Tricia, they created safety. When Janet heard what happened to Brad, she created safety. These parents banished the offending children from their homes and yards. They told their own children that they were not allowed to play with the offending children, not as punishment but as protection. With this rule in place, the children could simply say, "Mom said I can't," if the offending children asked them to play. In one instance, protecting the child led to confronting the parent and reporting the incident to state child welfare professionals. In the other, no confrontation of the other parents was attempted. All the factors must be weighed, but the safety of the child — emotionally and physically — must be the highest priority.

Protecting a child can force terrible choices. One of Stan's clients was sexually molested by her new stepfather, a pastor and former missionary. The abuse began during the first few weeks of the new marriage, when Cassie was thirteen, and continued until she left the home at age eighteen. The molestation mostly took the form of groping and fondling. Her mother, a devout woman, was financially dependent on her new husband, was struggling with the three uncontrollable stepchildren he had brought into her care from his former marriage, and was still grieving the death of her first husband. Cassie finally worked up the courage to tell her mother after almost a year of such molestation. Her mother exploded, called her a liar, and accused her of trying to break up her new marriage. Cassie never went to her mother again regarding this issue. She endured four more years of abuse and then abruptly married the first eligible boy to come along. She has paid for that choice ever since. Her mother would have had to pay a steep price if she had believed her daughter, but wouldn't Cassie's life have been worth it?

Creating safety is much easier when the molestation has occurred outside of the home. When it has been perpetrated by a brother, stepbrother, stepsister, father, or stepfather, it is much more difficult. It is a sad reality that women can be so financially dependent or emotionally, verbally, or physically intimidated by their husbands that it is easier to disbelieve the daughter's story than to confront and deal with reality. We cannot claim to have a simple solution to this dilemma. But we must protect our children. Confrontation of abuse within families may threaten the very stability of the family and the entire lives of family members. But not to confront it is certain to leave one of God's precious children defenseless. Would God want us to cling to marriage or financial security at that cost?

Reporting Abuse

Two terrible choices parents face are whether to report the abuse to state authorities and whether to make the abuse public knowledge in the family. Either of these actions is sure to create a firestorm in the neighborhood or family. Many of us tend to avoid conflict, especially by rationalizing an incident as a one-time occurrence. Sadly, such judgments are often wrong. One family we know found out after the death of a beloved patriarch that the old man had molested at least nine granddaughters, nieces, and grandnieces from the time he was fifty until he died. Most of the girls had tried to talk to their parents when it happened; every one of the parents held back from fully confronting the issue for fear of disrupting family relationships. Each of those girls, now adults, were scarred by the incidents.

There is no generally accepted rule about when to report and when not to report. But keep in mind, first, that sexual abuse by adults is unlikely to be an isolated incident. Any act that seems unquestionably improper should probably be confronted and reported. Second, in dealing with acts between children, it seems important to distinguish between sexual curiosity and exploration versus knowledgeable exploitation or more advanced attempts to mimic adult sexuality. The example above where children were acting out oral sex and intercourse undoubtedly involved children having knowledge and experience beyond their years. Such an incident should be reported so that the authorities can discover where these children found out about these acts and what sexual abuse they may have experienced themselves.

It breaks our hearts as parents to have to intrude on the joy and innocence of our children's lives by warning them about sexual molestation, but it is worth it to protect our children. It is also worth the pain and exertion to deal with it well when it does occur.

CHAPTER 8

Gender Identification and Sexual Orientation

Connie was worried. Her son Jay did not seem to be fitting in with the other boys in the neighborhood. Jay had always been different. He had always seemed a sensitive and caring boy. He was much more inclined toward art and creative play, and seemed uninterested and even offended by the rough and aggressive play of the other boys. He liked the other boys and would play with them one at a time at home, but he used any excuse not to take part in their wild play as a group around the neighborhood. Now Jay was refusing to take part in t-ball or any other sports, while the other boys thronged to these activities. What did this mean for his future? Was he going to grow up effeminate or to be homosexual? What should she do, and how should she think about this?

As a thirty-six-year-old cellist, Harrison had the following reflections on his life: "I grew up in a broken home with a withdrawn, sullen, and uncommunicative father and an overpowering and often hysterical mother. They divorced when I was ten. I always knew I was different from the other boys — I was left-handed, quiet, loved my music and art, hated sports and felt completely incompetent at them, and generally did not fit in. Other kids began calling me queer and worse very early on. The more I got into my music, the further I went in my musical education, the more homosexuals I was around. The combination of a broken home that made me very nervous about dating relationships, of feeling different and unaccepted by other boys, and of being around so many gays resulted in deep confusion for me about my sexual identity. People in the art community told me I was gay. My heart, and the Lord, told me I wasn't; that I was just different and that I was just fine being different. But my confusion and doubt ran deep, and it wasn't until I married at age thirty-four that I finally felt sure of my sexual identity. Getting married in the face of those lingering doubts was nerve-racking, but I felt it was what God wanted me to do. I feel incredibly blessed by that decision now."

Gender Identification

The term *gender identity* refers to a person's inner assurance that he or she is a boy or a girl, a man or a woman. The process by which a child's gender identity is formed is not well understood. Children begin to form their gender identity quite early. Parents typically make a big deal out of whether the child is a boy or a girl and tend to base expectations for the child on the child's gender (for better or for worse). Children learn the stereotypes for their gender both from parents and from their social environment.

The Beginnings of Gender Identification

Perhaps because young children are working hard to establish a sense of their own identity, they do not typically have to be taught purposefully about their gender identity. Rather they absorb a sense of it in the normal course of family life. They watch their parents intently, filing away what they observe. Often kids become a mirror of parents' attitudes and assumptions, a reality that for many of us may be either reassuring or unnerving as our prejudices are laid before us.

The final solidification of the child's identity as a boy or a girl typically takes place before the age of five. However, there is substantial disagreement over whether the most important period is early (focusing on the second year of life) or late (between three and five). Between ages three and five, children go through a period of intense curiosity about and investment in identification with their gender. This often comes out in clannish or competitive statements, such as "Girls are better than boys!" or "Dad, can just us men in the family go camping?" It can also be expressed in idealistic ways: "I hope I'm beautiful and loving like you, Mom, when I grow up."

It appears that the single factor most likely to encourage a secure and stable gender identity for our children in those early years is that they identify with the parent of the same sex; that the boy identify or see himself as like his father and similarly for the girl with her mother. This identification of the child with the same-sex parent, in turn, appears to be encouraged most by an ongoing, loving, and accepting presence of that parent in the life of the child. In other words, we do not typically do anything special to encourage this identification; we simply need to be available and have a positive relationship with our child. The same-sex parent needs to be a major force in meeting the relatedness need of the child to be loved, appreciated, and accepted. And this does not need to be completely or even primarily verbal. The father who enjoys having his son along as he works on the car or drives to the store is giving out important messages of acceptance to him.

Factors That Complicate Gender Identification

Many patterns can cause gender identification to be much more difficult or even cause the child to go awry.[1] The absence of one parent due to divorce or death can make this identification difficult. Even when the same-sex parent is present, if he or she is aloof, cold, and distant, or is an undesirable figure (such as an alcoholic or a chronically psychologically disturbed person), the child can begin to experience real doubt about becoming like the parent. Of course, the worst case may well be that the same-sex parent is present and actively harsh, rejecting, hateful, and demeaning to the child.

Additionally, the attitudes of the other parent can make a tremendous difference. For instance, imagine a mother who struggles with significant negative feelings about men in general and about her husband in particular. She makes snide comments about men and communicates a general emotional discomfort with things masculine. This can discourage her son's identification as a man.

Confusion about what it means to be a man or woman can also complicate the gender identification process. Gender distinctions and stereotypes of an earlier generation are falling by the wayside; there are hardly any commonly assumed gender-based ideals anymore. Nevertheless you should and can find ways to affirm your child's gender and to encourage a child to embrace being a boy or girl.

Consequences of Incomplete Gender Identification

The worst consequence of a failure to attain a secure gender identity is trans-sexualism, commonly understood as the phenomenon of a man feeling he is trapped in a woman's body or a woman feeling she is trapped in a man's body. Thankfully, this extreme condition is rare. It is also possible that some sexual perversions such as transvestism (cross-dressing for sexual stimulation) and exhibitionism (the "flasher" who assaults women by showing his genitals) may be related to diminished male gender identification. Three more common conditions are possibly related to an impoverished gender identification: sexual promiscuity, sexual addiction, and homosexuality.

Sexual promiscuity and its more extreme variation, which we have come to call sexual addiction, may have its roots in an insecure gender identification. Boys are often explicitly challenged in their teen years to "prove you're a man" by engaging in sexual intercourse. This may be an apt summary of part of what many young men and women are trying to accomplish by pursuing sexual conquest or addictive sexual release. The woman who is promiscuous may be trying to repair her damaged sense of womanhood by seeking affirmation from men. The man who compulsively masturbates to pornography may in part be trying to use his fantasy life and experience of sexual climax to achieve a stable sense of manhood. Rarely is there a single explanation for these types of problems.

Homosexuality

The evidence about the causes of homosexuality is inconclusive.[2] The causes may include genetic and/or biological factors such as brain structure differences that predispose some to move in the direction of homosexuality. The evidence here is mixed, though there is enough to suggest that genetic factors are a very weak causal factor, if a factor at all. The fact that a small minority of very young children show stark differences in behavior compared to their peers suggests that some significant innate influence may be at work for those cases. But it seems clear that there is no one cause of homosexuality. The phenomenon is too complex, too diffuse, for any one factor to explain it all.

The Gender Identification Factor

A great deal of evidence suggests that a disruption in the secure establishment of male gender identity is a problem for many male homosexuals.[3] Research consistently finds that gays report higher rates of having been viewed as a "sissy" or effeminate as children. A major study by a pro-gay psychiatrist studied boys who were diagnosed in young childhood to have strong tendencies toward effeminacy and found that many more than expected grew up to become homosexuals. It is unclear whether this finding represents cause or effect with regard to identity, but it could be both: A child who starts life less gender-typical may develop a more fragile identity and thus come to act even more in ways that are not typical of his gender, which leads to more identity disturbance and so forth.

Other factors may be involved in a young person being nudged in the direction of homosexual orientation. Disrupted relationships with the same-sex parent are common for homosexuals. Homosexual men are very likely to report feeling alienated from their fathers from early on in life.

The Molestation Factor

Early experiences with sexual molestation are not uncommon, especially among lesbians. Among the homosexual men we have known, many had experienced some form of masturbation or oral or anal sex with an older boy or man before they were twelve. Many homosexual women have been victims of heterosexual abuse, leading them to be deeply suspicious of and anxious about male sexuality.

Is There a Choice?

Some Christians naively assume that a person has a high degree of choice in becoming a person of adult homosexual orientation. Our main problem here seems to be simplistic black-and-white thinking: "Either gays chose to be the way they are or they had no choice." In light of modern research, choice appears to be a complex thing. It's likely that many factors give certain people a nudge toward homosexual identity. That nudge may be powerful for some and quite gentle for others. The presence of a weak or strong push does not eliminate human choice, however. It seems quite likely that the choices the child makes in childhood and adolescence in response to those influences, those nudges, will have a powerful effect on who he or she becomes. And the early choices may have powerful lasting effects; once homosexual preference is established, it appears very hard to change. The presence of influences does not make choice disappear. It is not either choice or causation. Additionally, becoming a *practicing* homosexual *is* a matter of choice.

What Does the Bible Say?

Regardless of the cause, the moral teaching of Scripture is clear. God condemns homosexual behavior in the Bible. Every time such behavior is mentioned it is condemned in the strongest terms (see Leviticus 18:22; 20:13; Deuteronomy 23:18; Romans 1:26-27; 1 Corinthians 6:9; 1 Timothy 1:10).[4] The modern arguments for changing the church's stance on homosexual morality all do fundamental damage to our understanding of the authority of God's revealed Word. Remember too that the same moral foundation that supports the traditional Christian understanding of heterosexual morality supports our understanding of homosexual behavior as immoral. As we argue in the next chapter, the true heart of Christian sexual morality is the notion that sexual intercourse is meant to bind a man and a woman together as one for life. Any other use of God's gift of sexual intercourse is an abuse of the gift. All of the arguments about homosexual relationships being loving and so forth may be true, but they do not touch the inner core of Christian morality: God gave us a gift, and we betray Him if we abuse that gift.

Guidelines for Encouraging Proper Gender Identification

All loving parents want to prevent their children from struggling with transsexualism, promiscuity, and sexual addiction. The very idea that one would want to prevent homosexuality sparks rage in the gay community, and yet most gays will say openly that they would not choose to be as they are had they been given a choice. Many Christians have no problem saying they would like to prevent homosexuality, since they view the homosexual lifestyle as immoral. Let us then explore a few tentatively offered guidelines for how we might help to steer our children toward a solid, comfortable gender identification and heterosexuality. There are a number of respected resources available for the parent who wants to read more in this area, most prominently Joseph and Linda Nicolosi's *A Parent's Guide to Preventing Homosexuality* (InterVarsity, 2002).[5]

Affirm Your Child's Gender

First, parents must take every opportunity to affirm their child's gender. From their first days, children should grow up regularly hearing, "I'm so glad God made you a girl!" or "I can hardly believe what a great job God did in making you a boy!" We should use every opportunity to make connections between the child's gender and his or her development. This may be in ways that fit common gender stereotypes, but can just as easily occur in ways that do not fit the standard stereotypes, as when we remark with pride about our son's musical gifts and remind him that he may follow in the footsteps of great male Christian musicians such as Bach, or when we praise our daughter's athletic skill and remark on the fantastic athletic skill God has given to both men and women. Encourage your kids to fully accept the gift of their gender that God has given them.

Encourage Identification with Same-Sex Parent

Second, encourage the child's identification with the same-sex parent. Fathers need to be available to their young sons and mothers to their young daughters during those critical first five years of life. Because parenting of young children usually coincides with the hardest period of establishing careers, the challenge of balancing work and family commitments will need to be a matter of considerable reflection and prayer. While there is some distinction between quality and quantity of time, parents cannot always create quality time when they have only a small quantity to give. Children have to be ready too for quality time, so providing a basic, dependable quantity of time is critical.

Express Affection

Above all, the honest and steady expression of affection by both parents is critical to gender identification. Love your child with abandon.[6] Remember from chapters 1 and 3 that parenting that provides both generous love and discipline produces the best outcomes in children's lives. In addition to meeting the child's relational need for loving acceptance, you are guarding your child against looking to have that need met elsewhere, possibly in a very inappropriate way.

Tim was a needy boy whose father was simply uninterested in his son. His mother, angry and hurt by her husband, was deeply involved in church and her own friendships. Tim was drawn into a "special friendship" with a grandfatherly neighbor at about age five. By the time Tim was seven, the relationship had become sexual, with the boy and the man regularly exchanging oral sex. The pattern lasted over four years, and Tim still struggles with homosexual urges today. Guard your child from having to go anywhere else to find love and acceptance.

Anticipate the Obstacles

We must address and solve obstacles to taking these steps. Conflict between the parents and negative attitudes of parents toward the other sex need to be honestly confronted and dealt with. Single parents raising young children should work through unresolved anger and frustration with an ex-spouse. Don't make the mistake of thinking you can hide powerful feelings from children. If you have strong unresolved feelings, take deliberate steps to resolve or manage them. You must also find within yourself the energy to give emotionally to your child when you yourself undoubtedly feel a tremendous need to have someone minister to you. A danger in single-parent homes is that children will be moved into the role of parenting the parent. They may be maneuvered into meeting the emotional needs of the parent rather than the reverse. If you're a single parent, encourage your child's relationships with same-sex adults who are loving and trustworthy. Sometimes this can be the ex-spouse, a grandparent, a neighbor, or a significant Sunday school teacher. Such relationships do not always have to be emotionally intense or involve huge amounts of time to be important.

We have reason to see as a danger signal behavior that is highly inappropriate for the gender of the child. If this happens in your family, be careful not to overreact. Work hard to accept the unique interests and gifts of your child who may not fit the easy stereotype of the rugged male or nurturing female. It is especially urgent that the same-sex parent offer acceptance; it is vital that the "all male" dad affirm and accept his artistically oriented or sensitive son and that the very feminine mom accept her tomboy daughter. If a child's departures from normal gender behavior become extreme, however, parents do need to be concerned. Deliberate and regular cross-dressing, boys wearing makeup, and any recurrent wish by the child to be of the other sex are of special concern. If you find yourself in this situation, encourage more appropriate gender behavior by having the child spend more positive time with the same-sex parent and rewarding the child for participating in gender-appropriate activities. If those patterns continue, consider contacting a mental health professional for consultation.

Parents must often deal with sex play between same-sex kids, boys with boys and girls with girls. Unless such behavior occurs along with the types of extreme gender confusion patterns described in the paragraph above, you probably should not be concerned. Handle it just as we suggested you handle all sexual play. It is not cause for alarm. Above all, such behavior should not be labeled homosexual. Kids today are aware at early ages of what it means to be gay. Unfortunately, it is common to believe (1) that any homosexual behavior means one is a homosexual person and (2) that once you are a homosexual person you are that way for life. While sexual orientation does not appear to be easily changed in men, it is vital to point out that sexual orientation is probably not completely set until late adolescence or even early adulthood. Thus any labeling of a child as homosexual is horribly premature and may become a self-fulfilling prophecy, a label the child takes into his heart and lives by for the rest of his life.

Sexual Orientation Concerns in Adolescence

Though the major work in establishing gender identity and influencing sexual orientation undoubtedly occurs in the early years, this does not mean that the adolescent years are irrelevant. Even if a young person has some leanings in the direction of homosexual desire, it is quite possible that the adolescent years are critical to that person finalizing his or her sexual identity as heterosexual or homosexual. Several realities complicate this process.

It's Not Black-and-White

First, we live in a society that thinks in absolute black-and-white terms about sexual orientation. A person is either gay or straight, they say, and if you have sexual feelings for the same sex, you are gay. But this is not a good description of reality, which is our second point: Homosexual thoughts and impulses are a normal part of adolescence for many young people who are not gay. Teenage sexual preoccupation and drive can be so powerful that teens find themselves reacting to any sexual stimulus. A very normal teenage boy may be secretly horrified to find himself aroused when he hears a description of oral sex between two men. A recent study that followed adolescents over several years reported that only 11 percent of young men who reported having same-sex attraction were still reporting that attraction just one year later.[7] The teen years are also a time of intense sexual curiosity, and so a teen may be confused by her own fascination about hearing of homosexual practice. We are very complex creatures!

Third, many public schools, under the increasing and relentless pressure of gay-rights groups, are establishing gay-awareness groups and gay-affirming events on campus that encourage early identification and acceptance of one's "gay identity." The message is often, "If you aren't purely and exclusively and conclusively straight, then you are gay; join us and settle the agonizing identity-formation process." The great danger here is of a premature leap into an identity that does not really fit. And yet some teens do already have a fairly stable orientation toward the same sex by mid-adolescence, and we should not minimize the pain that these people feel. To find oneself to be so different from most other teens, at a time when we crave nothing more than to be like everyone else and be accepted, is a kind of pain that many of us have never experienced.

Confused Adolescence

Earlier in this chapter we emphasized that the central psychological building block of sexual identity and sexual orientation is your child's identification with the same-sex parent. A child who enters adolescence confused about her sexual identity is most likely to resolve that confusion positively if she has a close and loving relationship with the same-sex parent or with someone who is like a parent to her (a grandparent, relative, older brother or sister, youth minister, scoutmaster, teacher, and so forth). Adolescence is no time to let down on the work of relationship building! The other-sex parent is also vital in affirming the gender of the adolescent.

It is vital for a father with his adolescent son and a mother with her daughter to talk about how confusing sexual feelings can be and how common sexual feelings for people of the same sex are. Whether it is a girl who feels powerful feelings of closeness and longing when she hugs her best friend or a boy getting an unwanted erection in the locker room when he is sneaking curious looks at how other boys' genitals are developing, we must help our children to see these confusing feelings as normal and no cause for alarm. Perhaps a father could say something like the following to his son:

> Lee, you are going into what is the hardest time of life for many people. I found junior high and early high school to be very difficult. You're changing so fast, you sort of want to stay the same but you sort of want to grow up, and sometimes it just seems that nothing is right. We have already talked about how powerful your sexual feelings can be; sometimes it seems like you think about sex a lot, and you get erections that are embarrassing, and on and on. It's tough.
>
> One of the things that can be most confusing is having sexual feelings that seem weird, that you don't want to have. I want you to know that it's normal to have such feelings. I remember other guys talking about sex in a way that was dirty and gross, but I felt turned on by what they said. I remember wanting to look at other boys in the locker room because I was curious, and it was kind of exciting too. I heard other kids being called a "fag" — I didn't know what that was back then, but I knew it wasn't a good thing to be, given how other kids made fun of anyone with that label. And I remember the first time I heard about homosexuals having sex, I was repulsed, but again curious and half excited by hearing about it, and I remember thinking, "Is there something horribly wrong with me that I think this way?"
>
> I want you to know that you will have many strange feelings that you won't be able to explain and that won't make sense. But I want you to trust that you're okay; what you are going through is what I went through and what most men go through. I want you also to thank God that you have a brain and a will; you don't have to act on any of the feelings you have. And decisions you make will help to shape the feelings you have — the more you trust in God and act rightly, the way God wants you to act, the more your feelings will go in the right direction. And I want you to know that

you can talk to me about anything. Is there anything you want to talk about now?

No Cause for Panic

Parents should not panic or make much about a child who seems uninterested in the other sex or who doesn't fit the gender stereotypes. The vast majority of people who don't fit those stereotypes turn out well. We have one friend who has given his life to painting and the visual arts. He was almost tortured in adolescence by other kids who were convinced that because he was introverted, gentle, sensitive, artistic, unaggressive, and highly verbal he had to be gay. What was particularly damaging was that he picked up clearly from his parents that they also suspected something was wrong with him. Kids should not be hauled off to a psychiatrist because they don't want to play football, try out for cheerleading, or date. As parents, we must trust and love and affirm them, and not undermine their confidence by catastrophizing.

A teenager may trust his parents enough to come and express concerns that he is homosexual. If this happens, first be very careful to distinguish between homosexual interest, homosexual experimentation, and homosexual orientation. Our society is in a rush to identify homosexual orientation and affirm it. But many kids feel homosexual feelings and experiment with homosexual behavior yet still emerge in adulthood with a stable heterosexual orientation. You should pray for wisdom to discern whether your child simply needs to be affirmed that he is okay (as well as urged not to engage in any further experimentation) or whether you should seek professional counsel of some kind.

If you do choose to get professional consultation for yourself as you deal with your child or for your child himself, carefully screen whom you see. Gay and lesbian groups in most major mental-health organizations have come to exert tremendous power, and the "official" position of all the major organizations today is that homosexual orientation is not problematic and is something to be embraced, affirmed, and celebrated. Yet a sizable group within each major profession still regards homosexual orientation as undesirable. Two organizations we would turn to for a referral are Exodus International (www.exodus.to) and the National Association for Research and Therapy of Homosexuality (www.narth.org). Ask the professionals you are referred to three critical questions:

1. Are they Christians themselves, or at least respectful and accepting of your Christian beliefs, so that counseling will not undermine the faith of your family?
2. Do they regard homosexuality as a normal and acceptable variation of human sexual practice?
3. And do they have any professional training and experience in dealing with matters of homosexual desire and interest?

One final caution: While you will hope to find a professional who can answer these questions in a way that fits with your beliefs, do not confuse Christian morality and religious belief with professional competence. We are concerned that some doctrinally conservative Christian "counselors" offer orthodox belief as a substitute for professional competence, rather than as a complement to it. They have the right moral views but no professional skills to actually help. We hope you will be able to find someone who combines both qualities.

What About Change?

Finally, what about change? It is commonly argued today that homosexuals can't change. Well-meaning Christians often naively argue back that change is easy — just a little repentance, prayer, and effort will have the person heterosexual in no time. Neither of these views does justice to reality. Some homosexuals are healed; some do change. Every scientific study that has examined the effectiveness of a treatment for homosexuality has reported that some homosexuals change, though the power of those treatments is not great. Spiritual healing appears to be a reality for some, but many report that such healing was at best illusory or partial for them.

We believe change is possible for some, but we never quite know for whom. The situation is rather like what we face in dealing with physical disease; our God is a God of healing power, but that healing power is not always extended in the way we might desire. Some give glory to God in their healing, while others can give glory to God in the way His strength is shown through their weakness. Christians must not be led into thinking that God always requires change to heterosexuality in order that the person might please God. God is pleased by a life of purity, whether that purity occurs in the context of loving heterosexual marriage or in loving celibate singleness. The path of chaste singleness is one that all Christ-followers, including homosexuals, have open to them.

PART 3

The Preparatory Years:
The Prepuberty Period

CHAPTER 9

"What Is Sex? Why Is It Wrong Outside Marriage?"

Kimberly, a twenty-one-year-old mother of children eight months and two years old, learned about sex from her boyfriend. "When you're in middle school and you run into a boy who's nineteen and cute, he can teach you about sex in a few minutes. You don't want him to be the one who teaches your kids about sex; but if you don't, he will."[1]

Why in the world would you as a parent explain sexual intercourse to young children before they even get near puberty? Isn't that pushing it? Aren't you forcing them to grow up too fast? Aren't you going to traumatize them? Do they really need to know? Wouldn't that encourage experimentation and premature preoccupation with sex?

We're glad you asked those questions!

The timing of telling your child about intercourse is a strategic decision, not a moral decision. There is no divine rule in this area. We do not know when children in ancient Israel learned about sex in their families. But remember, they lived in a culture dependent on breeding, raising, and consuming animals, a culture in which the fertility cycles, breeding strategies, and births of animals would be daily staples of existence. They also lived in a culture short on privacy. People lived in tents or small one- or two-room homes. In this culture, as best we understand it, young people married quite early by our standards.

This was also an earthy culture in which God spoke to His people in earthy terms. For example, through the prophet Ezekiel, God talked in a brutal and explicit way about His people's spiritual unfaithfulness (see Ezekiel 23). He compared them to two sisters who act like whores, even to the point of fantasizing that their immoral lovers have penises the size of those of donkeys and semen ejaculations comparable to that of horses. (Read verse 20; many "polite" English translations dodge the explicit meaning of the Hebrew words here, but, yes, the Bible actually talks of donkey penises and horse ejaculations.) And God's law, in all its explicitness (rules and stories about incest, adultery, prostitution, and the like) was read aloud every Sabbath for all to hear. So let's not assume that Victorian ignorance, silence, and embarrassment are godly behaviors.

Whether children will be traumatized by hearing about sexual intercourse depends entirely on how they are told. Lurid, sensationalized, or overly graphic descriptions are not healthy for children, especially young children, and can lead a child to be preoccupied with sex. And this is increasingly a risk for children in today's media-driven culture. Many teachers report that it is the rule rather than the exception that nine- and ten-year-old students regularly watch R-rated movies at home. The kids who don't see such movies themselves are regaled on the playground with vivid descriptions of those movies.

One of the best reasons for parents to be the first to tell their children about sexual union in marriage is to prevent them from getting an initial impression that is distorted or destructive. This is another application of our third principle: "First messages are the most potent." It is far more powerful to form a child's view of sexuality from scratch than it is to correct the distortions the child will pick up in the world. Trying to build a godly view of sexuality and sexual intercourse after children are exposed to the distortions of the world would be like trying to teach children good nutrition after allowing them to be raised for years on junk food. For this reason we urge parents to tell children about sexual intercourse between ages five and seven, between their kindergarten and second-grade years.

Tell Them Early; Tell Them Explicitly

Our next general principle is:

Principle 6:
Accurate and explicit messages are best.

Err on the side of providing too much information and being too explicit. By explicit, we simply mean being detailed, clear, and direct. We don't mean being indiscreet or lewd. Avoid using language that is figurative, too technical, or obscure. Typically, little damage is done by giving too much information if the information is true, sensitively described, and offered in a positive spirit. Children absorb the information they are interested in and can understand, and they seem to simply ignore or file away whatever they cannot grasp or are uninterested in. Strike a balance here; if we bore children by drowning them with detail they don't want, we discourage them from coming to us for information. But asking about sexuality is hard for children, and if we make them feel like they are pulling teeth to get information from us, they will get the information they want where it is easier to get.

Try to give children direct, simple, and explicit responses to questions, and give them about 20 percent more information than they seem to ask for. Then try to interact with them and keep talking about the subject as long as they seem interested. Quit as soon as they seem uninterested.

Elementary school kids are interested in sexuality, but parents sometimes don't know it because kids tend to talk more to their peers and less to adults about the topic, especially if those adults are nervous about such conversations. Kids are suddenly exposed to a grand vista of peer relationships in school through which they can learn new and fascinating information. This increased discussion about sex among peers signals the even greater need for parents to be the primary source from which their child learns about sex. If learning about sexuality early on creates problems, it's because children are being told the wrong things and in the wrong ways — often by their peers. Godly instruction early on by their parents is the solution to this problem. If our children are going to learn about sex at a young age in our sex-saturated society, it must be our responsibility for them to learn the right views and for God's perspectives to form the foundation for all they come to believe.

Why It's So Hard to Tell Them About Intercourse

First, we are unused to talking about sex at all, and when we do talk about it, it is usually in the abstract. Second, there is a natural privacy around our sexual lives that is difficult to deal with. When we begin to talk with our kids about sex, we have a sense of invasion of that privacy; the little people in the bedroom next door now know what we have been doing! Many parents feel conflicted about their own sexuality and sometimes feel unresolved guilt or shame about past choices or actions. Finally, we fear our own ignorance and are afraid our children might push us beyond what we know.

But none of these reasons must stop us. We must put aside our defenses and discomfort, work through our hesitancies, and risk not having the perfect answer or being shown not to know everything. Our children are worth it.

How to Tell Them

Our teachings as parents should be their first messages. Our teachings should be explicit and direct. And that leads us to our next general principle of sex education in the Christian home:

Principle 7:
Positive messages are more powerful than negative messages.

Romans 2:1-16 teaches that God's law is written on the hearts of all persons. We trust, on this basis, that in their hearts our children will be able to recognize the truth when it is presented to them. And the truth of the Christian view of sex is a good, positive truth: Sex is a marvelous gift of God. Christians believe that good is more powerful than evil. Because the Christian message about sexuality is fundamentally positive, good, and true, we can trust in the persuasive power of the positive message about the Christian view of sex. In fact, all other messages about sexuality other than those of the Christian faith diminish rather than enhance our understanding of sexuality.

Carolyn Nystrom's wonderful book *Before I Was Born* (for ages five to eight) is book 2 in the GOD'S DESIGN FOR SEX series. This is a marvelous introduction to the topic of sexual intercourse. After describing the nature of marriage, she offers the following direct, simple, tactful explanation of intercourse:

> Friends bring gifts to a wedding. God has a special gift for new husbands and wives too. It is called sex. God's rules say that only people who are married to each other should have sex. It is God's way of making families strong.
>
> Because the man and woman are married, their bodies belong

to each other. They enjoy holding each other close. When a husband and wife lie close together, he can fit his penis into her vagina. His semen flows inside of her and their bodies feel good all over. Husbands and wives want to be alone during sex so they can think only of each other.

This is the way babies are made. A husband can't make a baby by himself. A wife can't make a baby by herself. But God made their bodies so that they fit perfectly together. And together they can make a baby.[2]

We have had the following type of conversation after reading this description to our five- and six-year-old children.

CHILD: So that's sex, is it? When people talk about having sex, they mean the man's penis being inside the woman's vagina? That is so gross!

PARENT: You know, I felt just the way you do when I first heard about sex. I think maybe God makes us in such a way that when we're too young to have sex, it just sounds gross to us. But it really isn't gross. Someday, when you really love someone and you are physically ready to have sex, it won't sound gross anymore. Instead it will sound wonderful. I remember when your mom and I were dating, I wanted to have sex with her. But even when it sounds lovely, it isn't the right thing to do until you are married. God wants you to have sex only with your husband [or wife]. Since your mom and I weren't married, we didn't.

CHILD: Why does God have that rule?

PARENT: Well, like we read in this book, God made sex as a special gift for husbands and wives to share only with each other. You know how you feel about your most special toys — you really don't like to share them? Well, sex is a little like that; it isn't meant to be shared with anyone but your husband [or wife]. To share it with other people would ruin it. It's like two radios that two people can use to talk just to each other. If you break the radios into more pieces so that three or six people can all share the pieces, the radios are broken and they don't work. They were not meant to be shared like that.

CHILD: Oh.

PARENT: You know what? I like talking with you about this, and I'm glad that you want to know. Would you please tell me when you have more questions so that I can talk more about it with you? Sex is very beautiful, but a lot of people believe the wrong things about it, so you will hear other kids telling you really dumb and wrong stuff. And television will show you many people who have very wrong ideas about sex. So I want to talk with you about it so that you will know God's truth about sex.

Typically, knowing the most basic physical information — that intercourse is when the man's penis goes into the woman's vagina — satisfies the curiosity of the child. But over and above the physical facts, what children really need to get from their parents are the spiritual truths that sex is a good gift from God and that it is meant for marriage only, and they need to learn the relational truth that you as the parent are open to talking about sex with them and that you welcome their questions.

Sometimes kids may ask other, more detailed questions about intercourse, questions about positions, movement, exactly how it feels, and other embarrassing questions. You might feel an instinctive privacy reaction to such questions or simply have a firm limit of what you are willing to go into with your child. Balance such natural reactions with an awareness of what might lead kids to ask such questions. Are they hearing things about intercourse on the school playground? Are they seeing questionable movies at a friend's house? Respond in a matter-of-fact way, when possible, while protecting your own privacy. It is important to be comfortable with some limits on what information you give, as some things don't have to be known until marriage.

We also encouraged our children not to discuss the topic of sex with other children, because other parents may have different time schedules for telling their kids about sex. But we encouraged our children to speak up when they heard another child expressing misinformation, or at the very least to come back to us and ask us the truthfulness of what they have heard. We especially warned them that they would hear some kids talking as if sex is always a dirty and ugly thing, and alternatively they would hear other kids talking as if sex is the greatest and most important thing in the world and that anyone who doesn't start having sex at a young age has something wrong with him or her.

When you talk about sex, it is best to focus on human beings. "Birds and bees" and other animal examples can be helpful, but parents should be aware that using nonhuman examples can be a subtle way of depersonalizing and thus evading the implications of their discussion of sexuality. Also, such discussions tend to make sex a purely biological process divorced from its distinctly human meanings as an expression of committed love and the vehicle by which husband and wife are united. Within the context of its human meaning, Christian sexual morality really makes sense. Finally, animal examples make sex seem primitive or animalistic, which it is not. Children need to be able to connect sexuality with their own bodies and feelings, and an overemphasis on nonhuman examples can defeat this. Even young children know what it is to love deeply, to share pleasure, and to be committed to another for life.

The Heart of Christian Sexual Morality

If they are to influence the moral choices of children, parents need to be able to make a reasonable presentation of what that morality is and why it is valid. "Because I say so!" or "Because God says so!" will not suffice for most kids. In fact, such responses probably will undermine our case, because they make it look like Christian morality does not really make sense and has to be enforced by bullying.

But the traditional Christian sexual morality does make exquisite sense. Like all of God's wisdom, it's a thing of beauty and grace. God's law is a path that guides us toward wholeness; it's a lamp that shows us the way through the darkest night. How sad that so few of us can really give a reasonable defense of what we believe about sexual morality. Our goal in the next chapter is to equip you to be able to talk confidently with your child about God's will for handling his or her sexual choices. Communicate the essence of this message to children when they are young — early in elementary school — and then repeat and repeat the message in new forms as they move toward and through puberty. Our discussion here will give you, the parent, the big picture as you teach your young child about the morality of sex. Understanding God's will in the area of sexual intercourse is the foundation for building a complete system of sexual morality.

The Morality of Sexual Intercourse

We present Christian sexual morality by using three types of reasons or rationales. Each type serves a vital role today. Sadly, the tendency for most of us is to emphasize the first, mention the second, and totally miss the third. We regard each aspect of the support for Christian morality as equally vital. The three types of reasons for chastity are the caution about consequences of sex, the value of obedience to God, and respect for the uniting nature of intercourse itself.

Caution about consequences. Based on a spirit of caution, parents reason that teenagers should not have sex because of the risk of the serious consequences of pregnancy and disease for an unmarried person. The majority of arguments in Christian and nonreligious books exhorting teenagers to wait to have sex are about such consequences. These types of arguments can be extremely powerful because they are concrete and easy to describe. "Do you want to get pregnant and ruin your life?" "Do you want to get AIDS and waste away and die?" Some of the physical and emotional consequences of premarital sexual activity truly are devastating, and children need to be informed about these consequences. Because these consequences are important, we will expand on them in a later chapter. But putting the main emphasis on them is a mistake.

The problem with arguing by the consequences alone is that it suggests that the act of sexual intercourse in and of itself does not have moral implications. The moral problem with the act comes only in the distasteful consequences that can flow from it. Do you see how confusing this message can be for a teen? It essentially says, "Sexual intercourse in itself does not matter. Sex is neutral. What matters is that you not get a disease or get pregnant." When we place the brunt of our concern on the possible *results* of disease or pregnancy, we set ourselves and the child up for the forceful opposing argument: "But you can prevent unwanted diseases or pregnancies by using birth control, so you don't have to abstain from sex." In other words, the bad consequences become mere obstacles to be avoided; they are not really a solid argument for the immorality of the behavior. The consequences can be bad, but sex in itself does not matter. At its worst, this emphasis suggests that if physicians ever do wipe out sexually transmitted diseases and produce the perfect contraceptive method, Christian morality will be obsolete because the consequences are under control.

Thus these arguments, while powerful, can lose much of their punch when the child learns about ways of avoiding the consequences. The risk of sexually transmitted diseases can be reduced by proper use of condoms. The risk of pregnancy and abortion can be lessened by use of birth control. Guilt can be avoided by rationalizing behavior. Difficulties in breaking up and emotional distress can be avoided by simply growing up and being mature. And so forth.

Defending Christian morality by majoring on negative consequences of sex is a mistake. It puts the emphasis in the wrong place. The possible consequences of premarital sex are vital and of deep concern, but they are vital because they support the core of Christian morality about sexual expression; they do not in and of themselves form the core of Christian morality.

Value of obedience. The second major class of argument focuses on the value of obedience to God's commands. This approach is vital in any sincere expression of Christian faith. Unfortunately, this reasoning can be hard to express to a child or adolescent. It can easily degenerate into the type of interchange that we stereotype as "do it because I told you to do it!" And yet the deeper truth is that obedience is probably our clearest way to express our love for God.

"If you love me, you will obey what I command. . . . If anyone loves me, he will obey my teaching," Jesus said (John 14:15,23). God loves us perfectly and asks us to give our lives to Him out of love. God's will for our lives is perfect and perfectly trustworthy. To say we love God and then withhold our obedience to Him expresses that something is wrong with our love for and trust of Him.

Scripture speaks clearly about one specific way in which obedience pleases God: Obeying God's rules about sexuality is a concrete way in which we can honor God with our bodies (see 1 Corinthians 6:20). Christians so often are predisposed to think of their spirituality as disconnected from their bodies that it is a delight to know we can express our spirituality physically. We can incarnate our devotion to God. Using our bodies in the ways God intended is a concrete way to honor Him.

Why, then, is it insufficient to present this as our main emphasis in our moral teaching, to say in essence, "If you really love God you will stay chaste because that is what He wants"? This is insufficient because we all share a distaste for relationship demands that make no sense, for having to prove ourselves by behaving in a way that seems artificial or arbitrary. "If you love me, you will eat that grasshopper." "If you love me, you will stand on your head and scream." "If you love me, you will never say the word *blooper* in my presence." Why would God want us to refrain from sex until we are married? Is there any defensible reason for this request? Is God's will about intercourse just an arbitrary test of our loyalty to Him? No, it is not.

In His Word, God promises rewards for obedience, both in the present and in the hereafter (see Leviticus 26, Deuteronomy 28, or Galatians 6:7-10). These rewards are offered after obedience and have no explicit tie to the obedient behavior itself. In other words, the act of obedience itself may not be rewarding, but rather God will reward us for obeying. In this way, God shows us clearly that He values obedience. He wants us to obey so much that He will reward us for doing so regardless of the command. But if we stop there, we still have no idea that it makes sense to do what God is asking of us.

We read in Proverbs, "For whoever finds me [wisdom] finds life and receives favor from the LORD" (8:35). Not only does following God's wisdom in obedience result in reward or "favor from the LORD," it's also the right way, the way of life. God's law expresses a blueprint of what is in our best interest, of how we were meant to live (see also Psalm 19 and Proverbs 1–4). In fact, we have already heard this directly: "The LORD's commands and decrees [are given to you] *for your own good*" (Deuteronomy 10:13, emphasis added). We can have confidence that following God's rules about sexuality is the best way for us to act. But why is it best for us? The answer comes in understanding the nature of intercourse itself.

Respect for unity. The heart and foundation of Christian sexual morality is founded on the nature of sexual intercourse, on what God made sexual intercourse to be. The world wants us to believe that the physical act of sexual intercourse is a neutral, meaningless, biological act that is to be judged only by the consequences it produces (bad sex is sex that hurts people) or the intent that was in the heart (bad sex is sex that is based in selfishness). But by God's design, the physical act of sexual intercourse, and indeed all sexual activity, has an intrinsic, built-in meaning given to it by God. Sex has a fixed and objective meaning!

The scriptural view is expressed most succinctly in Genesis 2:24: "For this reason a man will leave his father and mother and be united to his wife, and they will become one flesh." The apostle Paul expanded on this truth in 1 Corinthians 6:15-17:

> Do you not know that your bodies are members of Christ himself? Shall I then take the members of Christ and unite them with a prostitute? Never! Do you not know that he who unites himself with a prostitute is one with her in body? For it is said, "The two will become one flesh." But he who unites himself with the Lord is one with him in spirit.

The truth here is that sexual intercourse has a meaning, and it is a meaning of union, of the uniting of two people.

No one has expressed this better than Lewis Smedes in his book *Sex for Christians,* where he says,

> It does not matter what the two people [who are having sex] have in mind. . . . The *reality* of the act, unfelt and unnoticed by them, is this: It unites them — body and soul — to each other. It unites them in that strange, impossible to pinpoint sense of "one flesh." There is no such thing as casual sex, no matter how casual people are about it. The Christian assaults reality in his night out at the brothel. He uses a woman and puts her back in a closet where she can be forgotten; but the reality is that he has put away a person with whom he has done something that was meant to inseparably join them. This is what is at stake for Paul in the question of sexual intercourse between unmarried people.
>
> And now we can see clearly why Paul thought sexual intercourse by unmarried people was wrong. *It is wrong because it violates the inner reality of the act; it is wrong because unmarried people thereby engage in a life-uniting act without a life-uniting intent. Whenever two people copulate without a commitment to life-union, they commit fornication.*[3]

This is a vibrant and important reality for Christians to capture. It's a positive truth woefully absent from most books about sexual morality. We need to teach children the positive truth and positive reality of what sexual intercourse is — a life-uniting act. Sexual intercourse glues two people together in such a way that their lives are forever different because of their union. For this reason God means intercourse for marriage. Sexual intercourse is meant to be and is a uniting event, a uniting force.

Union in marriage is both a one-time event and a process. Based on the Christian teaching of sexual union, it is true to say that a man and woman become one when they consummate their marriage by engaging in the fullest possible sexual expression of their love. A man and woman become one on the day of their wedding when they pledge their lives to each other and then seal that pledge by the exchange of their bodies. But it is equally true that becoming one is a process that is never complete; it is a process that we continue working on throughout our married lives. And sexual intercourse plays a role in that gradual process. Sex draws us together and unites us on an ongoing basis. The physical ecstasy unites us. The nakedness and vulnerability unites us. The gradual learning of mutual pleasuring and self-giving unites us. The bearing and raising of children unites us. But undergirding these relational developments that sex facilitates is the deeper truth that in some mysterious, spiritual way we can never fully understand, sexual intercourse makes us "one flesh." Something mystical and unexplainable happens when two people give their bodies to each other. We are bound together through sexual union.

We must be careful here; we must not create distortions that can haunt our children. An adolescent might interpret this to mean that two people are married just because they have intercourse. That is not true. Sexual intercourse does not create instant unity, as any nonvirgin can attest. A fifteen-year-old girl must not believe she can permanently seal her relationship with her current flame by giving in to his demands for sex. The nonvirgin must not be led to believe that her life is permanently ruined because now she can never become one in marriage. A man who has had sex with fifteen different women in his life is not "one" with fifteen persons permanently, forever fragmented beyond hope of repair. These are all distortions because they deny God's capacity to heal and restore the soul broken by sin.

The positive truth of the uniting reality of sexual intercourse helps us to see the beauty and blessedness of intercourse in marriage. It also helps us understand just how terrible it is when any of us abuses God's marvelous design. It's as if we take the wedding gift of a priceless painting and use it as a TV tray. We serve popcorn and spill soft drinks on a valuable painting.

We misuse the gift and desecrate it in the process. We can also better see the damage we do to ourselves when we abuse the gift. God meant sex to unite us in marriage. We are convinced that casual sex — any sex outside marriage — progressively makes it harder and harder for us to really bond with the person God means to be our life partner. If sex glues us together, but we spend our youth gluing ourselves to others and then prying ourselves apart from them, we are building up our own capacities to not really unite with anyone. We are training ourselves to be unable to bond in marriage. And thus the rise in divorce that parallels the rise in sexual permissiveness makes perfect sense. So does the body of research that shows that as premarital sexual experience increases, so do the tendencies toward marital instability, adultery, and lower satisfaction in marriage.

The Three-Strand Cord of Christian Sexual Morality

The writer of Ecclesiastes says, "A cord of three strands is not quickly broken" (4:12). The three general sets of reasons behind the traditional moral standard form a three-strand cord of great strength. If sexual intercourse is what Christians claim the Bible teaches it is — a life-uniting event — then obedience makes sense. God's command is not just an arbitrary standard; it's a rule that leads us to wholeness and blessing. For us who are married, this rule guides us into experiencing the best that God has for us — unity with our spouses. For us who are single, God's rule guards and protects us from linking our lives with those with whom we do not have a life union. The sexual ethic preserves us from acts that would be self-destructive.

If sexual intercourse is what Christians claim — a life-uniting event — the terrible consequences of illicit sexual intercourse make sense. The emotional devastation of bonds broken by unfaithfulness seems inevitable. The fact that we are relatively unprotected physically from sexually transmitted diseases makes sense when we consider that such disease would generally disappear in a single generation if all persons obeyed the Christian sexual morality. Bad consequences occur because we break God's creational design.

The three strands intertwine and mutually support each other in an exquisitely beautiful way. Sexual intercourse is a beautiful gift with built-in meaning. Its built-in meaning of union speaks to the deepest longings of our hearts for intimacy with another who loves and accepts us, one who is "bone of my bones and flesh of my flesh" (Genesis 2:23). And our union with another, in turn, mirrors and reminds us of our desire for union with God.

CHILD: But what does that mean, that having sex unites you? I don't understand!

PARENT: I don't either. Your mom and I have been married for fourteen years, and I'm still learning what it means. But let's think about it together. When you become a man, do you think you would like to have a wife whom you love with your whole heart and who loves you that way for your whole life?

CHILD: Yeah. I want to have someone to love like you and Mom do.

PARENT: Well, I think that is what everyone really wants. People who stay single can still have a wonderful life, because as Christians God will be with them and they can have special friends in the church. The Bible says that we were not meant to be alone. We are each made to love our children, our families, and our friends (our enemies too!), but we are each made to have one person in life who is especially close, so close that it is like the other person is part of us. Who do you think that special person is meant to be?

CHILD: Your wife?

PARENT: Yes, and your husband if you are a girl. But to keep two people that close, God seems to have decided to make a special glue to keep the husband and wife together. What do you think that glue is?

CHILD: Sex?

PARENT: That's right. It isn't the only glue, mind you. Having kids, sharing a home, and things like that also are like a glue that holds you together, but sex is so special because God made it to be that kind of glue. And you know what happens when you use glue in ways that it shouldn't be used!

CHILD: Yeah, you get really mad and punish me!

PARENT: Well, that's true, but I was thinking first that it ruins things, sometimes for good. Imagine that you couldn't get that clump of hair on top of your head to lie down, so you used your model glue to glue it down. We would have to shave the top of your head to get it off. Your hair would be ruined when you were hoping to make it better. Glue used the wrong way doesn't help; it hurts. Sex is like that — when a married couple has sex, they are using it the right way and it glues them together so they can love each other the best way possible for life. And you are right about my being mad and punishing you. I would be mad because I gave you the glue as a gift to use the right way. If you use it the wrong way, it is like you are saying to me that you don't care for me enough to use the gift the way I meant you to. Does that make sense?

CHILD: I guess. It's like if I used the baseball glove you gave me to scoop mud down at the pond.

PARENT: That's right. And it is that way with God. He gave sex to us as a gift. If we don't use the gift the way He wants, it's like we are telling God we don't like His gift, like we don't love Him enough to use it just the way He wants us to.

CHAPTER 10

Inoculating Your Kids Against Destructive Moral Messages

Planned Parenthood Federation of America, a secular group, offers the following example as an ideal moral or "values" dialogue between parent and child:

> A father one of us knows reported that one Saturday, when he was driving his twelve-year-old daughter to a flute lesson, she asked, "Daddy, how old do you have to be to do it?" He took a deep breath and replied, "Well, it seems to me that having intercourse — that is what you mean, isn't it? — is a real special thing that you don't do just because you're old enough or because it feels good. The most important thing is to be very sure of your own feelings and not do it because of anyone else or for anyone else. Your mother and I don't believe kids your age are ready to handle it, but if you decide differently, it's important to avoid a pregnancy you wouldn't be able to manage by using birth control."[1]

Even when dealing with a twelve-year-old child, Planned Parenthood does not recommend that parents give any solid messages about sexual morality. Instead, children's feelings should tell them when they are ready to have sex, and the really crucial issue is the use of birth control. In fact, Planned Parenthood explicitly says that it is useless for parents to communicate their moral views to their children; parents are "wasting their breath" in trying to teach what they believe to be right and wrong to the child.[2] Such are the views common in our culture today.

Our concern in this chapter is how we as parents can best prepare our kids to handle the messages they will be bombarded with from outside of our families. If we are going to raise children to live pure lives, we not only have to teach them what is right and true, but we also have to somehow protect them against the messages they get from elsewhere that undermine Christian truth.

The Principle of Inoculation

So, what are our options in protecting our kids? One is to try to shield them from all non-Christian influences. The problem with this approach is that it is impossible. It is doomed to failure, so attempting to totally shield them is a waste of time and energy. A second approach, simply telling them that other people will tell them bad things and that they should not listen to them, doesn't really seem to help. When kids hear the other messages and find them to be inviting, seemingly plausible, and much more popular than traditional Christian views, they may be unprepared to stand by what their parents have taught them.

What we can do is inoculate kids against the wrong messages and negative influences they will inevitably face. We feel this is so important that we have made it one of our core principles:

Principle 8:
We must inoculate our children against destructive moral messages.

A physical inoculation or immunization mobilizes the body's natural defenses that protect us from disease. To protect us against such dangerous diseases as polio, smallpox, or the flu, doctors isolate the virus that causes the disease, grow a culture of the germs, kill or weaken the germs, and then inject the inert germs into the body. The body's immune system responds to the foreign germs by manufacturing antibodies and other agents to find and destroy that type of germ. Because the inert germs posed no threat to begin with, our bodies thus develop a defense against the dreaded disease without ever having been at risk of developing it in the first place.

What we want to do, then, is *psychologically* immunize our children against the germs of the immoral messages they encounter in the world.

This inoculation work should begin early in life; it works best when you can get to the child before he or she has actually begun soaking in destructive messages from the media, school chums, or secular sex-education classes. Inoculation involves parents deliberately exposing their kids to the counterarguments and pressures they will be exposed to later in life, but in the safe environment of the family, where you can show them how those non-Christian influences are unconvincing, false, and destructive. For instance, rather than shielding children from the argument that having sex is essential to really growing up, we become the first to present them with this argument. Then we help them to reason against this destructive message, thus inoculating them against the argument.

A rich body of scientific research in the field of social psychology supports the effectiveness of inoculation.[3] When adults or children are sheltered from views that oppose those they have been taught, their attitudes on those subjects remain fragile and easily changed. But when they are challenged with accurate, strong, but not overwhelming counterarguments to the position they are being taught, and we show them that those counterarguments can be disputed, their beliefs will actually be strengthened. It's just like building muscle: If our muscles never meet resistance, we cannot become strong, but when we tax and strain our muscles, they respond by growing stronger.

How does such psychological inoculation seem to work?

Counterarguments Are No Surprise

First, being exposed to counterarguments leads children not to be surprised or threatened when others later oppose their views. Some kids raised in Christian homes are led somehow by parents and the church to think that Christian morality is self-evident and any reasonable person believes it. The first serious presentation of other views is unnerving. We must lead our kids to expect opposition; after all, they will be persecuted for what they believe.

Public Commitment Matters

Second, when exposed to counterarguments and challenged to come up with reasons to stick with the view parents have taught, children are led to publicly (in the presence of the parent) make a commitment to the view they have been taught. Research shows that few things are as powerful as making a public commitment for keeping a person faithful to the view he or she has embraced.

From Acceptance to Advocacy

Third, psychological inoculation helps children move from passive acceptance to active advocacy of the views parents are teaching. When we help our kids become active practitioners of what we have taught them, rather than passive listeners, they are more likely to make those views their own in the depths of their hearts.

Practice Thinking Skills

Fourth, this process gives kids a chance to develop and practice the thinking skill of making an effective counterargument; it forces them to be ready to defend the reasons they have for Christian sexual morality. They will need the skill of defending their beliefs all too soon.

To learn how we can inoculate our children, we need three things: (1) we must understand the heart of Christian sexual morality (which we explored in the last chapter), (2) we must understand the non-Christian morality systems that will challenge Christian belief (and here is where we turn next), and (3) we need examples of the actual process of inoculation.

The Destructive Moral Systems

Many different systems of values and beliefs stand in opposition to Christian sexual ethics. We will summarize them according to the following three types: playboy sensuality, the "ethic of intimacy," and the pseudo-Christian love ethic.

Playboy Sensuality

Hedonism, though not as popular as it was in the 1960s and 1970s, may be making a comeback among young people today, particularly among those who have lost hope in the meaning of their lives and the certainty of their futures. If the future looks bleak and if there is no God and hence no meaning, what is there to life but the gratification of the lusts of the flesh? And simple appeals to lust and pleasure may be the most forceful arguments teenagers in empty houses or the backseats of cars can make on the spot. Arguments like "You deserve to feel good" or "This is what your body was made for" are common. A girl can feel powerful pressure from exaggerated descriptions of the male sexual drive — that the boy has to have sex, that she is torturing him by saying no, that the drives have to be gratified or the boy suffers, and on and on. Finally, our kids will hear crude appeals to fitting in at all costs. "If you don't have sex, there must be something wrong with you." The core moral message here seems to be that being popular and accepted and fitting in are more important than virginity and sexual restraint.

Thanks to the stark contrasts between Christian morality and playboy sensuality, it is relatively easy to think of arguments to counter this view, though the counterarguments depend on your child accepting that Christianity is true.

The Ethic of Intimacy

Most "sophisticated" people today reject playboy sensualism. In many circles, promiscuity is out of fashion. What has replaced it is a more seductive and subtle distortion. Tim Stafford, popular Christian writer and longtime author of *Campus Life Magazine*'s popular column "Love, Sex and the Whole Person," has argued that the view that much of our secularized culture takes of sexual expression can be described as the "ethic of intimacy." He describes it as composed of seven basic ideas:

- *Sex itself is always viewed as positive; only sex by coercion, such as rape or incest, is intrinsically bad.*
- *Individuals are always independent; sex can't really unite people. Our first obligations are to ourselves and our own self-interest. People come together as long as it benefits them to do so.*
- *Compatibility is the key to good sex and good relationships. Compatibility just happens, so it is always best to "try on the shoes before you buy them." And people who are compatible at one time*

may not stay that way; after all, people change.

- *Sex, and ethics too, is a strictly private matter. If there is right and wrong, there is only right and wrong for each person. My life is none of anyone else's business.*

- *Sex does not change the person. Sex has no necessary consequences of any kind, good or ill. A virgin is not different in any significant way from a nonvirgin.*

- *There must be no double standard between men and women. Differences between the genders must be eradicated. If men are consumed with lust or promiscuous, women must try to close that gender gap.*

- *The magic element that makes sex okay is maturity. You must be able to "handle" sex, you must be "ready for it." Generally, this appears to mean that you should be able to take steps to prevent disease and pregnancy.*[4]

We see many of the elements of this ethic of intimacy in the works of Planned Parenthood and many school sex-education curricula. After telling parents that they are wasting their breath inculcating a morality in their children, the Planned Parenthood book for parents turns right around and prescribes its own morality that should be taught to children, saying,

To be ready for sex, persons must:

be sure they are not exploiting another person or being exploited themselves.

be able to discuss comfortably with their partners the cautions against unintended pregnancy and STDs and to share responsibility for taking steps to prevent them.

be able to accept the consequences of their own actions. Could they deal with a pregnancy or with contracting a disease?

be willing to make the emotional commitment and take on the obligations of a healthy adult sexual relationship.

understand that enjoying this aspect of sexuality involves the ability to make thoughtful decisions.

Without this the sex act is likely to produce far more stress and anxiety than pleasure.[5]

Planned Parenthood goes on to discuss various reasons teens would want to wait to have sex, all of which are stated in a negative and demeaning way. Sex is for the mature, so a major reason for young teens not to have sex is that "many young boys and girls are not emotionally experienced enough to deal with the strong emotions a sexual relationship can create."[6] Teens might want to wait because "early sex would make them feel guilty or anxious. Some may be afraid of becoming too emotionally dependent on a partner."[7] Others may be "late bloomers" who "may never develop a very strong sex drive."[8] Which of these reasons for waiting to have sex will the teenager identify with? Which teens want to be late bloomers, guilty and anxious, afraid, or immature? All of these, given as reasons not to have sex, are conditions any teen would be desperate to grow out of. And so, such reasons really do nothing to persuade the teen to wait to have sex, but actually create incentives to mature by having sex! Throughout this material from Planned Parenthood, the reader can easily see the very ethic of intimacy that Stafford has described. Inoculating your child to such views is critical for his or her future well-being.

The Pseudo-Christian Love Ethic

As if it were not enough to face destructive messages in the world, parents are often unwittingly sabotaged by destructive moral messages from within the church as well. Readers who are members of mainline church denominations must be especially cautious of views of sexuality that are circulating in seminaries, in popular "Christian" books, and in published sexuality curricula being used in churches. These views are often most clearly stated in the painful and highly visible discussions pushing for full acceptance of homosexuality in the churches.

What makes these views especially troubling is that they are the subtlest distortions of truth imaginable, requiring true discernment to detect and respond to. We have read these sorts of materials and arguments for years and believe the following are some of the core elements of the pseudo-Christian love ethic:

- *Sexuality is God's good gift to humanity. It is so good that to mix talk about sex with talk about sin is to diminish this good gift.*
- *Because God made us fundamentally sexual beings, the experience of*

full sexual expression is necessary for full development as a person. A celibate, sexually abstinent person is an underdeveloped person, a half person.

- *Because our sexuality is a good gift, we are all entitled to experience the gift of our own full sexual expression to the fullest extent. God would not give people a gift like a sexual appetite, or for that matter a homosexual orientation, and expect them not to experience to the fullest what God has given them a yearning for. Anything less would be unjust.*
- *Celibacy is a gift (see Matthew 19:10-11; 1 Corinthians 7:7). Because it is a gift, those without the gift are not expected by God to abstain from sex. If you aren't married and don't have the gift of celibacy, God must want you to satisfy your sexual longings.*
- *The declaration that "all of the law is summarized in the command to love" is taken to mean that loving feelings make sexual expression morally acceptable. It is argued that Christianity promotes an ethic of love that makes all mere rules (like "no sex outside of marriage") obsolete. We are to follow love, not law. Anything that we do out of genuine love feelings cannot be wrong.*
- *Because God is relational and our sexuality is relational in God's image, it is primarily when we are acting out our sexuality that we are closest to God and are in touch with the "God-force" within us. We are being relational, creational, and uniting (just like God) when we are having loving sex.[9]*

Children may be especially vulnerable to destructive moral messages that come sugarcoated with such "God-talk" and slightly twisted references to the Scriptures. It is vital that we inoculate our children against these messages as well.

How Do We Safely Inoculate Our Children?

If you expose your kids to these countervailing views, they will not be startled to find people who disagree with their Christian positions on sexual ethics. You can help them to expect opposition, even persecution. You can help them to think actively about what they believe and to put words to their beliefs. Help them to express their views so they are committing themselves to follow the traditional Christian way. And finally, help them to come up with sensible responses to these views.

Our core method in this area has been to watch carefully the messages given by television, billboards, popular music, and movies, as well as things that our own kids reported that other kids said on the playgrounds. We tried to catch these messages early, before our kids were even aware of the significance of what they were hearing or seeing. We then tried to use these messages as teaching moments with our children to inoculate them. Following are several examples:

CHILD: Dad, Clint [another ten-year-old] has a picture of a naked lady in his room, hanging over his bed. I saw it yesterday. She has her arms over her chest and her legs crossed so it doesn't show her private parts, but she's completely naked. Clint says he stares at it every night while he goes to sleep.

PARENT: [In shock] Do Clint's parents know he has that picture?

CHILD: Oh sure. He said his mom bought it for him.

PARENT: Well, what do you think about that?

CHILD: It seems kind of weird to me; after all, he's only ten. I wouldn't put up a picture like that.

PARENT: [Thinking, *You can say that again!*] I'm glad you wouldn't. What do you think a kid learns from having a picture like that in his room? Or, I guess what I'm really asking is, what do you think the people who made and sold that picture want the boys that buy it to think about women and about sex?

CHILD: I don't know. Maybe that it's okay for women to show their naked bodies and that it's okay for boys to stare at them?

PARENT: I think that's right. I think they believe it's okay for men and boys to stare at a woman's body and also to think about sex. They probably also believe that the most important thing about a woman is how she looks. And you know what else? That naked woman probably wants other women to think they have to look just like her to be beautiful. That probably makes her feel important and it will help her to get richer because those women will buy her exercise video and her diet books and all of the other junk she tries to sell. But how do you think God feels about that picture? Would God want you or me to have that picture on our walls?

CHILD: No way!

PARENT: Why?

CHILD: Well, because God made our bodies private and because being beautiful on the outside is not the most important thing.

PARENT: I think you made God very happy by the wise thing you just said. God made sex as a beautiful gift that helps make a husband and wife stick together for life. Sex and even the full sharing of our bodies is meant for marriage, not for posters on kids' walls. In the years ahead, Son, many people will tell you that you are stupid for believing what we have talked about today. They will try to tell you that it's okay to think about sex with anyone and to have sex with anyone as long as you don't hurt someone by giving her a disease or getting her pregnant. They will try to tell you and your sisters and your future wife that they are good people only if they are beautiful in the way that that woman is beautiful. All of this is a lie. All people are beautiful in their own ways because God made them. The most important kind of beauty has to do with whether the person is good. Is he or she beautiful inside? And part of being beautiful inside is loving God and obeying His rules about sex.

PARENT: Bill, did you hear what that TV news reporter just said? She said that the church would have to stop interfering with the private moral decisions of people today or it would become more and more irrelevant. Do you know what that means?

CHILD: No.

PARENT: What she was saying is what many people say today: Nobody, not even the church, has the right to tell people today how they should live their lives. People have to make up their own right and wrong in their own minds, and no one else can tell them if they decide rightly. So if I decide I can't have sex with anyone but your mom, that may be right for me, but another person can decide it's okay to have sex with a lot of people and that may be right for him or her. Do you think there could be different rules for different people?

CHILD: That wouldn't be fair. Doesn't God give the same rules to all of us?

PARENT: I think so. Do you think so?

CHILD: Yes.

PARENT: Why do you think a person might say that everyone's rules are different?

CHILD: Because that person doesn't like the rules?

PARENT: I bet that's it. If a person doesn't like God's rules, maybe it helps to say that they really aren't God's rules at all. You'll hear that in school soon — that no rules apply to everyone, because if they did, everyone would agree on the rules. But that has to be wrong. The Bible says that God made His rules for people, but right from the beginning people began to break the rules. Does that mean the rules aren't really good? No.

CHILD: You mean a lot of people don't think that God's rules from the Bible are good rules?

PARENT: Yes. Many people don't. They say that different rules for different people are okay. But Christians believe that God made us all and that He made rules for us all. It isn't our job to make others obey the rules or to yell about the rules. But we're supposed to live by the rules and urge others to also.

Note how in these dialogues we tried to (1) clarify the destructive message from culture to help the child to identify it, (2) encourage and help the child to articulate both the appropriate Christian truth and some objection to the destructive message, (3) fill in for the child other arguments against the destructive messages so the child can grow further in understanding, and (4) praise the child for his or her understanding.

We cannot, in this chapter, summarize a response to all the anti-Christian moral values discussed earlier. The heart of a parent's response, however, needs to be to clarify and make perfectly clear just what the opposing view is saying. Strip it of its sugarcoating and hold it up for the child to see in the clear light of the Christian view of sexuality. There is no absolutely irrefutable argument against any of the destructive moral systems. We must, in trust, proclaim as effectively as we can the Christian view that stands against the other views.

Sometimes we must not wait for an impromptu moment to teach but must initiate a conversation because we are concerned about what our kids are headed into.

PARENT: Sarah, now that you are twelve, I want to warn you about some of the things that others will soon say to you about sex, if they haven't already. You will hear boys saying that you have to give them sex to fit in or that you have to have sex because it's the greatest thing in the world and you are sick or crazy or a chicken if you don't. I think you're smart enough not to fall for that baloney. I don't think you will want to fit in with people who want to make you have sex to belong. We've talked about sex, and so I think you know that while sex is wonderful, it is wonderful in marriage, where it not only feels good but also helps to keep you in love with your husband for all your life. Those things don't worry me as much. One of the things that worries me the most is those who say that having sex is part of growing up, of being mature, of being an adult. Have you heard that?

CHILD: Yeah, there are kids who say that already. They say, like, "How are you going to know if you really love someone if you don't have sex?" And they say if you really love someone you will have sex with them.

PARENT: And what do you think about that?

CHILD: I'm confused. You have told me that sex is a way of expressing love. And I'm afraid of not knowing how to have sex when I do get married.

PARENT: Those are good thoughts. You see, that's why I was worried, because what you're being told is partly true and partly false. Sex and real love are meant to go together. That is why, when you start dating, you will feel excited about the idea of sex with a boy whom you really care for. There's nothing wrong with feeling that way. But real love is lifelong love. And that's what marriage is — a commitment to love each other for a lifetime. Some say, "Try sex and see if you're in love." God says get to know each other without sex, test your relationship by being patient and waiting, and then see if you really love each other by seeing if you are both willing to promise to love each other for a lifetime. Then you have sex when you are married to cement your relationship together. Do you hope to have one man to love forever?

CHILD: Yes! I would hate to wind up divorced and remarried three times like Aunt Kathy.

PARENT: I'm glad you feel that way. Did you know that people who do not have sex before marriage are more likely to have a happier and longer-lasting marriage than those who do and that they are more likely to enjoy sex with their husbands too? That takes care of your worry about learning to have sex — marriage is the perfect place to learn. Who would you rather learn with, a husband who is committed to you for life and loves you enough to wait for months or years to have sex with you, or a boy who tries to make you have sex on the third date and likes you only because he hopes to get sex from you?

This parent dives in and identifies a possible set of distorted beliefs to which her child might be susceptible, praises her daughter for expressing her thoughts and sharing her confusion, affirms the goodness of God's gift of sex, appeals to the basic desire in each of us to share love with a single life partner, and begins to offer ways to refute and resist contrary beliefs. This sample dialogue is more on the monologue side, with the parent doing most of the talking, but in this instance it was the parent who brought up the subject. This conversation sets the stage for a follow-up conversation in which the parent could draw out the child, giving her more of an opportunity to actively articulate what she has learned in the home.

Inoculation prepares your child to face the real dangers of a world that has lost its bearings with regard to sexuality. By actively working to inoculate our children, we participate actively with God in preparing them for the challenges ahead.

We close with a brief anecdote from our lives, our favorite memory of inoculation work with our children: During the time when our two oldest kids were eleven and nine, we were walking the streets of downtown Toronto on a warm summer vacation day. These two stopped, staring blankly with mouths open at a store window while we walked ahead, oblivious, with our youngest. Realizing we had gone ahead, we strolled back to see what had caught Jennifer's and Brandon's interest. Now it was time for our mouths to drop open. We were faced with a clever display of a shop specializing in sexual novelties, focused on condoms and leather goods. Our kids were staring at a rainbow array of condoms of all colors and styles (many blown up for better display) and an amazing array of harnesses, whips, thongs, handcuffs, chains, spurs, and . . . well, you get the idea.

All our instincts at that moment were to drag our children away in a rush and pray they developed amnesia. But in response to their breathless, "What's this store about?" we instead had one of our most memorable discussions ever about the meaning of sex. The discussion began when, between the two of us, we managed to say something like the following: "This is a store that sells things that some people feel will make their sex lives more exciting. You see those handcuffs and whips? Some people have fallen so far away from God's purposes for their sexual lives that they think it is fun to wear handcuffs and be whipped while they have sex, or to be the person who does the whipping, all as a way to make sex more exciting. The sad thing is that people who do this sort of thing are taking God's gift of love and turning it into something twisted and mean. We would never dream of acting like that, because what makes our sexual relationship so exciting is that it is rooted in our love for each other. Do you think punishing or hurting the other person as part of sex could ever be God's intention? What do you think these people think about sex?" The discussion that followed was a rich opportunity to reinforce, yet again, a Christian view of sex. Passing by that S&M/condom store has become a favorite family memory.

CHAPTER 11

Preparing for Puberty and Adolescence

Some children will begin the marvelous transformation process we call puberty as early as age ten; others later. We urge parents to take the lead before puberty begins to positively introduce children to the wonderful and amazing changes their bodies will soon be going through. Help them to anticipate with excitement the changes ahead, including pubertal growth and the onset of menstruation. Set the stage for their understanding of sexual attraction and excitement. And this is the period when you can do some serious preparation for the roller-coaster ride of adolescence.

Late elementary school is an easy time for parents to let down and not do their work of sex education and character formation. Kids may be so involved with their friends and with school that they ask fewer questions. We often dread the transition children will make from childhood to adulthood, and so we are reluctant to talk about it. We procrastinate. We fear the enormity of the challenges they will face. We feel a sense of loss as they cease being the little kids who depended on us so completely. And we can remember so clearly the confusion and pain of our own transitions through puberty and block out our own memories in part by ignoring the fact that our own kids are headed down the same road. And yet the late elementary school years are perhaps the most vital time to impact your child's character.

An important aspect of preparation is recognizing how crucial repetition is in parental sex education.

Principle 9:
Repetition is critical; repetition is really, really important.

Young children love repetition. They seem never to tire of reading the same favorite book or playing the same favorite game over and over. Family rituals become a bedrock of stability and security for them. Children learn through repetition; we all do. There is a comfort and joy in repetition. In many of our churches we repeat the Lord's Prayer and the Apostles' Creed, and if we allow ourselves, we continue to learn from such rituals, whose meaning is never lost but only deepens with repetition.

The lessons of Christian sex education also need to be repeated over and over. After all, the world will be repeating its messages about sexuality over and over to our children in movie after movie, joke after joke, television program and commercial after program and commercial. On and on the sexual messages of the world will come at our children. Our lessons cannot be offered to our children once for all, but must be renewed and revisited. The later elementary school years are a wonderful time for repetition before puberty, middle school, and social changes begin to introduce their confusions.

Explaining Puberty to Your Child

The age of onset of puberty has been steadily decreasing. The average age for onset of menstruation for girls is now under age twelve. Some girls, in fact, are beginning their menstrual periods as early as age nine, though others can begin their periods as late as age sixteen or seventeen. Boys are beginning to go through puberty between the ages of thirteen and fourteen. It is not at all uncommon for persons to be sexually mature for just as long in their life before they marry as they were sexually immature. The average boy spends thirteen years before puberty and then fourteen years after puberty before he marries, and the average young woman today spends twelve years before puberty and then thirteen more years as a sexually mature woman before she marries.

We summarize here some of the things you need to tell your children in the kind of language you might use with them during the late elementary school years. As you discuss these changes with your sons and daughters, work hard to be positive and affirming. Tell kids they will be receiving a gift in installments over the next few years, the gift of an adult body. God is the Gift-Giver, and He means them well with His gift. Explain that you as a parent are excited about that gift and that you want to help them know as much as possible about the gift and how to use it wisely and well. Start these discussions early, before the actual onset of puberty. With the acute self-consciousness kids feel going through puberty, discussions about their bodies and their experiences can be more difficult during puberty itself.

We have written two books for kids in the prepuberty period. *What's the Big Deal? Why God Cares About Sex* (book 3 in the GOD'S DESIGN FOR SEX series) is written for kids eight to eleven and is designed for a parent and child to read together. *Facing the Facts: The Truth About Sex and You* (book 4) is written for kids eleven to fourteen. *Facing the Facts* is designed so your child can read it alone, though we urge you to think about reading it alongside your child and talking about the issues it raises. Ideally, we think each of these books should be read early in its designated age ranges, particularly *Facing the Facts* in preparation for puberty, generally around age eleven or twelve. These books contain thorough examples of how to talk to your child about the changes of puberty, and so we will be brief here.

What to Expect with Girls

Girls typically grow through pubertal changes a year or two before boys. They go through unexpected growth spurts. In a society consumed with how much people weigh, girls often are concerned when they put on weight unexpectedly. Their hips, thighs, and shoulders begin to round out and broaden. Their breasts grow, beginning with development underneath the nipple (what is called the breast bud) and then spreading out from there. At times, a girl's breasts can feel swollen or tender. Under the influence of hormones, the quality of her sweat begins to change and she may begin to need to use deodorant. The girl has more body hair, starting with light pubic hair but including the development of underarm hair and possibly light fuzzy hair as a mustache. She can develop pimples and acne. She may experience extreme alternation between having a lot of energy and feeling deprived of energy.

In the year following the beginning of breast development, she begins to get more pubic hair, which starts to grow in straight and gradually grows coarser. Her labia, which form the outer part of her genitals, grow slightly larger and take on a deeper, ruddier color. Many people do not realize that just as boys experience spontaneous erections, girls experience spontaneous lubrication of the vagina. Girls thus may begin to be aware of a feeling of wetness in their vaginas and the creases between their labia. Some young women notice vaginal lubrication or wetness when they wake up from a dream (this is the female version of a boy's wet dream).

Menstruation typically begins between a year and a year and a half after the girl begins to experience breast development. She may experience backaches, tenderness of her abdomen, and a bloated feeling in her abdomen on an irregular basis for several months before menstruation begins. She should be well educated about menstruation before it begins. Initial periods tend to be irregular, and this is not a cause for alarm.

Some families celebrate the girl's first period. They make it a time of recognition of the girl's transition from childhood to the beginnings of adulthood. Whether you have a family party, a quiet and special dinner just for daughter and mother, or just a positive talk with your daughter, it's vital to make this a time of true affirmation. Starting menstruation is a symbol of her womanhood, of the totality of God's marvelous gift of femininity to her. Help her appreciate this great gift.

The earlier onset of puberty today creates a situation where a woman can get pregnant before she has the strength and physical stamina to tolerate a pregnancy well. Girls who give birth prior to age sixteen are much more likely to die in childbirth; their risk has been cited as being up to 400 percent higher than for adult women. Early pregnancy also creates tremendous health risks for the baby. Babies born to young girls are more likely to be premature, to have low birth weight, and to have more birth defects. Complications with birth and prematurity can lead to such conditions as mental retardation.

The girl's body is also more capable of being sexually aroused after going through puberty. Her clitoris and all of the tissues of her genital area grow more sensitive during this time. Some girls will notice this and experiment with masturbation by rubbing their genitals with their hands or possibly with an object such as a pillow. All of these changes take place in spurts over months and months; remember, puberty is a period of time, not an event. Girls and boys experience an increased capacity for sexual pleasure (and interest in such pleasure) as they go through puberty.

Tell them about the experience of orgasm, saying something like, "Honey, one of the changes your body will go through is that it becomes more able to experience pleasure from your sexual organs. Women and men both are able to have what are called orgasms. You've probably heard the word before. An orgasm is a brief burst of intense good feeling that every person can have when he or she has felt sexual pleasure for some time. Married people can feel orgasms when they have sexual intercourse if they learn to please each other. This is part of the joy of being together and sharing our bodies. Girls and boys may have orgasms in their sleep during a dream; the dream may or may not be about sex. Girls and boys may also have orgasms if they touch their own genitals or if they let another person touch them. The ability to feel orgasm is a gift from God; it really feels wonderful. But like all of God's gifts, we should use it the way He wants us to."

The girl's emotional development is influenced by her having gradually stronger sexual feelings and specific sexual thoughts. As with the boys, she experiences anxiety with these changes. With the onset of her menstrual cycle, she may experience significant mood shifts. Being conscious of her bodily changes and quite unsure about how she feels about them, she may become defensive and evasive about her body. Parents can ask about what is happening with her and receive extremely vague replies, if any at all.

Socially, girls often vacillate between avoidance of boys and fascination with them. They try out new social skills and styles for relating with boys, playing at being shy, coy, rowdy, or flirtatious. Girls are often more successful in school at this age than boys are and will take great comfort in their successes in this area. They can become very interested in femininity and work hard to fit whatever is promoted as the most influential ideal for being feminine.

What to Expect with Boys

Boys typically begin the transformation of puberty about two years later than girls. Teenage boys between ten and thirteen go through a period of general physical development. They get taller. Their shoulders broaden, their muscles get larger, and they get stronger. Many boys experience slight swelling of their breasts around their nipples and some tenderness there. This is a normal reaction that some boys have to the changing hormones in their bodies and is not necessarily a sign of anything being wrong in their development. Their perspiration begins to smell stronger, like an adult's, so most boys need to begin using deodorant. Their skin and hair gets oilier. They begin to develop hairier arms and legs, and hair under their arms. They get the beginnings of a beard and mustache. Pubic hair, which begins growing in straight, gradually becomes more curly and coarse. They can begin to develop pimples or acne, and their voices begin to change.

A number of changes are specific to the boy's sexual development. His penis and scrotum grow larger. Boys will often notice that their scrotum is looser and that the skin of the scrotum develops more wrinkles. With the onset of puberty, boys begin to have more spontaneous erections — erections that appear to happen for no particular reason. This is usually very embarrassing for them. It's essential to inform them that this will be happening and is no cause for alarm. Tell boys about orgasms in the way we discussed a few pages back. Many boys begin to experience wet dreams, where they ejaculate in their sleep. Sometimes this is in response to a sexual dream, but not necessarily. Many boys have their first ejaculation during a wet dream. Wet dreams are often a point of deep embarrassment for them. They have no voluntary control of this response and should never be criticized or disciplined in any way for it. It is best simply to tell your son ahead of time that this will happen, let him know that you understand that it might be an embarrassment, and give him permission to change his own sheets as often as he might like. Many boys will experiment with masturbation during this period of transition. Boys begin to think about sex during this time, including moving from general sexual feelings to more specific sexual thoughts.

Emotional changes are underway. The development of stronger sexual feelings and of sexual interest in girls can be intimidating and anxiety producing for boys. They worry about their normalcy and not being accepted, and they are sensitive to embarrassment with their peers and about anything they perceive as a failure or a mistake. Typically they have a strong interest in girls but attempt to hide it. They develop an intense interest in being "manly" and are likely to be overly concerned and defensive about this.

In their social relationships, most boys desperately want to be accepted by their peers. The struggle to learn how to relate to girls is difficult. They need to try out new ways of relating to them, but are afraid of failure. They can often overreact to their own perceived failures. The approval of their group of friends becomes very important, and no one wants to be perceived as less than a man.

The transition of boy to man should be celebrated too, even though this transition is harder to mark for boys than for girls. A father can acknowledge the growth and change he sees in his son and welcome his son into manhood.

What to Say About Uncomfortable Urges

You can tell both boys and girls that the sexual feelings and yearnings they will feel during and after the puberty period can be powerful, mysterious, and at times very uncomfortable. One of the most troubling but common experiences of many teens is to feel sexual arousal in unexpected ways. Boys especially can find themselves sexually aroused by girls they don't find attractive or don't like. They may feel sexual attraction to a cousin, sister, or friend of the family. They may get turned on by television commercials, magazine ads, or lewd jokes describing deviant sexual acts. The same thing can happen to girls — they can feel aroused by someone they dislike or by thinking about rape.

Because teenage sexual arousal can be unfocused, many normal heterosexual teens find themselves on occasion feeling a sexual response to hearing about homosexual acts or to thinking about another girl's or boy's body. Help teenagers to take this in stride by recognizing it for what it is. They are going through a period when identity as a sexually mature adult is being shaped. Remember the study we mentioned in chapter 8 showing that only 11 percent of young men who initially reported they had some same-sex attraction still reported those feelings one year later. Early on in this process, they do not have as definite a "form" to their sexuality as they will later. Warn them about these experiences, and tell them not to worry about them. Such occasional feelings are to be expected and will eventually resolve. Their job during this period is to be thankful for their awakening sexual feelings, make the right decisions that God wishes of them, enjoy their relationships, and be patient with themselves as they grow up. They do not have to act on any of the sexual feelings they experience.

Some children and teenagers engage in sexual experimentation, including same-sex behavior, and this needs to be discussed as well (we discussed these statistics in chapter 2). Same-sex experimentation can take the forms of guys wrestling and grabbing one another's genitals, girls practicing kissing or petting as they talk about dating, two boys watching each other masturbating, and so forth. It is vital to not label such behavior as homosexual; to do so is to brand the person on the basis of an action. If you discover your child engaging in any of these activities, never say, "Stop that homosexual play!" or "Are you trying to become gay?" Children can be branded with doubt by such statements. Instead discipline them for their failures to protect the privacy and sanctity of their own bodies, but always in the context of affirming their basic normalcy.

At the same time, we should talk with them compassionately about the feelings that might have been associated with their actions: curiosity, fear of not fitting in, loneliness. We might say something like this for ten-year-olds: "Bill, because you were engaging in sexual play with Jeremy, showing each other your penises, you are restricted from playing with him for one week. Acting like that is inappropriate. It is very normal to be curious about another boy's body. But you are meant to keep your body private, so that you will be able to make it a special gift to your future wife. Your body and its sexual feelings are a special gift from God to you. I'm punishing you now because you did not make a good choice of how to use that gift." If children confess such actions to us, we should again talk with them with compassion and help them to structure their lives to try to make sure it doesn't happen again.

Preparing for Adolescence

Scientific research[1] shows four factors to be significant predictors of teenage sexual experimentation (and each of these is rooted in at least one of the five aspects of sexual character we have been discussing):

1. the closeness of the relationship of the child with his or her parent (character factor: needs)

2. the amount of sexual experimentation that goes on in the peer group (character factors: needs, supports)

3. the teen's religious beliefs and practice (character factors: needs, values, beliefs, supports)
4. how intent on and confident of success and achievement in school the child is (character factors: needs, values, beliefs)

We discuss each factor and its implications for parenting below. Each exerts its powerful influence on sexual behavior in adolescence, but parents will be too late if they wait for adolescence to begin working on these factors.

The Power of a Close Parental Relationship

In elementary school, children begin to move outward from the family, building friendships and steadily coming under more and more influence of those outside of the family. They spend more time with friends in the friends' homes, thus falling under the influence of the values of other families. Relationships with their friends — their peers — become more and more influential. Kids begin to hear different messages from influential adults, especially their teachers in school.

Once the child is in adolescence, the closer the child says his or her relationship is with parents, the less likely the child is to be having sex. A close relationship between parent and child appears to instill in the child the desire to want to live out the values and moral beliefs of the parent. In other words, part of the power of a parent to influence the children's morality lies not so much in how loudly or eloquently that parent expresses his or her moral views, but rather in the power of the love relationship between the parent and the child. This makes sense, as part of our obedience to God is because we love the Lawgiver (see John 14:15,23). If we want to have a powerful impact on our children's morality, we must be close enough to them that they will want to follow in our moral footsteps. This is our next major sex education principle:

Principle 10:
Close, positive parent-child relationships are crucial.

Take advantage of the late elementary years. In elementary school, perhaps especially in late elementary school, you have an opportunity to either foster a continuing close relationship with your child or to let your child slip away. It's easy to let the child slip away as he or she becomes more independent, more involved with friends, and more difficult to communicate with. To continue to build a close relationship, put effort and creative energy into the relationship. Think of good opportunities to spend time with your child. These are not times to lecture or instruct, but simply to enjoy being with him or her. One of the great dangers of the busyness of our lives, of our investment in careers, church, and everywhere but the family, is that we simply will not be there for our children, available to be close to them and to enjoy them. Build a relationship grounded on encouragement and praise. Mindful of their fragile sense of self at this age, take every opportunity to build your children up; communicate your confidence in them and your excited expectation for what life has in store for them. Avoid unnecessary battles, which become more likely as kids move through puberty into adolescence; allow your love to cover a multitude of sins (see 1 Peter 4:8), and forgive as Christ forgave us (see Ephesians 4:32).

Be an askable parent. Continue during the elementary school years to work on being an askable parent. Among other things, try the following:

- *Praise your children when they ask questions, any questions, but especially questions about sexuality and relationships. Acknowledge how threatening it can be to talk about such things.*
- *Praise manifestations of their understanding of what you have been teaching. Ask, for example, what God would think about the way women are portrayed in a television commercial or the way sex is treated in a sitcom, and praise their insightfulness as they use what you have taught them.*
- *Restrain your impatience; give them time to develop their questions. Attempt to provide a good answer to any question a child asks, regardless of how confusing the question is. Often our discomfort leads us to hurry the child or demand clarification that the child cannot provide; this comes across as rejection or other negative reactions.*

In the turbulent adolescent years, a close personal relationship with a parent, especially between a young woman and her mom, can serve as a foundation for fundamental personal loyalty, so that when the girl is making sexual decisions on a date, she will see the morality her parents taught her not just as abstract rules but as an issue of personal loyalty. She will have to decide, not between a persistent boy and an abstract principle, but between her relationship with the boy and her relationship with her mother. Hopefully she will see her parents as representatives of God's character, and her relationship with them will reinforce the values and beliefs they have taught her.

Remember also that your child, like you, needs to be loved and affirmed. When the teen's relationship with one or both parents provides rich love and acceptance and praise, that child doesn't have as great a need to go into a dating relationship or a sexual relationship to get the love he or she needs. If we feed them full at home, we send them to the grocery store satisfied rather than starving. Beware, however, of letting a healthy relationship drift into becoming an unhealthy, clinging one. A close relationship is founded on respect, appreciation, and genuine care for the other, not on fear, mistrust, dependence, or insecurity.

Answer personal questions carefully. In this context of discussing having a real relationship with your developing child, you can best answer the daunting question, "What do I say if my child asks me what I did, what rules I lived by, before I was married?" Some parents will have the joy of honestly saying they followed God's plan for them. Others will not. Knowledge of the sexual actions of their parents may be too much for younger children, so parents might want to tell a younger child (perhaps twelve or younger) that they will talk about their own pasts when the child is closer to adolescence. A good time to talk with the child may be when he or she begins to experience stronger interest in the opposite sex.

True, close relationships are grounded in honesty. Honesty is essential. No parents, especially those who have pasts involving extensive promiscuity, should feel compelled to disclose details of their pasts or describe them in ways that compromise their own privacy or the imaginations of their kids. A simple statement such as "I made very foolish choices in a relationship when I was in college" or "No, I was not a virgin when we married. I was not a Christian then and really lived by the rules of the world rather than of God" should be enough. Kids' requests for more details should be turned down.

Your response should also include the following elements.

Choices and feelings. First, discuss how you feel now about your choices then. Statements like "Well, everyone has to sow a few wild oats" will obviously not help your cause, whereas "I look back now and see that I felt as if no one loved me, that I had to give sex to be liked, and that I took horrible risks with my life" will be helpful.

Choices and consequences. Second, discuss the consequences of your choices, both the clearly negative consequences (emotional pain, feeling cheated, realizing that you used people, disease, pregnancy, abortion) and the consequences that seemed positive at the time — "You know, I really felt as if sex made my relationship with that man into true love, and I enjoyed sex, but when the relationship ended I realized that having sex made it harder to see that this was not a marriage relationship of real love but just an infatuation that could not last. I also realized that the good feelings physically did not make up for all the pain and regret I felt later."

Choices and challenge. Third, you should challenge your children to do better than you. Challenge them to not let your failures become their failures. Finally, discussing such an experience is a perfect time for a powerful lesson in God's forgiveness and redemption for your child. It gives you a chance to testify to how God can bring healing and good, through His grace, even out of our failures.

We know such a process strikes fear into the hearts of many a parent. But we should have the courage of the gospel in sharing with our children how God can make all things new. We should have the courage displayed in the Scriptures themselves, which show the saints of God throughout the ages — warts, sins, and all — as they grow in grace. We are in good company in taking on such a daunting task!

The Power of the Peer Group

The sexual activity of a teenager's peer group is another factor that predicts a teenager's sexual activity. We all want to fit in and be accepted. If a child is not close to her parents and if she is seeking the approval of a sexually active peer group, she is very likely to begin having sex. Based on this, it's vital you work to strengthen your relationship with preteens and take a vigilant role toward your child's involvement in a group of peers. The easiest time to influence a teen's choice of peer group is before she ever becomes a teen.

Stay close. You can have the most powerful influence on your child's selection of friends by simply working hard to stay close. The child who has a strong relationship with parents, who is closely attached to the parents, is going to tend to seek out a group of friends whose values, morals, and activities would tend to meet with the approval of the parents. Use positive praise and encouragement to foster involvement in church youth groups and to steer them toward friends who come from healthy, involved families.

Kids who feel distant and disconnected from their parents are more likely to choose peer groups at odds with the morality and wishes of the parents. If you sense a distance in your relationships with your children and are worried about the peers that they are choosing as friends, your task is much more difficult. Under these circumstances, be very careful not to instigate terrible power struggles that further alienate your kids from you. This calls for the wisdom of Solomon and fervent prayer.

Decide about boundaries. If you are really worried about a child's selection of friends, you may have to take direct and decisive action to break him or her away from those friends. This can be extremely difficult; really count the cost of taking this gamble. First, realize that there are large areas of your child's life that you cannot begin to control. Kids can spend time with undesirable friends at school, at school activities, and so forth, and you may have little to say about this. Second, while to some extent you can prevent them from associating with certain undesirables, you cannot create friendships with desirable kids for them. Your own children have to be actively involved in that process.

Sometimes you will be more likely to meet with success if you don't try to separate your kids from an undesirable peer group, but rather encourage them to also be active in other, different peer groups. You may not get them to stop hanging around with one group, but if you can also get them in a church youth group or other more desirable group, at least you will have begun to blunt or diffuse the influence of the negative peer group. You don't create friendships for kids by encouraging them to be involved in groups, but you can at least encourage them to be in the right place at the right time, where they are more likely to form the right kinds of friendships. Also, talking with other parents who are involved in the same dilemma can be extremely helpful.

The Importance of Personal Faith

Adolescents who have a firm, personal, religious faith are less likely to be sexually active than their peers. A firm faith in Christ does at least four powerful things for our children:

1. Above all, it places them in a relationship with the living God, who through the work of the Holy Spirit can plant His law in their hearts and give them His own strength to face their trials and temptations.
2. A relationship with God is perhaps the most critical relationship every person needs to meet his or her need for relatedness and significance.
3. A living faith reinforces the moral beliefs that we have advocated teaching throughout this book.
4. A living faith helps to place our children in a community of faith, a fellowship of fellow believers who are together trying to live according to God's will. This peer support is essential.

For all of these reasons, we should work diligently during the elementary school years to build up the living faith of our kids, that they might be strengthened for the challenges of adolescence.

The Value of Academic Achievement

Children who have academic goals, especially those who are confident of going on to college and who believe that school is an exciting place to work hard and achieve, are more likely to delay their sexual experimentation than academically discouraged or hopeless kids. It seems that children who have lost hope of success in their preparation for meaningful work are more likely to pursue physical pleasures. If their future is dark, why not?

The real issue here is not whether the child values and gets high grades. This would sound like kids who make As will remain virgins and kids who get Cs are destined to fall into promiscuity. No, the real issue here is whether children have hope for meaningful lives where they have something constructive to offer to the world that gives them a reason not to fall into the empty pursuit of pleasure wherever they can find it. We can forgo the satisfaction of our selfish desires when we have a higher purpose that calls us beyond ourselves. In the absence of any higher purpose, we naturally move toward the simple gratification of our own wants and desires.

We should encourage our children's performance in school and their having goals to work to their best abilities. But at a deeper level we need to give our kids hope for the significance of their lives regardless of how well they do in school. We do this by having an attitude that respects the dignity of all work, an attitude that suggests that they can serve a purpose in God's kingdom regardless of whether they are a theoretical physicist or a ditchdigger.

If we build up our relationships with them, gently guide the formation of their peer groups, and give them a deep sense of hope and significance for the future, we will be laying vital foundations for their living sexually pure lives.

Conclusion

The late elementary school years, before puberty begins, are a vital time for positively introducing children to the wonderful and amazing changes that lie ahead of them. So much rides on the crucial decisions they will soon be making. We must carefully continue our work of building the foundation of character they will take into their adolescent years. In addition to what we have just discussed, we remind our readers that this period is also the optimal time to work on developing the critical skills we discussed in chapter 3, the skills of empathy, assertiveness, self-control, delay of gratification, and decision making. At this age, your kids are still close, but they are experiencing more and more challenging situations. Use every opportunity to encourage their growth in strength in these critical areas.

PART 4

The Transitional Years: Through Puberty

CHAPTER 12

Preparing for Romance, Sexual Attraction, and Dating

"Mom, a guy named Dirk asked me to go to the football game with him and then to go hang around afterward. He is, like, a really cool guy. Some of the other guys call him Snake, but I'm not sure why. He says that dropping out of school was a big mistake, but he's so smart that I'm sure he'll get back into school after he gets a job and gets his really cool car paid off. He said getting the tattoos was, like, a big mistake, and the parts of his head that were shaved are growing out. He doesn't go to church, but he says he's really spiritual. I don't think his being five years older than me is a problem, because I'm, like, about as mature as him. And he promised not to smoke or drink while we were out. I can go, right?"

Words to chill the heart of any parent.

What do you plan to do about your child and dating? In this chapter we will outline the kinds of issues parents should think through and talk about with kids during their transition through puberty, in preparing for dating. We should gently but firmly surround our teenagers with a supportive framework of rules about romantic relationships that will allow them time to mature and grow in strength before they face the challenges that adulthood will offer them. Hopefully, as they move into readiness to form and experience such relationships, the following are increasingly true:

- *You have built a history of helping them meet their needs for relatedness and significance in healthy and godly ways. Teenagers who enter romantic relationships with a deep sense of love and acceptance from parents and from God and with a sense of confidence in the meaning of their own lives and ability to serve God well with their gifts and abilities are strong young people. These teens also understand their deepest needs and can make mature decisions about how to get those needs met.*

- *You have supplied them with the most important core beliefs about sexual morality, with accurate information about sexuality, and with a growing understanding of what love between a man and a woman is like.*
- *They have come to value the right things. Adolescence is when we begin to truly discover whether we have taught them by example and word to value conformity, approval of others, and self-gratification, or rather chastity, strength, independence, purity, and obedience.*
- *They have the skills to handle themselves well. They can resist peer pressure, say no, defend themselves, think through situations and risks, and articulate their beliefs.*
- *They have supportive relationships. Your support as parent, provided in the forms of affection and encouragement but also rules and limits, can give your children moral strength at a time when other relationships are depleting that strength. They also have positive and supportive peer relationships.*

The Realities of Romance and Dating

Research shows clearly that over 90 percent of adults will marry during their lifetime. The average age at which they marry for the first time is now above twenty-five and twenty-seven for women and men, respectively. Thus teenagers experiencing the first blush of romantic attraction are typically facing many years before they will commit themselves in marriage to another. You can help your children to think in godly, positive, and long-term ways about how they will handle their romantic feelings and relationships in order to honor God and experience His best for them for the rest of their lifetimes. Speak candidly with them about how their actions in their teen and young adult years will set the stage, for better or worse, for what they will experience for the rest of their lives.

Dating or Courtship?

Perhaps the first thing you'll have to settle in your mind is what you believe about dating. In the first edition of this book, we took a positive stance toward dating, trying to provide suggestions for how a teen could honor God in dating relationships. What we said generated some strong negative reactions. We discovered what we had previously been unaware of: that some Christians believe that dating itself is a corrupt social practice that fosters immorality and relational confusion, a practice that should be replaced in Christian families by what they argue to be a biblical pattern of courtship.[1]

Courtship relationships are modeled after what is understood to be a biblically mandated approach to establishing marital relationships. There are no examples in the Bible, they argue, of emotionally intimate male-female relationships outside marriage. Advocates of courtship tend to argue two points based on Numbers 30 and on those biblical passages that describe how biblical figures married. This means, first, we should reject the invalid, failed, and fictionalized notion of the lightning bolt of "true love" telling us that we have found "the *one*." Instead we should embrace a biblical understanding of marital love that grows in the context of mutual submission to Christ and of utter and complete devotion to our spouses based on obedience to Christ. Second, romantic relationships between a man and a woman should happen only when the man and woman are actually considering marriage and should be under the spiritual authority and practical oversight of the woman's parents (primarily her father).

We resonate with some of the deepest concerns of courtship advocates. Many young people do have an unrealistic view of romantic love. They think that we are passive as love strikes us and then perhaps later dries up, leaving us free to fall in love with another. Hence we must wander from relationship to relationship seeking the desired bolt from above. Christian marriage is undergirded with something much stronger and enduring. Perhaps no one has said it better than C. S. Lewis:

> Love as distinct from "being in love" is not merely a feeling. It is a
> deep unity, maintained by the will and deliberately strengthened

by habit; reinforced by (in Christian marriages) the grace which both partners ask, and receive, from God. . . . "Being in love" first moved them to promise fidelity; this quieter love enables them to keep the promise. It is on this love that the engine of marriage is run; being in love was the explosion that started it.[2]

We also agree that dating is unhealthy if understood as a revolving door of emotionally (and sexually) intimate couplings. Further, dating should not be utterly isolated from one's family, especially in the teen years. Finally, we agree that one does not best prepare for marriage by forming and breaking a long series of romantically intense and exclusive relationships.

But these agreements do not take us to the place of rejecting dating in favor of courtship. The core reason is that we do not see the pattern described in the Bible for establishing marriage as necessarily mandated by God as the only way to establish marriages. Just because the Bible never describes democracy as a form of governmental rule in the Old Testament does not mean it is an invalid form of government today, and similarly we do not believe that relationships between single young people today need to follow Old Testament courtship patterns precisely. What we must preserve are the biblical moral absolutes for relationships, which have been the focus of this entire book.

Changing Realities

It is very hard today to speak with any confidence about a general picture of the romance scene for young people. Dating as it was practiced in the 1970s and 1980s has become much less common. Young people today are much more likely to do things in groups and less likely to have formal dates. One study on college campuses found that two-thirds of women had five or fewer dates in their entire four-year college experience. Dating has been replaced by informal hanging out, but also increasingly by hooking up.

Hooking up today means casual, relationship-less sex where the two individuals involved gratify each other's sexual appetites but without commitment and without any perception that their sexual interchange means they have a stable relationship. Parents need to encourage and challenge their preteens and teens to conduct their relationships in a way that runs counter to the culture and honors God.

We'd like to sound specific cautions.

Discourage early romance. Given the realities today of when marriage tends to occur, parents should discourage early involvement in romance. There is strong evidence that adolescents who start dating early are more likely to begin having sexual intercourse early.[3] Those who mature early are more likely to get into trouble with premarital sex than are "late bloomers." Because of the influence of peers, kids who are in groups that start dating early are at greater risk. Early dating is not harmless.

Beware of dishonesty. There is a high level of dishonesty in many adolescent dating relationships. Studies continue to show that teenage boys, in particular, feel it is okay to exaggerate or even lie about their feelings for the girl, especially to get sex. Lying about one's sexual history (previous partners, STDs — even HIV) is also rampant. We need to give our kids a clear sense of the extent of trust that is reasonable and communicate with them that when it comes to sex, both men and women have many incentives to be dishonest.

Warn of date rape. We must warn our girls in particular about the growing prevalence of date rape and forced sex; we discuss this at the end of this chapter.

Expectations for Teen Relationships

Begin your discussions with teenagers by talking about the purposes their teen relationships should serve. Too much of what kids pick up on their own is destructive. Boy-girl relationships can be presented wrongly as the place where you prove your value as a woman by pleasing a young man or by being the woman the guys pursue — even if you pay for that pleasing and pursuit with your own sexual purity — or as the place where a boy shows his manhood by domination and manipulation of a woman, by "getting all he can." Parents can discourage any sense that dating in the teen years is likely to result in marriage. While this does happen, the statistics suggest that it is unlikely. Also, one statistic in particular should urge caution for parents and teens: Couples who marry early, before age nineteen, are more likely to divorce than those who marry in any other age category. As we will argue later, the best test of true love is the test of time and restraint.

Teen Relationships Are Valuable

Teenagers need positive expectations for teen relationships. We must try to strike a balance between on the one hand giving them positive expectations that will serve them well later and on the other hand encouraging caution and restraint in building romantic relationships while they give themselves time to mature.

Teen relationships present opportunities for teens to have fun, to enjoy different activities, to get to know a wide variety of people, and to learn better what they really like and respect in people. They are a great place to enjoy friendships with and learn more about the other sex. Good marriages are built, in part, on friendship with one's spouse and on an understanding of the other person. Our kids can begin the process of becoming good spouses by learning to be friends with people of the other sex.

Peer relationships are also opportunities for teens to grow in confidence and skill at handling themselves in challenging situations. When friendships and dating relationships are handled rightly, teenagers will be able to gain self-assurance as they slowly move out from the family and successfully handle the challenges they will face: peer pressure; confusion; how to stop, slow down, or deepen intimacy; and how to put a stop to a relationship that is no longer healthy or helpful.

Sex Is Not Everything

Parents often do their kids a disservice by focusing so much on the sexual dimension of romantic relationships that they ignore the greater significance of the emotional dynamics. We feel strongly enough about this to offer it as our next principle:

Principle 11:
Sexuality is not the most important thing in life.

What do people ultimately want from their human relationships? Sexual thrills satisfy only the most superficial levels of our yearnings. We must keep our sexuality in proper perspective. It is a vital and beautiful gift, but it is itself a signpost pointing us to a deeper reality—our capacity to love God and to love and become one with a special person. All of the smoke about sexual feelings can hide the real fire creating the smoke. The adolescent finds out in his or her heart what each of us must ultimately discover: We are made to be incomplete by ourselves, and we long for union with God and another special person to be made complete. In their awakenings to a desire for a romantic relationship, our kids will experience the powerful emotional awakenings of their true selves, the selves that are restless until they rest in a relationship of union with God and spouse.

These relationships are thus an opportunity to feel strong feelings of interest and infatuation, or even to fall in and out of love, and thus over time to learn what true love really is. Teenagers must understand that they will experience such ups and downs many times before they learn what real love is — though no one really understands this until they go through it. These relationships are a great place to learn that "love at first sight" is mostly an illusion; teens learn this reality as feelings come and go. They can learn that it is not really easy at all to distinguish infatuation from real love but that the best test is simply to be patient and see if the feelings endure. Another of the differences between infatuation and true love is that true love can see flaws in the other and still love. Any real relationship can stand the test of time, and if it can stand the test of time it can also stand the test of sexual restraint. We should never interpret for our kids that what they are feeling at age sixteen is not true love. Rather we should rejoice with them that they feel love and encourage them that if what they are experiencing is true love, it will be deepened and made yet more beautiful by sexual purity and exercising the patient discipline of allowing the relationship to develop slowly. James Dobson has a helpful discussion of many other myths of "love" in his book *Preparing for Adolescence*.[4]

Tell Your Stories

Remember the power of stories. One of the most helpful things you can do as a parent is to tell your stories to your kids. Tell them of the ups and downs you experienced. Tell them what the power of infatuation felt like when you were sure it was lifelong love. Tell them about the obsessive way you wrote your flame's name over and over, the way your whole day revolved around when he would call you, or the way you got an electric thrill to see her smile at you. Tell them about your confusion and pain as a relationship died a lingering death. Tell them about the agony of betrayal. Tell them about the fear of asking out the one you thought you adored. Tell them of the boredom and frustration of discovering that you were not enjoying the one you were with. Tell them how your powerful feelings blinded you to his flaws and led you to exaggerate his perfections. Do all this to give your children a wider range of experiences, namely your experiences, to serve as vantage points from which they can see their own experiences more clearly.

In their relationships with the other sex, teens will experience feelings of sexual attraction and have opportunities to learn how to handle those feelings rightly and glorify God in the process. It's a normal and good thing for them to feel sexual excitement for someone they care for, to want to kiss, to touch and be touched, and even to want to be united with someone sexually. But we must also tell them, again, that they do not have to act on those feelings, that it will not hurt them *not* to act on those feelings, that if it is a godly relationship it will not hurt the relationship either, and that God wants them to follow His rules. They also have the opportunity to learn that sexual attractions to other people do not disappear when we feel infatuation and love and that sexual purity requires discipline. A dating relationship is a wonderful place to follow God's commands and see how He will bless obedience and purity.

Dating is an opportunity to grow to love your future spouse. We probably should not utterly separate teen dating from its connection to marriage; after all, some people do begin dating their spouse-to-be in the teen years. But we should balance this possibility by gently letting teens know that many long dating relationships do not make it to the altar.

Guidelines for Romance and Dating

Parents should not think of romantic relationships and dating in an all-or-nothing way. Kids' romantic relationships take many different forms today, and you need to have rough ideas of what you judge to be healthy at different ages and hence of what you will allow and approve of. Some patterns of dating have more potential than others to move adolescents toward more sexual experimentation: the more individual and private the pattern, the more likely it is to cause trouble.

Set Wise Limits

It is probably wise for both parents to have in mind the youngest age at which you will let your child begin a romantic relationship of any kind. We have discussed how kids who mature early and start dating early are at particular risk for early sexual activity. It is vital that you spend enough time setting limits with your kids and supporting them so they don't get in over their heads in adolescent sexual relationships. For instance, be clear with a precocious thirteen-year-old that she will not be allowed to date until the time you have determined, regardless of how aggressive the boys pursuing her are.

And if you're going to set limits, you'd better have the energy and resources to back them up; it's no use setting limits on dating and then leaving the child unsupervised three evenings of the week. It's not enough just to enforce limits; we also need to help our children to find other ways to get their needs met. The parent who sets limits but is not there to help and support the child is likely to be perceived by the child as cruel. We need to set the limits and provide the support.

How old is old enough? Decide at what age you might allow your child to attend a group activity or school function with another kid who is a romantic interest. For instance, parents might be willing to tell a fourteen-year-old boy, "If you want to spend time with Pam, you can invite her to the youth group or to go with us to church or to join the theater and drama group you're in at school. That's a great way for young people to get to know each other."

We did not let our children go on solitary or independent dates until they were sixteen. Our sense was that children can wait until they're old enough to drive before taking on the full responsibility of being out and on their own with another person. We always had curfews and restrictions on activities for such dating in high school. Remember, kids who operate under reasonable dating rules imposed by caring parents whom the kids are on good terms with are less likely to experiment with sex than kids from permissive homes. Be ready to talk about the rules, but also be ready to support your child by having limits.

The trust issue. Parents who set up guidelines for dating are likely to get hit with the trust issue — "Why don't you trust me?" Assure your kids that you do trust them and will continue to do so until proven otherwise. But that doesn't mean you similarly trust all of their friends or all the situations they might get into. It may be a good strategy to give an example from your own life when you had good intentions but got into a situation that was beyond your ability to handle.

Brenna experienced a terrifying and instructive example of this. At age sixteen she was set up on a blind date with a college basketball player who, thanks to her naiveté at that age, manipulated her to go up to his dorm room. He clearly took the fact that she had gone there as consent to have sex. In that situation, she could have easily been raped, but thankfully this enormous and powerful man had enough moral scruples not to victimize a younger girl. You may deeply trust your child's integrity, but your trust does not extend to situations and people your child does not control.

Remember too that you must be honest about your trust levels. If you don't trust your kids, tell them so. Trust is earned; it cannot be established on demand. Give your children opportunities to show they are trustworthy, but don't play stupid or blind when they violate your trust. When trust has been violated, it has to be rebuilt, and that rebuilding is a slow and painful process.

Make Teens Accountable

Teens should be accountable to definite plans and guidelines.[5] "Hanging out" is not a good plan, especially in early dating. Specific activities at specific locations should be the rule. Having the couple engage in deliberate forethought about what they will be doing can help prevent disastrous, spontaneous "doing what comes naturally." Parents today should beware of the illusion that cell phones establish accountability; just because you can reach your child does not mean you know where he or she is.

Couples should avoid sexually explicit media as part of their activities. Urge teenagers to choose activities wisely, and set limits on the kinds of activities they can pursue.

Urge Teens to Dress Modestly

Teens, especially young women, should dress modestly rather than provocatively. Everything a young woman does in a relationship, from mode of dress on, communicates some message about her moral standards. Young women from Christian families should not send out mixed signals.

Remind Teens to Choose Companions Carefully

Teens should choose all of their companions, especially those they date, very carefully. Our companions will shape who we are (see Proverbs 13:20; 28:7; 29:3).

Clarify Moral Standards

Teens should be prepared to state their moral standards with someone they are dating. They should set their physical limits and standards early and firmly. No infringements of their standards should be accepted. Many Christian boys today are having problems with sexually aggressive girls who push the young men to experiment sexually; teenage boys need to be prepared with their limits every bit as much as girls. We will discuss where to set these limits in the next chapter.

Introduce Prayer in Dating

Christian teens can include prayer in dating, both before and during a date. Our first date was actually to a talk given by Josh McDowell in 1973 entitled "Maximum Sex" (much to Stan's horror, who asked Brenna to go with him without knowing what the topic was going to be). Josh challenged Christian singles to include prayer in their dating relationships. As a result, we prayed together on our first date, and prayer has ever since been a source of strength and guidance for us as a couple. And remember from chapter 1 that praying together as a couple is one of the best predictors of marital happiness. If that is so, why not get in the habit of praying with people you care about?

Blast the Obligation System

If boys pay for the activities of a date, girls often feel obligated to the boys, that they somehow "owe" them. Many boys subtly encourage this feeling of obligation and have a specific repayment plan in mind for their monetary investment in the date. The place to start dealing with this problem is awareness — we should warn our daughters (and sons) about this occurring and make it very clear that they never owe part of their bodies to anyone. If the date seems to want something back, have your teen tell her date that you, her parents, will be more than happy to refund half of the cost of the date, with interest.

Steer Kids Away from High-Risk Situations

Teens should be urged to avoid high-risk situations. Parking alone in a car miles from anywhere is very risky, as is being alone in a house or apartment with no responsible adults around. Situations where men drastically outnumber women should be avoided or a hasty departure made. Perhaps the most risky situations are those where alcohol and drugs are involved.

Take an Absolute Stand on Alcohol and Drugs

Parents should take an absolute stand that their children not consume alcohol or drugs or be around others who are consuming them. Not only are alcohol and drugs problems in themselves, but numerous studies have found that kids who take risks with alcohol and drugs are also very likely to be involved with sexual experimentation. Unfortunately, the teenagers who are most likely to take risks with alcohol, drugs, or sex are the very ones who are least likely to recognize the dangers of the behaviors they are engaging in. One implication of this for our parenting is the need to be vigilant not only about the child's sexual behavior but also about any of the behaviors that fall into such risk-taking categories.

Urging a Pledge to Stay Chaste

An increasingly common aspect of many church-based and even school-based sex-education programs oriented toward encouraging abstinence is the "virginity pledge." The widespread "True Love Waits" campaign of the Southern Baptist Convention is one prominent example, but many other church curricula for youth groups encourage such a pledge, and books encourage parents to include a chastity pledge as the culmination of the sex talk with the younger teenager.

The core of the idea is this: Following a discussion about sex and morality with a young teenager, the parent asks the child to make a covenant, a solemn vow or promise, before the parent and God, that the child will remain sexually pure until marriage. When the child agrees to make this covenant, the parent is often encouraged to give the child a symbol or token of the agreement, usually a ring or necklace, which can serve as a constant reminder of the commitment the child has made.

The strengths of such an interaction include the following:

- *It appears generally true that one way to create commitment is to make commitments. Part of growing in belief and commitment is to vocalize our commitments, to take that step of faith of raising our hand or going to the altar or joining the church or agreeing to share what God has done in our lives. The strength of the chastity pledge procedure is that it challenges the child to make a commitment publicly and decisively.*

- *We applaud that such commitments are made in public and not in private. One of the most pernicious anti-Christian moral messages in our world today is the notion that sex is a private decision with only individual implications and dimensions. The reality is quite the reverse. The way we handle our sexuality has tremendous public ramifications. The choices our children make about their sexuality are intimately interwoven with all of their other choices of what they do with their lives. How they express their sexuality is intertwined with their public and private character. There is something right about the Christian adolescent being called to make a public commitment to the sexual morality standard that God calls us to.*

The weaknesses or potential problems, though, include the following:

- *Perhaps the greatest weakness of this approach is its seeming emphasis on one solution to the premarital sex problem. Often this emphasis on a pledge is promoted without a connection to a lifelong conversation between parent and child about sexuality, and such a relationship is the optimal one from which a young teenager will be best positioned to make a sincere chastity pledge.*
- *The chastity pledge method runs the risk of being artificial and heavy-handed. Teens who have such opportunities for pledging sprung on them may feel manipulated into making an insincere pledge. One of two bad outcomes could occur: The child could angrily reject the idea of making such a commitment when with greater patience and conversation he or she would have, or the child could make the commitment but feel that he or she has either lied to God and to the parent or has been trapped into making a promise unfairly.*

A recent excellent and widely debated scientific study suggests both the strengths and weaknesses of such pledges as a part of effective sex education.[6] The researchers studied a huge sample of adolescents, including a significant subpopulation who had taken a chastity or virginity pledge (mostly in the context of a church activity). They found the following:

- *Chastity pledges work in that those teens who made pledges were 34 percent less likely than their peers to be sexually active at every age.*
- *Those who were sexually abstinent were better off on an array of emotional (for example, self-esteem) and behavioral (for example, GPA) measures than teens who were sexually active.*
- *Despite harsh predictions by critics of the chastity pledge movement that those teens who violated their pledges would experience negative emotional consequences, teens who broke their pledges and became sexually active experienced no worse emotional outcomes than teens who never made such a pledge.*
- *Chastity pledges worked most effectively when the teens who made them were neither just one of a large crowd making such pledges nor utterly alone in doing so. If "everyone else is pledging," the effect of the pledge is minimized, but the effect of the pledge is also minimized if the teen feels no one else is doing it and he or she is alone.*
- *Pledgers do sometimes break their pledges, and when they do, they are 33 percent less likely to use contraception at first intercourse than if they had not taken a pledge. It appears that those who take pledges and later break them are unlikely to be honest with themselves that they are moving toward sexual experimentation and thus are more likely to have risky sex. It is this last finding that critics of abstinence approaches to sex education have trumpeted.*

In light of all this, we feel the strengths and potential benefits of asking a child to make a commitment to purity outweigh the dangers of doing so. Having a commitment talk with an adolescent can be a very helpful thing to do. But we recommend this with some cautions.

First, such a commitment talk must be seen as one more point in a long process of shaping a child's sexual character, a process that began in earliest childhood.

Second, such a talk should occur only if the following conditions are met:

- *You have a track record of openness and dialogue about the spiritual, moral, relational, and physical aspects of sexuality.*

- *The adolescent voices a genuine personal commitment to the Christian faith, one that goes beyond a passive submission to the parents' religious wishes.*
- *The parents feel sufficient readiness to go into such a conversation with the ability to back off if they sense hesitancy or ambiguity on the part of the child.*

Third, it's important that children not be put in a situation where they think they've been forced into making the covenant. We suggest that you raise the idea of a covenant, expressing the wish that your child make such a covenant. But explicitly tell your child that it is the child's decision and that you would like the child not to make the covenant on the spot. Rather urge the child to pray and reflect on the magnitude of his or her commitment for at least two days and then report back to you if he or she has decided to make the covenant with God. Describe the covenant as being between God and the adolescent.

The commitment talk begins with a summary of why you believe sexual purity to be God's will for your child's life. Remember, repetition of key lessons about sexuality is vital. Tell your child exactly why you think God wants him or her to be chaste. Discuss the coming struggles to stay pure, reminding the child of both the arguments others will use to encourage him or her to have sex and the pressures the child will feel to go along with the crowd. Pay special attention to the emotional side of relationships, of how the desire to be physical goes naturally with caring for another person. Be ready to answer, or find the answers to, any questions about the physical, emotional, relational, or spiritual aspects of sex.

The conclusion of the commitment talk, as we discussed it above, might go something like this:

Beth, your dad and I have always told you how strongly we believe that it is God's will that you save your sexual purity for marriage. This talk isn't the beginning or the end of our talking about sex. Sexuality is an important part of life for everyone. But now that you are a young woman, now that you have started your period and are capable of having sexual intercourse and of becoming pregnant, now that thinking about and being interested in boys and dating are going to become important parts of your life in the next few years, you are at a point where you have to decide what sort of life you will live.

Dad and I believe that what you will do with your body, whom you will share yourself with and when, is not an accident that happens to you. It's a decision. And while the world will tell you that sex is just good fun or that you have to have sex to fit in, God's ideas are different. He wants you to stay pure for the sake of His glory, your future marriage, and your own safety and welfare.

And so, I want to invite you to decide now what kind of life you will live sexually. And I invite you to make a commitment, a promise, to God and to some other person you respect. I would be glad to be that person. But I ask you not to make that decision and commitment now; it's too important to do on impulse. I ask you to really pray and think for the next two days what you really believe about sex and how you will live your life. Then I ask you to make a commitment based on what you decide. I won't pester you about this; if you don't come back to me I won't harass you. But this is too important a decision to make on a date or at a boy's house. Whatever you decide will shape your life forever. I pray you will make the right choice.

A process like this will help the child to internalize the covenant that he or she is making and maximize the impact of this technique.

Date Rape

This has largely been a positive chapter about an exciting development in the life of your child. We hate to close the chapter with a downer, but we must face potential problems. You should discuss the realities we cover in this chapter with your daughter as she moves out into more independent relationships with young men.

Defense Against Date Rape

The majority of rapes do not occur in the way so many of us imagine — a violent ambush by a total stranger with a weapon. Instead most rapes occur on dates or in male-female relationships where the rapist is known by the victim (so it is also called acquaintance rape). Estimates of the frequency of date rape are unclear, as this problem is underreported and in some cases hard to define. Based on surveys of college women, date rape may occur to as few as 3 to 4 percent or as many as 15 to 20 percent of women.

We need to take steps to prevent this from happening. First, prepare your daughter with the right understanding of male sexuality and human nature. Again, do not think of date rape as a violent ambush but rather most often as happening through persuasion, manipulation, blackmail, force, or even drugging. Teach your daughter that a man's sexual drive is not uncontrollable, that she is not there to meet the needs of a man she is dating, and that she is not harming him by remaining chaste and denying him sex. Men at their worst (indeed all of us at our worst) are capable of great selfishness and cruelty, and the godly response to such a reality is to prevent something evil from happening by exercising godly strength and forcefulness.

Communicate clearly. A woman's first defense against date rape is to communicate clearly about her sexual limits and standards. A woman must also be prepared to say no with every ounce of forcefulness. In addition to being prepared to repulse pressure with her words and even to threaten police prosecution of the man, young women should also be prepared to fight back physically if words are not enough. While physical resistance is not advised when the rapist is a stranger with a deadly weapon, in date rape situations a woman should strike out or gouge his eyes or break his finger to force him to back away. Girls are often afraid of physical violence, but the pain of a physical blow or two fades much more quickly than the emotional and physical pain of a rape. She should strike and yell, "Fire!" if anyone can hear, or strike and yell, "I'll keep fighting and you will go to jail if you touch me!" if no one can hear her.

Recognize danger. To prevent date rape, a woman should be able to recognize when she is in danger, to trust her instincts, and to act decisively to get out of danger. The research is unclear here, but the danger signals point to certain predictable characteristics of the woman, of the man, and of the situation.

Women who have been victims of date rape are often described as naive or vulnerable. Discussing this can quickly sound like blaming the victim for what happened, and we do not wish to do that. But no one should ever be able to describe our daughters as naive — the best cure for naiveté is information. A perpetrator is often simply taking advantage of opportunity, and so any perception that the woman he is with is isolated, unsupported, needy — in short, a good potential victim — makes that woman a target. Parents can help by being involved and communicating that they are there with their daughter. One small example: fathers simply being there when a boy picks up a girl from home to meet and shake hands (sometimes quite firmly) can make a difference in perception. Parents can also encourage girls to be strong and confident, and to conduct themselves to stay within their limits and protect themselves; if we do, they will be much less likely to become a victim.

Know the predictors. Two predictors indicate a man is likely to be the kind who would attempt a date rape: domineering and aggressive attitudes toward women and use of alcohol or drugs on dates. Girls need to listen carefully to the reputations of boys at school; they should do some homework on the person who has asked them out. Is he respectful, polite, and sober? They need to know the importance of avoiding like the plague risky young men and of exiting quickly if alcohol or drug use begins. Women should have a backup plan and ideally have a cell phone contact plan with parents who can extricate her if needed.

We need to train young women to look for danger signals and high-risk situations. Among the factors that predict rape will occur is one that is perhaps the most chilling — simple opportunity. Some men who would otherwise have no predisposition to rape will seize on the opportunity to coerce sex. Therefore, women should stay out of situations where there is the opportunity for the men to get away with rape, that is, they should not agree to go to isolated places or enter any situation where there is no accountability and no escape route. In the last two decades there has been an escalation of rapes perpetrated with the assistance of various drugs. Women should be aware that this happens and discreetly insist, in any suspicious or new situation, that they get their own drinks from unopened bottles and cans or other uncontaminated sources.

What If Date Rape Occurs?

Though we pray this does not happen, we must be prepared for action. Your first concern must be for the well-being of your daughter. Attend immediately to her physical and emotional needs. Also have a concern about punishment of the man who forced himself on her to prevent him from victimizing other women. The hours after a rape can take a terrible toll on a young woman, especially if she reports the rape to the police and has to endure questioning. In the long run, though, the sense of victimization is best overcome if she has taken steps to report and prosecute the crime, so the short-term discomfort and anguish of reporting it are well worth the extra pain.

Preserve evidence and prevent infection. The best course of action would probably be something like the following. The woman should not wash or clean up in any way, as this destroys evidence for prosecution of the rapist. She or her parents should call the police and have them meet her at her medical clinic or hospital emergency room. She will be able to decide whether or not to press charges later; she can talk to the police immediately and not press charges, but if she does not talk to the police and later decides to press charges she is much less likely to be successful in having the man convicted. In the clinic or emergency room she should get a complete physical exam; the attending physician should take physical samples that will stand as evidence later. She should answer the questions that doctors or police ask her as directly as she can. The medical professionals can advise about current medications that are quite effective at preventing possible infection from HIV or other STDs as a result of the rape.

Be an advocate and support. A parent can be the young woman's advocate and support during this process and should protect her from insensitive, demeaning, or inappropriate questions. She will probably be offered a "morning-after birth control pill," which will make implantation of an egg fertilized as a result of the rape unlikely. The young woman and her parents may be forced to make an agonizing and major moral decision in a very short and difficult time — such a pill must be taken within seventy-two hours of intercourse to be effective, but it is more effective if taken sooner. And remember, in the long run she will have to be tested for sexually transmitted diseases, especially AIDS. During this time, make use of the support of a rape-crisis team or counselor. Pray that in the midst of chaos you will receive God's own counsel.

CHAPTER 13

Developing Moral Discernment About Masturbation and Petting

"Dad, is kissing okay when you're dating? What if he wants to kiss me good-night? If all we're doing is kissing, what's the big deal?"

"Is it all right for a boy to touch the girl's breasts if they are going steady?"

"Mom, what is oral sex? Some of the girls at school say it's okay, because the guys really like it, and if you do it you're still a virgin."

"But how far can I go?"

"Is masturbation okay? After all, you're not having sex with anyone."

We have now set the framework for kids to think about romantic relationships and dating. As a parent, hopefully you have prepared your child to understand powerful sexual desires as a reflection of God's gift of a sexual nature. But what, exactly, should they do with their sexual desires short of intercourse? What about sexual release with themselves in the form of masturbation?

Scripture does not give us a direct answer for either of these issues. Dating, as we experience it today, did not exist in the ancient world. By and large, marriages were arranged by one's family. On average, people were getting married very close to the time of puberty, so the need to deal with sexual desires for years before marriage was not typically an issue. Courtship did not involve time alone in the back seat of a chariot or in a deserted house. The independence of modern dating would have flabbergasted parents in biblical times. For all these reasons, Scripture is silent on petting. Perhaps for these same reasons, the Bible also does not give us a direct word about masturbation. With couples marrying young and growing into their experience of sexuality together, perhaps it was just not much of an issue.

How early should we talk with our kids about the morality and realities of masturbation and petting? Our kids could or will be exposed to sexual situations and temptations early on. On average, over 25 percent of teens have had intercourse at age fifteen. We must prepare our kids to handle the challenges they will face. The puberty period, between ages eleven and thirteen, is the time to tell our children about masturbation and about what young people do short of intercourse in physically expressing their affection and/or sexual drives. In this chapter, we will assume that you will be talking to a twelve- or thirteen-year-old.

We have worked the kind of reasoning embedded in this chapter (and the next on pornography) into our book for kids ages eleven to fourteen, *Facing the Facts: The Truth About Sex and You*. It will be a helpful source for more examples of how to speak directly to your kids about these issues or to give them as a resource to read to encourage discussion with you.

Setting the Moral Framework

Perhaps we can move toward greater clarity by first being certain what the Scriptures do and do not say. Scripture clearly condemns certain acts while expressly commending or approving others. We do not often think of the Bible commending or approving sexual actions, so let's look there first.

Commended Patterns

Scripture approves of and speaks of with forcefully positive words two patterns of sexual behavior. The first approved behavior is sexual intimacy in marriage. Hebrews 13:4 says that "marriage should be honored by all, and the marriage bed kept pure, for God will judge the adulterer and all the sexually immoral." The marriage bed — sex between a husband and wife — is pure, but it can be made impure when the marital relationship is violated by sexual intimacies outside the marital relationship. Marital sex is pure; it is commended and blessed by God. In 1 Corinthians 7:3-5, the apostle Paul gives the down-to-earth advice that spouses should meet each other's sexual needs in marriage. He is a realist here who portrays marriage as a supportive relationship that can help preserve us from temptation and meet our needs. God approves of marital sex.

The second approved pattern is celibacy, abstaining from overt sexual expression. Paul urges believers who are content with single life and not torn with temptation to remain celibate for the sake of the greater focus and energy they can devote to service of the kingdom (see 1 Corinthians 6–7). His words echo those of our Lord Himself, who commended the life of celibacy both by His words (see Matthew 19:12) and by His perfect example of living a celibate life.

Condemned Patterns

The condemned acts list contains more items than does the commended acts list, thanks to our human creativity in violating God's will.

- *Adultery, the sin of a married person having sex with someone other than his or her spouse, is condemned in the Ten Commandments (see Exodus 20:14) and in numerous other places.*
- *Sexual immorality or fornication, understood as sex with anyone other than your spouse, is condemned in many places, such as Acts 15:29, 2 Corinthians 12:21, and Galatians 5:19. We discuss this more in the paragraph that follows.*
- *Incest is condemned in such passages as Leviticus 18:6-18 and 20:11-22.*
- *Rape is condemned in Deuteronomy 22:23-30.*
- *Homosexual intercourse is condemned in such passages as Leviticus 18:22 and 20:13, Deuteronomy 23:18, Romans 1:26-27 (note that this is the only passage that refers to female homosexuality), and 1 Corinthians 6:9.*
- *Bestiality, acts of sexual intercourse with animals by both men and women, is condemned in Leviticus 20:15-16.*
- *Cross-dressing, where men and women deliberately mimic the other gender, is condemned in Deuteronomy 22:5.*
- *Sexual intercourse between husband and wife during the woman's menstrual cycle is condemned as unclean in Leviticus 18:19. However, most evangelicals see this as a function of the Jewish ceremonial law, which Christians are not under obligation to obey.*
- *Lust is condemned in Matthew 5:28.*

Most of these condemned patterns are easily and clearly understood, but there is some legitimate uncertainty about the meaning of the terms *sexual immorality* and *lust.* The Greek word *porneia* is translated as "sexual immorality" and its synonym "fornication." Biblical scholars agree that, at the minimum, this term refers to all sexual intercourse outside the bonds of marriage, such as premarital sex. Does it mean more than that? *Porneia* is associated with "sensuality" and "impurity" in 2 Corinthians 12:21, Galatians 5:19, and other passages. This has led many to interpret all petting and masturbation to be instances of *porneia,* of sexual immorality. We cannot know for certain, however, that the word really was meant to include such actions. And if it includes petting, does it include everything from simple kissing to oral sex?

Lust is equally hard to define with precision. Our Lord declared in Matthew 5:28 that "anyone who looks at a woman lustfully has already committed adultery with her in his heart." Surely our understanding of what lust is should not be so extremely strict that any noticing of another's sexual attractiveness is lust, but surely also our definition should not be so liberal that anything can go on in our minds as long as we don't act on it.

We do not have precise answers to these moral dilemmas, but we think that the closest we will get to an answer is by being clear about God's ideal for our sexuality: God wants us to live pure lives. He wants us to live with our sexuality submitted to Him, held up for His approval, lived out under His lordship. He wants husbands and wives to be passionate toward each other and not toward others. He wants the unmarried to live chaste, sexually pure lives where neither their actions nor their thought lives are consumed by immoral deeds or thoughts. Every action and every thought should honor God and be pleasing in His sight.

Discussing the Morality of Petting

So, what do we teach our children about petting? What is God's will about it? Is it surely a sin for a boy to touch a girl's breasts? Does God look at that action the same way if the couple are thirteen-year-olds and barely know each other as He does if they are in their early twenties and one month away from getting married? If we say it is sinful, what is our justification for our stand? If we say it's not sinful, what is our basis? What is God's will for how a couple should express themselves physically before marriage?

Our starting point is that sexual intercourse is out of bounds for the dating couple. More, given the beauty of the gift of sexual union in marriage, we will strive to act in such a way that will guard that gift so that when we marry, we will be able to experience the fullest joys conceivable of what God meant sexual union to be.

So, what do we say to our kids? We urge that you as parents think through the range of physical things that two people can do with each other without having intercourse. What do you believe is a level of physical expression that can be honoring to God for a teenager in a dating relationship? Have your own inner limits in mind as you read further on setting the framework.

Acknowledge Desires

We must acknowledge the basic goodness of the sexual desires of the teenager and of his or her desire to express them in a loving relationship. This may be extremely hard for us as parents; it involves coming to see our beautiful, innocent little ones as sexual beings entering adulthood. But we are all — parents and teens — made by God to want to be physically close and intimate with someone for whom we feel love and affection. We should tell our kids to expect such feelings and to be glad they feel them. Our fundamental attitudes as we talk of sexual feelings and desires should be positive.

Teach How to Sort the Good from the Bad

We should warn our children that not all sexual desires are good; many of our sexual desires are not good — they are predatory, foolish, selfish, obsessed with sensual pleasure, insincere, and dishonest. We should give our kids a way to understand their own experiences so that they can sort the good from the bad. It's part of our fallenness that we may want to use other people for our gratification. We may want to dominate others. We may care for certain parts of the other person's body but not about the person. We may use our infatuation with another to alleviate our own boredom or loneliness.

We must lead our kids to see that their sexual feelings and those of their boyfriends and girlfriends are impure mixtures of good and bad, of genuine affection and sinful lust. Their feelings, at the most basic level, are a gift from God but also a trial and temptation to sin.

Ask the Right Question

Urge teens to recognize that "How far can I go?" is the *wrong question*. The right question is "How can I honor God with my body and my choices?" We will develop this explicitly in just a moment.

Be Clear That Refraining Hurts No One

Don't hesitate to tell children that no one is hurt by refraining from sexual expression. Teens do not have to act on sexual feelings, despite what the popular culture tells them. As parents, we have to acknowledge that not giving in to sexual desire can sometimes produce frustration, but also suggest that the frustration is a small price to pay to please God, to prepare for a lifetime of love with a marital partner, and to avoid the consequences of sex outside marriage. This means, in part, that we will urge our children to err on the side of caution. Physical affection can be a blessing in a loving and mature relationship. But a mature, godly dating relationship will be hurt much more by going too far into physical expression than it could ever be hurt by not enough physical expression.

Keep Judgment Clear

Teens need to be aware that expressing physical affection probably makes it harder, rather than easier, to understand the true character of the partner and the real status of the relationship. The strong feelings of sexual attraction that are aroused by any level of physical expression cloud our judgment about the realities of the relationship.

Suggest Concrete Limits

We would urge you to prayerfully reflect on and then to suggest concrete limits that you want your child to hold to. Ground your discussion in a broader discussion of God's purposes for sexuality. As you discuss what you feel to be God's will about petting, don't worry about having moral absolutes or revelations of divine will that you do not in fact have. Be able to say honestly, "This is what I believe is right for you. I have put a lot of thought into this, and I hope you can find my views to be trustworthy as a guide. If you feel I have been right in other areas, I ask you to trust me here."

Urge Caution

Urge teens to exercise caution rather than an attitude of experimentation in expressing themselves sexually. Urge them to make a personal commitment to explicit limits that they choose. Clearly discuss how some sexual expression typically leads to further sexual expression. It's hard to go back behind the line you had previously drawn, and after you pass over that line, it's that much easier to lurch forward two more steps. "Light petting" (no one agrees what this means) may be inadvisable not because it is wrong itself but because of what it may lead to. As we develop this theme, however, we must not plant in the minds of our children some sort of pessimistic sense that if they violate the limits we discuss with them once, they are rapidly sliding down a slippery slope toward promiscuity from which there is no return. With God's help, people change patterns of life all the time. There are no actions for which they cannot be forgiven and enabled to start anew.

Reinforce Themes About Dating and Romance

Discuss how transitory adolescent dating relationships tend to be and how much dishonesty and game playing happens in teen dating relationships. This is a good opportunity to reinforce the themes we discussed in the last chapter.

Encourage Clear Moral Communication

Urge your teens to communicate their moral standards clearly in their dating relationships. Teenagers should be able to talk about their standards with each other and live by those standards. Encourage your teen to believe that a dating partner who cannot communicate about the reality of the relationship and who does not abide by the standards that both partners agree to does not deserve loyalty or affection.

Two Sample Monologues About Petting

We offer the following as one side of a dialogue with a thirteen-year-old on "what's right and wrong in petting" that includes most of the elements above:

> Christopher, I hope that, as you feel more and more attracted to girls and begin to really have special feelings about some, you will

realize what a precious gift those feelings are. Those feelings will probably allow you to someday fall in love with the woman you are to marry. God made you to have those feelings, including the feelings boys have of wanting to kiss, touch, and even have sex with a girl. But He did not make you so that you have to act on those feelings by getting physical with a girl.

Many of the feelings we have about sex are not from God, though. When I was your age, I remember feeling real affection for some girls, but I also remember feeling selfish, feeling that I wanted to touch and feel a girl's body because it would be fun for me, would excite me, and would make me seem cool with my friends. I sometimes would not think about the girl as a person, but only about her body. Those feelings were wrong. Girls have sinful selfish feelings too and may also be ready to do anything to get boys to like them as well. That's not what God wants either.

Son, many kids in high school will have sex with people they are dating. Many of them who don't go all the way into sexual intercourse will be much too intimate, so intimate that they might as well be having sex. You know that intercourse is wrong when you are not married, but what about other things like kissing and touching? What's right and what's wrong?

"How far can I go?" is really the wrong question; it's like asking, "What can I get away with?" The real question is, "What is best for me and the girl I am dating? What does God want me to do?" I don't have the perfect answer for you. There isn't an absolute rule in the Bible. But here is what I think:

Sex outside of marriage is wrong because the joining of our bodies makes us one, and we're supposed to be one with a person only in marriage. I should be one only with one person, my wife. You should be one only with one person, your wife, after you marry her. Oneness is something that happens immediately when you have sex, but it is also something that happens gradually in many other ways, and sharing bodies without having intercourse is one of those ways. If you get involved with a girl and enjoy just about every part of her body and she yours, but without having intercourse, you have begun the process of becoming one with her. You will have started down that road when it is very unlikely you will marry her. You will have also put yourself in a situation where, because of the excitement of the moment, you will find it very hard to make the decisions that Jesus would want you to make.

I think then that you should decide not to get very physical with the girls you date in high school. You probably will not meet and date the woman you will marry until college or after. If you meet and date her in high school, you probably will wait a long time to marry. I would urge you not to go beyond kissing in your dating relationships while you are a teenager; no touching of girls' breasts or genitals, and no letting them touch your genitals. These experiences are too intimate, too close, too powerful to play around with when you are so far from marriage. Enjoy your dating. Enjoy the respect and fun and appreciation you will find in your relationships.

I want you to understand that if you choose not to get into sexual intercourse or into heavy petting, you will be in the minority. Guys may razz you for being a virgin or for being a prude; girls you date may want to do more with you than you feel is right. You will also find it frustrating sometimes not to have sex and not to do petting. But this is a frustration you can live with; no one ever died or went crazy from not having sex. You will need a lot of strength to live your life by God's rules. But it's no more of a difficult task than any that God has given to His saints.

Kids hear about petting at school and from friends, but usually in the form of slang terms that no one defines for them. They are often very confused about what exactly happens physically between initial introductions and full sexual intimacy. We can help them to make better moral decisions if we help them to know what others are talking about. We urge that you talk with your teen about what happens in petting, after laying the kind of moral framework we have just discussed. The monologue on the next page is very close to the kind of instruction we gave to our children at this age. You as a parent may set the limits differently; that is your role and obligation as a parent.

How do we tell our children about the realities of sexual involvements in dating that fall short of intercourse? What should we tell them? Perhaps the following monologue, framed in terms for a thirteen-year-old to understand, will help.

A word of caution: Some will find this monologue to be overly explicit. Others may feel strongly that it represents what should be said, but could not imagine saying this to their children. Friends, we must talk explicitly with our kids about sexuality; if we don't, they'll get their explicit instruction from their peers and on dates. We urge you to try talking about these matters and to trust that any progress in talking about petting is a success that will bear fruit in helping your child make a commitment to chastity. But is what follows too explicit? The following monologue even brings up oral and anal sex. "Why?" you might ask. Because research continues to suggest these actions are becoming more and more common among teens (see chapter 2). With the kind of statistics being reported for oral and anal sex, how can we not warn our kids about engaging in such behaviors? We must help them to think about them as a Christian.

Julie, I want to tell you a bit more than I ever have before about the ways people who are dating might relate to each other sexually. I want you to understand exactly what can and does happen. I want to tell you about these things for several reasons: so you will firmly make up your mind now, ahead of time, about what you will and will not do. I also want you to know what can happen so you can see the warning signs if a boy is trying to get you to do something you shouldn't do.

Some of what I'm going to talk about I think is fine in the right relationship and at the right time. Much of what I'll talk about I regard to be very wrong before marriage. I've already told you why I believe as I do about the rights and wrongs of petting. Now you need to know what can happen.

The physical relationship usually begins with a kiss. But there are kisses and there are kisses. Kisses range from a quick smack on the lips to the kind of kissing where people's mouths are open and they stay kissing for a long time. You have heard already that when people kiss like this they often put their tongues in each other's mouths; you asked me about French kissing years ago. This idea is really gross when you have never done it, but it is exciting and lovely with a person you really love and are attracted to. I would urge you to be cautious about whom you kiss and that you save kissing passionately for when you are older. You're thirteen now and will have a good amount of time to learn whom you really care for and can trust.

The boy or girl who finds his or her partner attractive and exciting will want to touch that person. Touching often begins when a boy and girl hold hands or put their arms around each other while walking or give each other a hug. These can be very nice ways to express affection with someone you really care for. Some boys think that going out even on the first date means that you will touch like this, but you don't have to. Even these kinds of touching can be really exciting.

I hope that you will never think that the feeling of excitement means you are in love, because it doesn't. You may feel sexually excited with someone you just have a crush on for a few days. Boys can and do feel sexually excited even with girls they don't know or don't like at all. Feeling sexually attracted does not mean you are in love.

After kissing and hugging, the couple may move on to touching other parts of the body. You know that your genitals are the most sensitive and sexually exciting parts of your body. They are for a boy too. A girl's breasts are the next most exciting area. But your whole body becomes more sexual as you grow up and especially as you are attracted to someone or feel you are in love. Some parts of your body are more sexual than others. That is why after kissing, some couples begin touching other parts of the body. A boy may want to kiss not only a girl's lips, but also her face, neck, ears, or arms. Even more intimately, couples may want to touch the thighs and the bottom. This can feel good, but it can make it harder to make good decisions because it is more sexually exciting.

Couples sometimes then move to touching the most sexual parts of the body on top of or through the clothes. Julie, I would urge you to have this be the point where you choose not to go along; I would urge you not to let a boy touch your breasts or any of the other things I'll tell you about. It is too close, too intimate, and it can make it harder for you to say no to what could come later.

Some couples may not do this kind of touching until they are ready to get married after dating for years, and some guys may try to do it on the first date. It can happen suddenly when the boy brushes his hand over the girl's breasts. Remember, you never really know for sure what the other person is going to do. You have to know your limits and make your choices and be ready to handle things you do not agree to. If she lets him, the boy may touch and feel the girl's breast for a long time; he finds this really exciting and she does too. If they both want to go further, the boy and girl may move to touching their genital areas by touching each other between the legs; the boy may rub the girl's genitals through the girl's clothes, and the girl may rub the boy's penis through his pants. This can be so sexually exciting to them that one or both may have an orgasm from this kind of touching. I think this is sad, as I believe that kind of sexual pleasure is something only a husband and wife should give each other.

If they go further they will move to touching under their clothes. As I said earlier, this can happen quickly or slowly. It can happen as quickly as the boy suddenly slipping his hand under her shirt to touch her breast. Couples can go even further to touching their genitals under their clothes or with their clothes off. Here, clearly, they are getting so intimate, so close with their bodies, that they're really sharing just about all of themselves. This is far too much intimacy when you aren't married.

I must warn you that a girl can get pregnant doing this even when she doesn't have sex. If she is excited enough that her vagina is wet and if the boy has an orgasm so that his semen spurts out, any semen that touches her wet area around the vagina can get her pregnant. The sperm will actually swim into her from the outside of the vagina even if his penis was never in her vagina. This doesn't happen often, but it's not unknown.

Some couples move from there right into having sexual intercourse. At this point, they have already been so intimate, they have shared and given so much of themselves to each other, that it is only a small step into intercourse. If they don't have sexual intercourse for some reason (maybe one or both believe that it is the only thing they won't do, or perhaps they are very afraid of pregnancy), sadly there are still other things that some unmarried couples do. One is oral sex. Most kids find this gross to hear about, but many kids now do this and so we have to talk about it. You've probably heard about it. When couples have already touched with their hands all over their bodies, they can move the kissing from the lips to kissing the skin, to the boy kissing the girl's breasts, to "kissing" each other's genitals. This may not actually be sexual intercourse, but you can hardly get more intimate than this. You are totally sharing your bodies. That is why it is wrong outside of marriage.

Another thing that couples do is called anal sex. This is where the couple has intercourse, because the boy's penis goes into the girl's body. But it does not go where it was intended to go, into the vagina, but instead it is put in her rectum, where her bowel movements come out. Apparently more couples are doing this today, in part because they think this is a smart way to have sex without the danger of pregnancy. Unfortunately, having sex this way is the very best way to transmit HIV, the AIDS virus. Because the rectum was not made for sex, it usually causes tearing and bleeding of the girl's rectum. Anal sex also can pass bacteria that are in the rectum (and are harmless there because it is designed to handle them) to other areas of the body where they can cause terrible infections. I believe God did not make us to have anal intercourse.

And that summarizes the kinds of things people can do between the time they first kiss and when they have intercourse. Sadly, some couples can experience almost all of these in one evening, when they rush from a first kiss through touching to intercourse. A couple who would do that have totally trashed God's gift of their sexuality. Another couple may date for two years and only kiss before their wedding day, saving all touching and sharing of their bodies until their wedding day. Some couples date a long time before doing some touching, but go no further than light touching.

Julie, your body is one of God's most miraculous gifts to you. He has given you the capacity to feel attraction, feel love, feel sexual excitement, get pregnant and bear children, be a wife and mother. This is a great gift. Any good feelings you would get from enjoying intercourse or lots of sexual touching outside of marriage would not be worth you disappointing God and making it harder for you to experience all of the joys God wants for you in your marriage or your single life. I pray you will set the right standards for yourself and make the right choices. I would like you to pray and reflect on what I have said and decide what your standards should be.

Discussing the Morality of Masturbation

What do we teach our children about masturbation? The following thoughts set the framework:

- *We must again acknowledge the goodness of the sexual desires of the teenager.*
- *Masturbation is common, but clear statistics are hard to come by. It is more common for men than women, but it seems to be increasing among young women.*
- *The Bible appears to be silent about masturbation.[1] For instance, attempts to connect masturbation to the sin of Onan (this is why masturbation used to be called onanism) in Genesis 38:1-10 are unconvincing. It is not surprising, then, that Christians are quite divided over how to think about the morality of masturbation. One poll of laypeople and clergy by* Christianity Today *found that almost exactly one-third of each group reported that they believe masturbation is wrong, one-third believe it is not wrong, and one-third believe "it depends."[2]*
- *Masturbation does not involve the kind of overt harm, to the teen or anyone else, that sexual experimentation does.*
- *Some Christians argue for tolerance of masturbation on a very practical basis. They say masturbation is a way to handle sexual urges and desires. Therefore, they argue that, if a kid gets sexual release through masturbation, he will be less likely to press for sexual intimacies with the person he dates. The crucial issue in this argument is whether the practice of masturbation increases or decreases teen sexual acting out.*

Is masturbation a way of managing sexual tensions by oneself or does it lead one to be more preoccupied with sex and hence more likely to push for more intimate sexual experiences with others?

- *There are people who struggle with compulsive masturbation and sexual addiction. Some people feel addicted simply because they continue to masturbate occasionally, but others really do engage in this behavior in a compulsive manner (three or four times daily, or more). This is likely not the result of masturbation itself but of addictive or other problems.*

- *Masturbation is necessarily incomplete. Full sexual gratification is meant to be relational, to unite a man and woman together. Masturbation is solitary. One author argues that for most adolescents, masturbation is a step of learning about oneself and of handling the intense sexual urges of the teenage years.[3] He argues that it is not all that God wants for that child, but until he or she is married, it is a partial and neutral experiencing of the gift of sexuality.*

- *What we do with our imaginations and emotions matters morally. Jesus condemned lust (see Matthew 5:28). Are people committing adultery in their hearts when they masturbate? It appears that men almost always use vivid and arousing sexual mental images to accompany their masturbation. Women, on the other hand, do not do so as frequently. When women masturbate, they often simply touch themselves because it feels good. Much of a woman's fantasy, when she does fantasize, tends to be vague thoughts of romance with the man she loves. Is a man's vivid fantasy lust, but not a woman's? And could masturbation encourage a person to be self-centered and thus less rather than more capable of truly giving to another?*

So, what do we tell our children? Can we be honest? We are of mixed opinion about the morality of masturbation. After musing about it for years, we can regard it neither as an unquestionably and intrinsically evil act nor as a blessing from God that we are meant to enjoy with clear consciences. We would fall in the decisive third of the *Christianity Today* groups who said, "It depends."

What does the morality of masturbation depend on? The worst kinds of masturbation seem to us to be those that cultivate a heart of selfish preoccupation with personal pleasure, those that involve fantasy about immoral acts with others, those that channel one's energies away from loving relationships with others, those that make one more rather than less preoccupied with sex, and those that drive a wedge between the person and God by becoming a focus of guilt and shame. The least questionable kinds of masturbation would seem to be those that are a phase in adolescence rather than a life practice, those that do not use mental images of immoral acts, those that somehow contribute to the person maintaining a resolve to stay chaste, those that contribute to the person's positive appreciation of the body and sexuality as a gift from God, and those that help the person positively anticipate eventual sexual union with a spouse in marriage.

It would seem that masturbation is not itself lust, but it certainly can and often does involve lust. And we should actively urge our children not to cultivate a habit of lust.

Masturbation is not the fullness God desires. But perhaps in a sexually saturated and overstimulated world, it may be an expedient way for the teen to cope with his sexual urges along the way to becoming an adult person ready for marriage. Overreaction to masturbation probably causes more suffering in Christian circles than the practice itself does. Many people, men especially, who have grown up in the conservative Christian church have been deeply scarred and hurt by overly zealous crusades against masturbation. At summer camps, masturbation is too often the easiest subject on which the preacher can stir up guilt and thus generate more seemingly sincere conversions and rededications. It can take a long time to heal from such guilt, especially when one struggles for years about whether the guilt was legitimate in the first place.

Perhaps in trying to formulate one key message to give to our young adolescents, we can do no better than to quote James Dobson, who addressed this issue speaking to young teenagers:

> It is my opinion that masturbation is not much of an issue with God. It's a normal part of adolescence, which involves no one else. It does not cause disease, it does not produce babies, and Jesus did not mention it in the Bible. I'm not telling you to masturbate, and I hope you won't feel the need for it. But if you do, it is my opinion that you should not struggle with guilt over it.[4]

We have a substantial section on masturbation in our book for kids aged eleven to fourteen, *Facing the Facts: The Truth About Sex and You.* This material, where we talk directly to young teens, can serve as one example of how to discuss these issues.

CHAPTER 14

Clear and Present Dangers: Pornography and Cybersex

While cleaning out unused files on the family computer, Kevin was puzzled to discover several files of a type he did not recognize. A bit of research brought him to a shocking conclusion: these files were video pornography of the vilest nature, which had been downloaded and hidden on the family computer. The culprit had to be his thirteen-year-old son. When confronted with part of the proof and a clear statement that there was more proof yet, his son confessed that he had been viewing porn with some regularity for five months. He had been introduced to it, and told how to hide it, by kids down the street.

Consider this: "Last year, one in five kids aged ten to seventeen received an Internet sexual solicitation."[1] Americans live in a society immersed in eroticism. In the premodern world, erotic images existed, as nude and sexually explicit paintings and sculpture show. Today, though, we are bombarded with sexual images on television, in movies, in glossy photographs in magazines, and so forth. And pornography of the most graphic sort is only a few clicks away on the Internet.

Most secular experts today make a distinction between the erotic and the pornographic. Erotica is defined as that which is designed to stimulate sexual interest and excitement. The United States Supreme Court has defined pornography, on the other hand, as material that meets three standards: it has no artistic merit, appeals to a "prurient" (wanton or excessive) interest in sex, and violates community standards of decency. The material in question must meet all three standards to be classed as pornography, and all three standards are difficult to establish in a court of law. We might think of erotica as a very large circle and of pornography as a much smaller circle inside the larger circle; all pornography is erotica, but legally not all erotica is pornography. Many Christians may be surprised to learn that what they consider to be pornography, such as explicit nude pictures in *Playboy* or *Penthouse* or even explicit hard-core videos of sexual intercourse available on the Internet, are not legally pornography but rather erotica. The circle of material that can be classified *legally* as pornography has been shrinking steadily, while there has been an explosion of the availability of erotic materials.

In this book, we have used the term pornography to refer to all of the types of sexually explicit materials that most Christians would regard to be morally offensive. We are thus using the term in a way lawyers and many sexual libertarians would view as too broad and repressive.

Most popular sex-education books take a neutral and permissive stance toward sexually explicit materials. For example, one popular book stated, "When parents come across this kind of thing, what should they do? Nothing. What harm can the pictures do if they are looked at in private?"[2] This is a good example of the privacy dimension of our modern sexual ethic (see chapter 10). Sex, it is implied, can only be wrong when another person is directly harmed, while anything that occurs in private must be morally neutral. We feel this is utterly unacceptable for Christians, for reasons we will develop below.

Many parents are naive about the kinds of sexual materials that are popularly available, which go beyond what many from earlier generations could even conceive. Depictions of such sexual acts as group sex, homosexual practices, rape, the infliction of pain and torture (especially on women), and the sexual victimization of children are all common.

And make no mistake — pornography is widely available to children. In local schools, it is common for children as young as first grade to be exposed to pornography on the playgrounds as older kids bring printed materials to school from home. Distribution of pornography is an enormous part of the profit margin of cable and satellite television companies, making a wide array of sexually explicit movies and programs only a remote-control-button push away from our kids. Hidden pornographic scenes are built into some computer games. Pornography is increasingly easily downloadable onto home computers, video iPods, and other digital devices. At the changing rate of technology, new venues for the distribution of smut will no doubt continue to surprise us in the years ahead.

Are our kids exposed to this material? We have no formal statistics to report, but we have heard some frightening anecdotes. We recently discussed teens and pornography with a group of college students who had served as summer camp counselors at Christian camps. The campers they had worked with would likely be classed as those least likely to be exposed to porn, as they came from families of means where the parents cared deeply about the welfare of their kids and their proper nurture. The parents of these kids were involved, vigilant, and concerned. Yet these camp counselors reported that of the eleven- to thirteen-year-olds they worked with, almost *all* had direct exposure to Internet pornography to some extent. Few of the kids had deep exposure, but they knew of it and had some awareness of how to get it. This problem is widespread.

Is Pornography Wrong?

We Christian parents should forbid our children from using pornography, and we should do our best to shape our children to utterly reject its usage when they are no longer under our control. We have several fundamental concerns.

Pornography universally depicts immoral acts. There is no market for pictures and images of married couples lovingly meeting each other's needs in mutual tenderness and submission. Immoral, promiscuous, and degrading sexual acts are presented in pornography in such a way as to make them seem thrilling and alluring. These immoral acts are powerfully imprinted on our minds. People appear to remember vividly images they see when they are emotionally aroused. Pornographic images arouse sexual desire, especially in men, who tend to be more visually oriented than women, and thus are vividly remembered. Kids digesting pornography are filling their minds with immorality, and the images can be indelible. At a time in life when it is vital to be filling the teenage mind with what is good and true and holy (see Philippians 4:8), pornography programs it with what is evil and false and dirty.

Pornography presents people's bodies in ways that are likely to result in harmful comparisons with our married partners. Pornography often presents idealized bodies doing fantasized acts under ideal conditions of lighting and makeup, with the resulting pictures touched up to remove any final flaws. How can a real marital relationship with a real person under the normal demanding and distracting conditions of life stand up to comparisons with such depictions? In reality, loving marital sex is better than pornographic sex, because it fulfills the intimacy goals that God built into us. But as couples are trying to develop their relationships, comparisons with idealized physical acts (which ignore real relationship) can be devastating. Taking these first two points together, we say that pornography is likely to undermine a Christian view of marriage and of sex.

Pornography almost universally presents a degrading view of women. At the minimum, pornography presents women's bodies as passive objects of men's sexual desires. Women's bodies are violently torn from the totality of who they are as people and made to stand apart as objects of lust. Pornography that presents women as the objects of violence, degradation, and torture are particularly repulsive. Given that so much pornography is of this kind, is any wonder that scientific studies are suggesting a possible connection of the viewing of this type of pornography with the victimization of women? One study, for instance, found that men who viewed a few hours of violent pornographic movies were more likely to believe statements like "Women who are raped really enjoy it" or "Many women secretly want to be raped," and were even likely to agree with a statement saying that they would commit a rape if they were certain they would not be caught.[3] Pornography likely contributes to the victimization of women.

Beyond Pornography: The World of Cybersex

Pornography is not the only problem your child could encounter on the Internet. We are increasingly aware of sexual predators prowling online, seeking victims. It is not just the adult pervert to be feared, but also other young people who would be willing to lure another teen into seductive circumstances for a sexual encounter.

The Internet provides an increasing array of forums for conversations between people who have never met: instant messaging, chat rooms, FaceBook and MySpace, and other "social networking" programs. New technologies are probably just around the corner. It is quite common for conversations in these contexts to turn sexual. The anonymity and lack of accountability of the medium fosters lewd conversation and gives license to those who would victimize others. This technology has been rapidly evolving; parents need to do their research to find out what they need to be concerned about. One of the best sources of information is older, responsible Christian teens; they are often aware of the dangers and willing to share their perspectives on how to identify and protect younger teens.

In the worst case of the Internet predator, an individual haunts the chat rooms, posing as a young person and presenting false personal information, striking up conversations and using all of the proper slang and abbreviations (for instance, LOL means laugh out loud). He searches for the curious, lonely child who is vulnerable. He works to build a wall of suspicion and resentment between child and parents by asking about past arguments and difficulties, and he picks at the relationship to undermine it. He draws the child into sharing secrets by seeming disclosure on his part. He uses guilt to manipulate the child into feeling obligated to share more information and to keep it secret. Eventually, he seeks a face-to-face meeting.

What Should We Do?

Inoculate and prevent. Anticipate that children will be exposed to pornography and cybersex, and attempt to inoculate them against this. In the spirit of inoculation from chapter 10, help them to avoid such contact by discussing the kinds of temptations that will come their way and then help

them to build up some immunity to these temptations by developing solid reasons to avoid them. This conversation should probably take place well before the teen years. Perhaps a dialogue with a preteen boy might go something like the following.

> **PARENT:** Have you ever heard the kids at school talking about looking at sexual material online or at dirty magazines or movies that show people having sex?
>
> **CHILD:** Yeah, there are a lot of kids who watch R-rated movies at home on cable. Some have even seen really dirty movies that their dads have on their computers.

PARENT: What do you think about that? [a risky question that puts the boy on the spot, because he knows the parents disapprove]

CHILD: Oh, I don't know; I don't think about it very much.

PARENT: Let me share some of my thoughts on stuff like that with you. I would really like to hear your thoughts and answer your questions if you have some. It is completely normal for men to be interested in women's bodies and to find women sexually attractive. It's normal to really want to look and to feel excited. But I think pornography is not right and it is not good for you. Do you think sex was something that was meant to happen between strangers without real love or between a husband and wife who truly love each other?

CHILD: Married people, of course.

PARENT: I agree. Sex in marriage is wonderful, and it helps your love grow stronger as you live out your lives together. But pornography usually depicts sex between people who really don't know each other, between people who aren't married. That's the way animals have sex; it's not what God meant for people. Pornography is also unrealistic; it shows people acting like they are really having a great time when the actors are probably lonely and unhappy people. It shows women who do nothing with their time but make their bodies look good. What is even worse is that pornography usually makes the person watching interested in sex, especially in thinking in his mind about having sex with the woman he is looking at. Can you see how a kid who looks at pornography is being led to thinking about sex with a stranger, sex without love or commitment? If a young man sees a lot of pornography, he is filling his mind with pictures of and desires for sex with strangers. He is also filling his mind with images of experiences he has never had, and that can make him more unhappy with where he is in life. Last, I think pornography degrades women.

CHILD: What does that mean? My friends say it makes them look beautiful.

PARENT: Maybe physically beautiful, but not beautiful as a person. A woman is beautiful only as a whole person when you appreciate all of her. When you focus only on her body parts and don't think of her the way God thinks of her, as a person with a body but also with a mind and emotions and dreams and thoughts and beliefs and relationships, when you make a picture of her that says she is there to be used as a thing to lust after for the men who buy the magazine or look at the movie, then you are making her into a thing, an object. And that, I believe, is wrong. For all these reasons and more, I urge you to resist the temptation to look at pornography. It will be hard when the guys say it is great and call you names if you don't. But by being strong, you will be pleasing God and making your chances better of having a beautiful and exciting and loving sexual relationship with your wife someday. And when they tell you that you're missing out, you'll know they are getting some thrills sinning now, but they are really hurting themselves and hurting God by what they are doing.

A dialogue with a daughter would cover many of the same elements, but might pick up the following distinctive aspects:

PARENT: Some of your friends may like to look at pornographic pictures. There is a lot of pressure today for girls to be sexually aggressive. Movies regularly depict the really cool female figures in aggressive ways. Watching pornography is often presented as part of what it means to be "with it" sexually. But even if you don't want to be like that, girls are often also tempted to watch as a way of finding out what the mystery is all about. You might think you can learn how to conduct yourself in a way that is sexy and competent. Girls also have just as much curiosity about sex as guys.

But the dangers are very real. When you expose yourself to pornography, you let the people who make this filth dictate and portray for you how a woman is to be attractive and sexually appealing. You are also programming your mind with images that stay with you a long time. Many women later struggle with comparing themselves to these mental pictures and feeling like failures. Pornography shows women as existing to gratify men, instead of being valued by God the way we've talked about before. This can damage your self-esteem. I don't want that for you. I know you may be curious, but I urge you not to give in to this temptation.

Teach your child appropriate skills for Internet use. Teach the child that he or she may stumble across or into pornography or cybersex on the Internet. Search engine (Google or Yahoo!) results for searches on innocent topics may occasionally include links to inappropriate websites. An innocent misspelling of a website address may also lead to a pornographic site. In part, this can happen because many pornography providers on the Web intentionally choose names that are slight variations of common search topics to lure customers in.

Also teach your child that purveyors of pornography are actively recruiting interest from anyone using the Web. Teach the child to recognize spam e-mails from porn distributors by their sexually explicit addresses, such as hotsexbabe@pornshack.com, and by their lewd or suggestive subject lines. Kids should recognize and avoid opening such messages.

Inform your child to be alert to Internet conversations through instant messaging, chat rooms, message boards, MySpace, or other "social networking" programs that turn in a sexual direction. Conversation over the Internet tends to be more unguarded and crass than normal modes of communication, and kids need help discerning the difference between direct and alarming. Remember the quote at the start of this chapter: 20 percent of teens have received a sexual solicitation over the Internet in the last year; you must prepare your child to recognize and reject anything leading in such a direction. Also, kids should be taught to *never* release personal information of any kind over the Internet. Predators are experts at easing a child into sharing more and more information. Kids should stick with their screen names and never disclose their real names, addresses or even hometowns, information about their families, and so forth. The best idea is for kids to communicate on the Internet only with other kids they know personally — and whom you know.

Purify the environment. Do what you can to purify the environment your children live in. By doing this, you build supports around them. Some simple steps can help control what comes into your home via the television. Cancel cable channels that broadcast questionable shows and movies. Consider implementation of the V-chip technology that allows for strong parental control of what comes on your television.

In someone else's home. Controlling what your kids see in the homes of other kids is more complicated. Staying informed and knowledgeable about where your kids are, whom they are with, and what the arrangements are for supervision is a start. Asking parents hosting your child what they do to monitor, control, and prevent exposure to pornography can get a good discussion going and may create some shared responsibility for protecting kids from porn.

Visible computers. Purifying the environment for the Internet is a more complicated undertaking. Start with accountability. Make use of the family computer a more public affair by moving it into a public place, such as in the family room with the screen facing outward to make it as widely visible as possible. Having private access to the Internet (a computer in the privacy of a child's room) is likely an invitation for real problems. Ask about or encourage your child to report and talk to you about incidents on the Internet that are inappropriate.

Filters. Consider the use of a filter program that makes access to pornographic materials harder. There are two types of such programs. One functions as an Internet service provider through which you connect your computer to the Internet; the second is a program you put on your computer to filter out material that comes through your Internet service provider. These programs and providers change often, so we cannot make recommendations of specific ones. Some research on websites dedicated to fighting against pornography can give helpful advice here, such as the website jointly sponsored by Focus on the Family and the National Coalition for the Protection of Children and Families, www.FilterReview.com. Talking to computer-savvy church members can help you find out where to get the latest information.

Activity logs. Consider also the use of a program that logs and records all activity on your computer, keystroke by keystroke. Make no mistake about it, these programs spy on other users (your kids). Parents we know who have used such programs are thankful they did. One parent discovered that her thirteen-year-old daughter had e-mailed nude photos of herself to an Internet site; another discovered long transcripts of her fourteen-year-old daughter engaging in sexually explicit dialogue with her anonymous conversation partners. The parent confronted with such material then has to work through this seeming violation of trust and intrusion into what the teenager meant to be the "private" part of her life. This is a small price to pay for intervening a serious problem early to protect and redirect your child. You probably would not implement such a program if you were confident you could trust your teen and had no hints of problems, but you may choose to implement it if you were anything short of absolutely confident.

Respond to problems. Be very careful of your response if you discover your child has or is using pornography or is involved in cybersex. If this happens, do not overreact and tear down your child's character. As in the previous dialogues, remember to affirm that curiosity and sexual interest are normal. Make the issue the unacceptability of the pornography itself, the values portrayed, and the meaning of the messages presented.

If you discover a problem, it may be the sort that simply requires direct discipline and renewed focus on accountability and the other strategies discussed above. But you may discover more serious problems. Most Internet addictions are really pornography addictions; the Internet is just the delivery system. And we hate to say it, but the problem that gets discovered might be the husband's problem (or even the wife's). Sexual addiction problems are serious indeed. They create deep wounds in a marriage, wounds of broken trust, betrayal, shame, loneliness, despair, and jealousy.

Hiding or denying such addictions does not help. They require confrontation, confession, and resolution. In this area, it is best to move immediately to engagement with others who can help provide resources, information, and structure for dealing with this terrible problem. Again we hesitate to suggest specific ministries and organizations because of the inevitable changes they go through, but the following are a few of the current ministries (in 2006, by their website addresses):

- www.faithfulandtrueministries.com
- www.teensagainstporn.com
- www.settingcaptivesfree.com
- www.pureintimacy.org
- www.higher-calling.com
- www.xxxchurch.com

PART 5

The Pivotal Years:
Adolescence

CHAPTER 15

Supporting the Adolescent

We begin with a word of encouragement. We are now on the other side of adolescence with our three kids, and we enjoy close and loving relationships with all three as young adults. We enjoyed their adolescences immensely. One of our three children, however, went through a terribly difficult time for about two years; we knew it was hard at the time, but only afterward did we understand just how bad that period was. We witnessed God's faithfulness in the lives of all three of our children and would not change anything we went through: none of the many times of joy and closeness nor any of the occasional times of pain and difficulty. God is good!

We want to focus here on the most important task of parenting adolescents: maintaining loving relationships and giving them the support they need as they go through this most challenging period.

Providing Loving Support

During the adolescent years, parents are not as likely to feel that they are having fruitful times of teaching their teenager. You are more likely to be met with cool indifference or bored impatience. If you have built the proper foundation, your major role now is to give strength to your child by being available and being a listening ear, an askable resource, an affirming voice, a source of affection, and a fair, firm, but compassionate limit-setter. The time has come for the teen to choose to live by the lessons you have taught. You help the teen make and live by those choices by providing the kind of supports we discussed as elements of character in chapter 3.

Affection

Affection is the cornerstone of your relationship with the teenager. Expressing affection with teenagers can be a challenge though. They are often disgusted by the idea of public displays of affection—forget a good-bye kiss at the curb in front of school! Even so, don't be discouraged, and continue to give them the love that you know they need. Never stop being physically affectionate with your teens. Even when they are standoffish and difficult, a pat on the back, a shoulder rub, a quick hug, or a kiss on the cheek can all be vitally important.

As parents, we must constantly remind ourselves of what our kids really need—relatedness and significance, acceptance and purpose. Continue to remind them how those needs can be met genuinely, rather than in a counterfeit fashion through sex. You as the parent can no longer fill up their needs; they are now beginning to move more definitively out beyond the family to have many of their needs met. But you can guide them as they try to get those needs met, and you can take the edge off their needs enough to allow them to make good choices. As a full grocery shopper makes better decisions in the store than a famished one, so too your children will make better decisions if their needs are partially met by you than if they're famished. Your affection and acceptance, your encouragement about the significance of their lives in God's eyes and yours, can send them into the world strong rather than weakened. If their needs for love and affection and for meaning and significance are insufficiently met, those needs will be more likely to overwhelm their moral commitments.

Praise and Encouragement

You can help meet your kids' needs for significance by being as lavish with praise and encouragement as possible. What can you find in their schoolwork to praise them for? Forget their grades if you must! Sit down with them and read the essays they wrote for a test or the papers they composed and find things to praise about their insights and knowledge. Affirm the skills they are developing, whether they are in calculus or auto mechanics. Praise their diligence in their part-time jobs. Praise any initiative or self-discipline they show. Affirm any signs of sensitivity to friends. As you do this, you will have to endure their teenage mood swings. You just have to tolerate and love them through those moods, continuing to find ways to praise them.

Personal Example

Don't give up on teaching your children, but now you must think much more about teaching through your example rather than lectures. Whereas teenagers may be unwilling to listen to you sermonize, they may be open to you as you share from personal experience. By sharing about your own triumphs and struggles in adolescence and young adulthood, you not only continue to instruct them about your views, but you also show them that you have struggled with similar issues. You know what it is like to have the feelings they are experiencing, even if they find this hard to believe. By sharing your stories, you may give them better skills in expressing their own struggles. Your talking gives them words to describe some of what they are going through. Can you tell them about times when you were lonely, pressured, despairing, angry, tempted, content, in love, confused, or hurt? Showing that you have experienced some of what they are going through can build the bond between you.

Religious Faith

In chapter 11 we discussed how teens' personal faith has a powerful influence on their sexual choices. We urge you again to do everything possible to encourage their religious faith. Pray for them diligently (as if you aren't already!). Continue to share about your own faith and walk with God. Be willing to sacrifice time, energy, and money to boost their faith. Be a youth-group sponsor, offer your home as a meeting place for the group, sacrifice to support your children's desire to go to a church camp or youth rally. Be as creative as you can in supporting their continuing development as Christians. By supporting their involvement in church, you are also helping them to form their peer groups in a way likely to encourage their sexual purity.

Reasonable, Firm Limits

Finally, support your adolescent by providing reasonable but firm limits. Family rules such as curfews, regular chores and family responsibilities, and restrictions on the kinds of activities he or she can be involved in are vital for the teenager. These supportive structures can give the teen a sense of safety. What makes our job as parents so difficult on this point is that our kids rarely praise us for providing such structures. Instead they fight against and complain about the limits. But it is one of the fundamental rules of parenting adolescents that such limits are good for them — even if they don't know it! One recent study found that not only did close parental relationships decrease the chance that kids were sexually active, but so did the kids' awareness that their parents would not approve of them having sex.[1] Discuss with other parents what limits are reasonable. Limits also can provide "a way out" for our kids. Brenna found that one comforting thing her parents did during her adolescence was to tell her that if she was ever in a situation where she was unsure or uncomfortable, she would be wise to get out of that situation, using her parents' "unreasonable rules" as her alibi. She used this excuse on more than one occasion.

Continuing Your Teaching

Of course you can do more in adolescence than just provide support. One of our principles with our kids was repetition. Continue to rehearse well-worn lessons. In our family, it became a joke — a meaningful joke — for us to say, "Remember, God made sex, and it's a good thing, so use it right!" Often our kids said it to us in a teasing way, but even the teasing was a rehearsal of a basic lesson from the past.

Continue the work of instilling them with godly beliefs and values. Continue to inoculate them against the destructive messages they will be soaking in from the media and popular culture. What else can you work on?

What Can Parents Do to Improve Adolescents' Decision Making?

Many school-based sex-education programs are not succeeding. The most likely reason is that these programs are all premised on the assumption that teenagers are more mature decision makers than they really are. This assumption seems wrong in two important ways. It attributes a greater rationality and maturity to teens than many are developmentally capable of. And it ignores the fact that human beings are not morally neutral calculating machines, but rather are sinners with a bent for doing what is wrong.

Point toward long-term consequences. You can do some things to help your kids make better moral decisions. First, remember that their thinking tends to be influenced most by concrete, visible examples. So the teenage friends who engage in sex without using birth control and who don't become pregnant are much more powerful influences than a hypothetical discussion in class about "the percentages of girls that become pregnant within a year of initiating sexual activity." Parents and churches have to try to even the score with concrete examples. Strive to make long-term, intangible consequences more obvious and powerful by showing those consequences in ways that are hard for kids to ignore. One way to do this is to make sure they see examples of the difficulties and devastations of pregnancy and disease. Discuss such examples in your community, not for gossip but for instruction. See if you know people willing to share testimonies of the challenges they have faced or mistakes they have made.

Put a personal spin on consequences. A second way to encourage greater teenage rationality is to walk your adolescent through the consequences of sexual activity and pregnancy. Ask how friends would respond if he or she got a sexual disease. Follow this by these sorts of questions: What would you look for to know that you had the disease? How would you make a doctor's appointment? How would you pay for the doctor's appointment? How would you eventually handle telling the person you were going to marry that you had had — or still have — a sexual disease? How would you handle the possibility of never being able to have children due to having the sexually transmitted disease?

You can ask kids some of the same questions about pregnancy.[2] Say, "I want to help you think through what teen pregnancy would be like, so that you can understand the consequences for yourself and anyone else you know who gets pregnant." Then follow with questions of how your child thinks his or her life might change with pregnancy. Flesh out their responses, asking, "How would having a baby affect your going out with your friends? Would you be able to finish school? How much do you think it costs to raise a baby? What kind of job would you need to get to adequately care for your baby? If you had to work to support your baby, how would you be able to spend enough time with it to give it the love and care that it needs? How old do you think the baby would be when you graduate from college?" These and other questions like them can be a way of making the hypothetical quite concrete.

Emphasize God's rules. Finally, continue to emphasize the enduring value of God's rules for our lives. Christians believe in a God who is perfect, loving, and just, a God who has chosen to reveal to us how we are meant to live. His laws are based on the true love and perfect justice that only He can perfectly embody. But we cannot throw out His laws and live by the abstract principles of love and justice; to do so is to trust too much in our own abilities and to set ourselves up as little gods. His laws can never be replaced by abstract principles.

> Blessed are they who keep his statutes
>> and seek him with all their heart.
> They do nothing wrong;
>> they walk in his ways.
> You have laid down precepts
>> that are to be fully obeyed. (Psalm 119:2-4)

> The law of the LORD is perfect,
>> reviving the soul.
> The statutes of the LORD are trustworthy,
>> making wise the simple. (Psalm 19:7)

How Can You Enhance Their Skills at Saying No?

Kids need confidence to be able to say no in a dating situation. As we said in chapters 3 and 7, being able to say no is a skill that has to be built up and encouraged, principally through practice. Do we want our kids to get that practice "on the job" (trying to fend off pressure from their dates) or would we prefer that they get some practice beforehand? We can't answer for you, but we would prefer the practice come before the live test. Psychologists and educators have developed techniques such as role-playing and behavior skills training to provide such practice. These techniques basically amount to having kids watch others show them practical ways to handle tough situations, having them pretend they are in those tough situations and practicing their own responses, and giving some coaching on how they could do better on their responses. Such role-playing is best handled among peers in a context such as a youth group. Speak to your youth-group leader at church and see if he or she can work into the youth curriculum some way for kids to practice getting out of tempting or potentially destructive situations.

Parents can do a lot to prepare their kids to resist peer pressure for sex. Most important, we can help them bring to adolescence a lifelong pattern of having been encouraged for speaking their minds and standing up for what they believe. Are we building up the strength of our kids as we lead them toward the teen years? Or are we chipping away at that strength by demeaning their ability to stand up for what they believe, criticizing them as "mouthy" or "uppity" when they assert themselves, and robbing them of any opportunity to think for themselves by always telling them what to do?

Say no. Several elements are important in encouraging an adolescent to be able to say no.[3] We focus here on the young woman. First, encourage her to be able to simply say no and to keep repeating her commitment to no. She doesn't have to give reasons or justify her decisions to her date or anyone else. She can learn to say, "No, I don't do that. No, I am not going to change my mind and I don't have to give you a reason. No, I don't wish to discuss my reasons. My answer is no," and so forth.

Next, the young woman, instead of being a somewhat passive victim of peer pressure, can be encouraged to reverse the pressure. You can teach your daughter to say things like, "Why do you keep pressuring me? Are you trying to make me do something against my will? Why do you keep pressuring me when I've told you no? Why do you think what you want is more important than what I want? Don't you think I have the right to say no? Don't you respect me enough to take a no as no?"

It can also be helpful to encourage teens to express their anger or frustration when they are pressured. "I'm getting angrier and angrier — you keep ignoring what I'm saying. You're trying to manipulate me and I don't like it and I am not going to do it! You keep pressuring me to do something I have clearly said I don't want to do. That means you don't respect me and that makes me angry."

Of course, young men need to be prepared to forcefully say no as well, both to pressure from male peers and from aggressive young women. Of course, peer pressure is easiest to resist when you have strong peers standing with you in your moral commitments, so encouraging and supporting your son (and daughter) to have the right peers is crucial. Locker-room bragging and tales of sexual exploits by other boys can make your son feel deficient, and the wear and tear of harassment (such as accusations of being gay) can be considerable. Preparing boys for such interactions through inoculation is crucial. They should expect to stand out, to be different, and at some level to be persecuted.

In terms of pressure from aggressive young women, though our sons are unlikely to face the risk of being overpowered physically, they are in danger of succumbing to manipulation ("Show me you care for me!"), to intimidation ("I will make sure word gets around that you are a sissy [or gay]"), or more directly to temptation (young men are more likely to have great difficulty resisting a flagrant "Don't you want this?!" display than a young woman). We should prepare our sons to stand firmly by their refusals to be involved in sexual immorality.

Get out. Don't suggest that kids simply stop at saying no, however. Prepare them to rescue themselves from bad situations. "That's it. I demand that you take me home right now. If you don't, I and my parents will make sure that your parents know just how you're acting." Help your daughter by giving her a threat she can use to regain control, such as, "If you do anything more, my father and mother will take me to the police station to file charges of criminal sexual assault against you. My father has sworn that anyone who pressures me to do what I don't want to do will go to jail!"

How Can We Help Them to Not Feel Alone?

For teens, as for adults, the cold statistics do not matter as much as the personal realities we surround ourselves with. For most of us, cold numbers like "fewer than 32 percent of adults take biblical authority seriously today" make little impact on us if we are surrounded by a few fellow believers who take biblical authority as seriously as we do. Three living people we respect and who believe as we do can outweigh all the percentages and ratios in the world. After all, under pressure we can remember and be inspired by people much more than by numbers.

The same is true in the area of sex: By surrounding them with people who believe as they do, we enable our teens not to feel alone in their pursuit of chastity. The statistics do matter; telling them that "if only 20 percent of teens remain chaste, that still means that 20 percent of 20 million — 4 million teens — are fighting the same battle you are; you're in good company" may make a big impact. But we would guess that abstract statistics can never have the impact of a peer group that is committed to the same standards as your child.

Try to draw on older teens and young adults who can serve as role models for your teen. Speakers in youth groups, older teens who can disciple your children, movies that depict the meaningful pursuit of purity — all of these and more can be ways of giving our kids good models to follow and of reducing their feelings of being alone in their battles.

Support of this kind is crucial for helping young women, but particularly young men, to stand strong morally. One of the great dangers for young men (but women also) is that of succumbing to peer pressure. The best defense against such pressure is twofold. First, build peer support to counter peer pressure. It is much easier to stand against peer pressure when we know someone — hopefully lots of someones — stands with us. Encourage your teen to connect with other teens who share their moral commitments through youth groups, Christian organizations at the school, and so forth. Second, we are better prepared to resist peer pressure when we are confident and informed in where we stand. The parents who have been following the patterns advocated in this book of developing all facets of Christian character are pursuing the best path possible for preparing their child to stand firm.

CHAPTER 16

Teaching About Contraception

Anne had a sinking feeling that she had botched it in teaching Becca about sex. She had told her daughter the basics about menstruation and the "facts of life," but she had done so late. Becca had complained bitterly that she had heard it all already in school and had acted embarrassed and ashamed to be talking about it at all with her mom. That was three years ago. Since that time, Anne had tried several times to inquire about Becca's relationships with boys, but had received evasive answers. What frightened Anne most was that Becca never asked her any questions and never disclosed anything. She had not started really trying to tell her daughter about God's sexual rules until Becca was fourteen, and Becca had clearly acted like her mother was speaking Russian. Now, in the last six months, she felt a change in her daughter. Becca was clearly disenchanted with church and the youth group; was hanging out with a crowd of surly, haughty, and sneaky sixteen-year-olds; and was pushing her parents' limits with ever-greater frequency and defiance. Anne had just overheard Becca whispering to a friend out on the front porch that one of the girls in the group was going to have an abortion. "I really have no clear sense that Becca has any commitment to Christ or to God's standards for sex. What if it's Becca getting an abortion in six months? What does God want me to do?"

What does today's teenager really need to know about sex? According to many secular experts, since most teens are "sexually active," what they need is to know how to stop feeling guilty or ashamed about their sexual activity, how to not catch one of the many sexually transmitted diseases of today, how to prevent getting pregnant or causing a pregnancy, and how to get access to a safe, legal abortion if they do get pregnant.

The faithful Christian parent will have a different agenda entirely. We desire for our children to grow to be women and men of God, to know the fullness of God's mercy and grace, and to be consumed with a desire to be like Christ. In the sexual arena, that means they abstain from all forms of sexual impurity and prepare for a life of sexual enjoyment and union within marriage or for a possible life of healthy, disciplined, and fulfilled singleness.

If our goal is that our children abstain from sexual intercourse, why would we ever consider telling them about contraception? Is it right or wrong to teach our children about ways of preventing pregnancy and sexually transmitted diseases in case they choose to become sexually active? We will briefly clarify what we mean by the terms *contraception* and *birth control* and discuss the main methods of each. We will then examine the thorny issues surrounding whether, and what, Christian children should be told about contraception, then draw our best conclusions.

Methods of Contraception and Birth Control

Birth control does not mean the same thing as contraception. In many human sexuality textbooks, the terms are treated as synonyms, but they are not, and the confusion of the terms is in part intentional. *Contraception* means literally to prevent conception at the first moment of life from occurring. *Birth control,* on the other hand, refers to anything that prevents the live birth of a healthy human infant from occurring from conception up to the last moment before normal birth. By this confusing definition of birth control, a condom is a form of birth control, but so is abortion, even in the eighth month. Using such confusing definitions, researchers declare public school sex-education programs that teach "birth control" to be successful, even though sexual activity rates and pregnancy rates go up. As long as the end product, *live births,* goes down due to increased abortion, you are still doing "birth control." Though disease prevention is not the same thing as either birth control or contraception, we will be including disease prevention in our discussion of contraception.

Birth-control methods can basically be classified into three types. The methods that prevent conception (the joining of the egg and the sperm) are the only methods that can truly be called contraceptive. A second group of methods prevent implantation of the fertilized egg into the wall of the woman's uterus (which occurs several days after fertilization). The final group is those methods that interrupt or terminate the pregnancy and thus kill the fetus at some stage in its development.

Contraception

Contraceptive methods that prevent the fertilization of the egg by the sperm fall into four major groupings.

Natural planning. First, there are the Natural Family Planning (NFP) methods.[1] Secular authorities often denigrate NFP ("What do you call women who practice NFP? Mothers."), but the reality is that these methods have been dramatically improved in the last three decades and can be remarkably effective when used rigorously. The essence of NFP is twofold: (1) the woman learns to accurately predict the time during her menstrual cycle when she is fertile and (2) the couple refrains from sexual intercourse for several days before, during, and after her fertility phase. At the heart of the method is the under-appreciated reality that a woman can often learn the reliable signals of ovulation her body gives off. Two such signs occur reliably.

- *Basal body temperature. Because her body temperature goes up slightly before and during ovulation, a woman can use a sensitive thermometer (Basal Body Temperature, or BBT, thermometer) to chart these changes.*
- *Secretions. Noticeable secretions of mucus from the cervix reliably occur with ovulation. With careful attention, ovulation can be predicted with fair precision, and then the couple can refrain from sex for the days when conception is possible.*

Barrier methods. Second, there are methods that put a physical or chemical barrier between the sperm and the egg.

Physical barrier. A condom worn over the man's penis catches sperm (when the method works) and does not allow them to get near the woman's egg; this is a physical barrier. Similarly, the female condom, diaphragm, cervical cap, and cervical sponge all put a physical barrier over the woman's cervix that does not allow the sperm to pass into the woman's uterus and fallopian tubes, where the egg could be fertilized.

Chemical barrier. Spermicidal foams kill the sperm, thus rendering them incapable of fertilizing the egg. This is a chemical barrier. The diaphragm and cervical cap are often used with spermicidal foams, and cervical sponges contain spermicidal agents, thus imposing a double barrier.

It is vital to know that only the condom (both male and female versions) provides some protection for both partners against the transmission of diseases. Neither the pill nor the diaphragm, two popular methods for married couples, provide significant disease protection; they are contraceptives only. The spreading of disease is every bit as much a concern as pregnancy, and many teenagers are confused, thinking that any method that prevents pregnancy must of necessity also prevent disease. This is not the case.

Oral contraceptives. The third category of contraceptive methods that block fertilization are oral contraceptives (the pill), contraceptive patches and implants that deliver the same hormones as the oral contraceptives but through the skin, and vaginal rings that distribute ovulation-blocking hormones. There is some ambiguity as to exactly how these hormone-based contraceptive methods work. The consensus of medical opinion is that they block ovulation, so that a woman never releases a fertile egg while she is on one of these drugs. It is possible that these methods occasionally allow ovulation to occur, and thus the woman's egg might be fertilized by the man's sperm even when she is using one of these methods. Artificial hormones may have the additional effect of preventing implantation in the uterus, so that the woman never becomes pregnant and never knows that she did release a mature egg.

Surgical sterilization. The fourth group of methods of contraception that actually block fertilization are the surgical sterilization methods: vasectomy in the man and tubal ligation in the woman. Vasectomy surgically prevents live sperm from getting into the semen a man ejaculates during intercourse. He has a seemingly normal ejaculation, but if his semen were examined under a microscope, it would be found to contain no sperm. A tubal ligation prevents a mature ovum from passing from the ovaries through the fallopian tubes into the uterus. The tubal ligation severs both fallopian tubes so that ova cannot get into the uterus, and the man's sperm cannot get out of the uterus. Thus sperm and egg are prevented from joining together in both methods.

It should be noted that the physical and chemical barrier methods and the hormone-blocking methods are obviously reversible. Couples can get pregnant by stopping using those methods. The surgical methods are meant to be irreversible.

Anti-Implantation Methods of Birth Control

The second category of birth-control methods includes those that block the implantation of the fertilized egg in the uterus of the woman. Here the woman's egg may be fertilized by the man's sperm in the beginning of its journey down the woman's fallopian tube, but then the zygote (the cluster of smaller cells that the fertilized egg has already become) fails to implant into the wall of the woman's womb, or uterus.

Two types of methods disrupt this natural implantation. The first is the various "Plan B" or "morning-after" pills, which are thought to render the woman's uterus "inhospitable" to the fertilized egg. The second is the IUD (or intrauterine device). While neither of these methods involves any direct action to damage or kill the zygote, the methods do artificially cause what might be called a miscarriage for the woman. The zygote thus dies because it fails to implant. There is scientific debate about exactly how the various "Plan B" or "morning-after" pills work.

There is substantial argument about the morality of these anti-implantation methods in Christian circles. A significant percentage of all pregnancies naturally end in miscarriage anyway, with many occurring so early that the woman never even knows she was pregnant. On this basis, some argue that these methods parallel natural development. Further, because the woman never knows for sure whether or not an egg was fertilized, a life conceived, she can take comfort in having made no deliberate choice to "end a pregnancy."

However, for those who believe that life begins at conception, these methods are unacceptable. They constitute deliberate action that results in the death of any child who was conceived as a result of sexual intercourse. We personally regard these methods as morally questionable at best for general use, especially given the availability of methods to prevent conception from occurring at all. For that reason, we classify them as birth control and will not discuss them further as options in this chapter. A number of Christians feel that these methods may be questionable in general usage, but that they are acceptable when a woman has been raped or a victim of incest.

Abortive Methods of Birth Control

Finally, there is a range of abortion methods that will "terminate the pregnancy," the politically correct term for killing the living fetus inside the pregnant woman. Some of these are designed to work early and indirectly, forcing the uterus to reject the implanted and developing embryo. Others are designed to work later and more directly to destroy the life of the developing fetus. Because abortion is the deliberate termination of a human life, we regard it as an immoral and unacceptable form of birth control. In the remainder of this chapter, we will not have the anti-implantation methods and abortive methods in mind.

The Morality of Contraception Itself

Before we can weigh other factors, we must first ask if contraception is itself moral.[2] If one believes that contraception itself (all methods except NFP) is intrinsically immoral, as many Roman Catholics and some conservative Protestants do, this is reason enough not to talk to children about this option. Most Protestants and many Catholics, however, do not appear to take this position. Let us take a brief look at the moral issues involved in judging the acceptability of contraception within marriage.

Procreation and the Nature of Sexuality

We must carefully think through what place procreation — childbearing — has in sexual life and in the nature of sexuality. Let's look at several views.

Every sexual act should have the potential to create a child. The traditional Roman Catholic view is that every sexual act is meant to have the potential to result in a child; sexual intercourse by its very nature involves the potential for procreation. Any separation of the sex act from its potential to generate children is judged to be unnatural and a basic betrayal of God's intent for the nature of that sexual act. Further, the more artificial the method to prevent conception, the more discordant that method is with the basic, potentially procreative nature of sex. Hence, NFP is acceptable to the Catholic Church, but condoms are not.

Marriage should have the potential for children at some time. A second, less severe view would argue that sexual relationships — marriages — should have the potential to result in children *in general,* but that it is excessive to argue that every sexual act must have the potential to generate a child. In this view, if a couple is open to having children at some point, this validates their choice to exercise control over reproductive potential at any given point in time. In other words, we can use contraception now because we are open to children later.

Potential for children is optional for marriage. Some would take a third view that the potential for generating children is a purely optional part of marriage and of the act of intercourse. Given the dense population of our world and the pressure that ever-increasing population is placing on our ability to meet human needs, they would argue that there is no reason to necessarily intertwine sexual expression with generating children.

You can see that the first view would make all contraception immoral, the third view would make contraception always acceptable, and the middle view would make contraception acceptable at times, depending on the motives of the couple and other factors. It would seem to us that the third view, that procreation is purely optional, separates intercourse too drastically from its natural potential to create children. The first view, the traditional Catholic view, may go too far in making the possibility of children a necessary part of every single sexual act in a marriage. So in our view, contraception can sometimes fit in with the general nature of our sexuality, which leads us to the next issue.

Is Procreation a Command?

Some claim that God's statement to Adam and Eve to "be fruitful and multiply, and fill the earth" (Genesis 1:28, RSV) was a command. But many biblical scholars have suggested that this is a misrepresentation of the intent of Genesis 1:28. This statement appears to be a blessing, not a command. In Hebrew society, blessings were often stated in ways that in English sound like commands. For instance, Rebekah's family responded to her plans to go off and marry Isaac as follows: "They blessed Rebekah, and said to her, 'Our sister, be the mother of thousands of ten thousands!'" (Genesis 24:60, RSV). Clearly, it is not their command that Rebekah have thousands and ten thousands of children. This is their hope for her blessing stated in emphatic language. We are not commanded to procreate, but rather the possibility of having children is an enormous blessing from God.

God's Sovereignty

The issue of contraception is another area where we confront a seeming conflict between God's sovereign will and our human capacity for choice. Could we, by using contraception, frustrate God's sovereign will that we conceive a child by a particular sexual act? But if God wants it to happen, can any human strategies frustrate Him? This is a complicated question with implications for all of our Christian lives.

Our sexual behavior may be an area where God has a specific intent and design, and He will carry out His purposes regardless of what we do. It may be an area where He has an intent but is willing, out of respect for our human freedom, to allow us to block what He intends and desires in our lives. Even further, our procreation of children may be an area where God's will is completely permissive; we may be allowed to have children if we choose to do so and to choose the number, spacing, and timing of their conceptions. These are deep issues each of us must grapple with. Each of us must decide if the use of contraceptives is more like Jonah running in the opposite direction in response to God's command or rather like Paul's choosing escape from Damascus in a basket even though he had total faith that God could protect him (see Acts 9:25).

Motives

Finally, in considering the morality of any use of contraception, we must think through our motives for using it. At one extreme is the couple in their midforties who have six children and, after serious deliberation and prayer, have chosen not to take the increased risk of a problem pregnancy or child with physical deformities. They decide God has given them all the children they should have, and so they prayerfully choose to begin using contraception. At the other extreme, we might have the couple who, out of a selfish commitment to a materialistic lifestyle and their own spiritual and emotional poverty, decide there is no room in their lives for children, who are expensive, inconvenient, draining, and unrewarding. They thus use contraception to remain childless. There are all sorts of potentially sinful and problematic reasons for using contraception, though there are also sinful reasons for choosing to have children.

We conclude from the above that contraception is itself, for the married couple, an acceptable option when used in response to prayerful consideration of God's call on your life as a couple and to sober self-examination of your motives for its use. But what about your children? Surely it's not a good thing for a teenager to conceive a child or to contract a sexually transmitted disease. What are the reasons against and for teaching an unmarried teenager about contraception?

Contraception and Your Child

Many Christians reject the notion of telling young people about contraception as part of sex education, whether in the family, church, or school. The core of this view is the belief that instructing teenage children about condom or other contraceptive usage undermines their commitment to abstinence. This is a powerful and important argument. Fear of the consequences of illicit sex is part of a responsible deterrence to having sex. There can be no doubt that it is horribly counterproductive to tell our children that we don't want them to do a certain thing and then to tell them how they can bail themselves out of their difficulties if they disobey us. We would never urge a child to study for a test and then teach her how to cheat to get a good grade in case she doesn't get around to studying. We would never tell a teenager not to get drunk and then tell him how to avoid getting caught by us and the police if he does get drunk.

Specific elements of the argument that are also important include the following:

- *Contraception methods (particularly condoms) are presented as if they make sex safe when the truth is that, compared to abstinence, condoms still leave teens profoundly vulnerable to pregnancy and STDs.*
- *To teach abstinence and then contraception is to say to a teen, "I think you can stay abstinent; well, no, I really don't." It is a very destructive contradictory message that suggests kids are incapable of remaining abstinent.*
- *Suggesting contraceptive use constitutes approval of sex as long as negative consequences are avoided, another destructive contradictory message.*
- *Providing teenage girls with contraceptives robs them of the protection of the fear of pregnancy and disease, leaving them utterly vulnerable*

*to male pressure. As one author said, "'Baby-proofing' [young women]
increases the odds that they are being sexually used by, and sexually
using, men."[3]*

Of course, some Christians argue for teaching contraception to kids in
Christian families. The core argument is that all sins are not equal.[4] True, at
one level Christ taught that all sins are equally heinous in the sight of God.
All sins, big or small, mark us as fallen and disqualify us from meriting
or deserving God's love and acceptance. In this way, unrighteous anger is
equivalent to murder and lust is equivalent to adultery (see Matthew 5:21-
22,27-30). Rage and lust, like murder and adultery, amply demonstrate how
far we fall short of God's standard of righteousness and how much we need
God's merciful forgiveness.

But only a fool would argue from this that it makes no difference
whether we simply lust or lust and also commit adultery, whether we simply
get bitterly angry or also take a shotgun and blow someone's head off. In
terms of the damage they wreak on human beings and the world God made,
sins definitely differ, with some worse than others.

And so it is with sexual sin. It is a serious matter, a terrible affliction, to
struggle alone with lust. That person is defiling his or her own mind. But
when that lust issues forth in actual physical immorality, another human
being is being hurt as well, and the bodies of both persons are defiled. When
the sexual partner is married, a third person is being ravaged — the innocent spouse. When multiple sexual partners are involved, the damage is
spread further. When diseases are transmitted, even greater damage is done
and the temple of the Holy Spirit, the human body, is further devastated.
When the immorality results in a pregnancy that is brought to birth, that
child may have to be raised by a single parent or be given up for adoption,
either of which may turn out well but neither of which can be described as
God's ideal will for that child. Finally, when fornication results in pregnancy
and the child is aborted, as so commonly happens today, the sexual sin has
borne the fruit of death — the very opposite result that the life-giving gift of
sex is meant to produce.

This line of argument suggests that if we cannot guarantee that our
children will remain chaste, we should give them enough information
to encourage them not to compound their sexual sins against their own

bodies and those of their partners with even more grotesque sins against their partners' bodies (in the form of disease transmission) or against a child they conceive. Further supporting this argument are the following:

- *While sex using condoms is not safe in any absolute sense and not as safe as abstinence, it is safer than unprotected sex.*[5]
- *We already discussed the empirical finding that teens who have taken a chastity pledge (and perhaps other teens from religiously conservative homes) are less likely to use condoms when they do first have sex, thus increasing their chances of pregnancy and contracting STDs.*

Based on the above, we have concluded that parents must talk to children about contraception. We don't regard contraception in itself to be immoral within marriage. The couple who has sex outside marriage is engaging in fornication, a sinful act in the eyes of God. But if that couple fails to protect themselves and other innocent persons (a future spouse, a child they conceive) by not using contraception, that multiplies the damage they are causing. Our children are likely to learn about contraception anyway in school sex-education programs, through the media, and in peer conversation; by parents taking the lead in teaching them or even in reexamining what they have already learned, we again have the opportunity to give them a godly perspective on this topic. In doing so, we can take care, in light of the concerns expressed about this topic, not to give mixed messages, not to pretend to be morally neutral, and not to inadvertently undermine our message of abstinence.

Explaining Contraception in the Christian Family

Secular experts say that an important part of getting children to effectively use contraceptives is to reduce their sense of guilt and anxiety about their sexual behavior. Many secular sex-education programs are targeted at decreasing guilt at any cost, even if that cost is the loss of the religious faith of the teenager. Can the Christian parent participate in such a program? No. We, or our children, may convince ourselves that what we are doing is acceptable, but we deceive ourselves if we go against God's revealed law. If we break God's law, we are objectively guilty. Christian parents regard premarital sexual intercourse to be sin, so how can we be party to assisting a child to feel less guilty about sin? We cannot. And so a part of our paradox is how to faithfully proclaim God's standards and to talk about contraception without eroding the value of those standards.

Insist on Moral Absolutes

The world's way out of this dilemma is to throw away our standards, assume that teens are going to be sexually active, and encourage them to feel good about using contraceptives. We cannot cooperate; we must continue to hold up God's ideal. But we can inform our children about contraceptive methods and tell them that we pray they will never use the information until they are married, except perhaps to counsel a friend who may be acting foolishly by engaging in unprotected sex. We can challenge them to courageously decide what they are going to do with their lives. We can challenge them that if they decide to go against God's standards, and we pray they don't, that they use an effective contraceptive method so that a disease is not transmitted and/or an innocent child is not conceived. What, then, is the essential information we should convey to our children about contraception?

Myths to Dispel

In talking with teens about contraception, confront the many absolutely erroneous myths that circulate among young people about pregnancy, which include the following:

- *You can't get pregnant or contract a disease the first time you have intercourse.*
- *You can't get pregnant or contract a disease unless you have an orgasm.*
- *The woman can't get pregnant if she is having her period (rare, but possible).*
- *You can't get pregnant in certain positions (such as having sex standing up, in a sitting position, or with the woman on top).*
- *The woman can't get pregnant if she urinates right after sexual intercourse.*
- *You can prevent pregnancy and disease with a homemade condom made of such materials as Saran Wrap or a baggie.*

- *Douching with any number of substances (soda pop, baking soda, and so forth) will prevent pregnancy and disease.*
- *Withdrawal of the boy's penis before he has an orgasm will prevent pregnancy.*
- *The woman can't get pregnant if the man's penis does not enter her vagina.*

Contraceptive and Disease-Prevention Methods Fail More for Teens

One of the elements parents must factor into decision making about teaching teens about contraception is the reality that all contraceptives appear to have higher failure rates when used by teenagers. Even Planned Parenthood acknowledges that effective use of contraceptive methods needs to be a habit cultivated in a stable relationship for the methods to work. They also acknowledge that such habits and patterns are difficult to develop in the unstable, transitory relationships that tend to be the staple of teenage romances. Even the contraceptive method that is regarded as most foolproof, the pill, has a higher failure rate with teenagers.

Condoms appear to fail more often for teens than for adults. Most adult married couples require a time of adjustment to learn to use a condom properly, a luxury that the teenage couple struggling with guilt and in a hurry does not have. Condom breakage is also more likely to occur among teen users. To work well, condoms need to be handled with care, put on correctly, removed carefully after intercourse to not allow the escape of semen, used with an artificial lubricant to reduce the amount of friction they are subjected to in intercourse, and protected with proper storage. Finally, they must be used in a disciplined and regular way. Few of these conditions hold for teen users. So, condoms work — they make it less likely a teen will get pregnant or get a disease. And condoms don't work — many people still get pregnant and get diseases while using them.

There Is No Failsafe Protection Against Disease or Pregnancy

There is no safe sex. No method utterly prevents all pregnancies, and no method utterly stops the spread of sexually transmitted diseases. It should be of grave concern that condoms do not completely stop the spread of HPV, for instance.[6] But while there is no safe sex, there is safer sex. Flawed as the use of contraceptives is, especially the use of condoms, their use does help to lower the chances of pregnancy and disease.

One of our most powerful messages to kids must be that premarital sex is not worth the risk of disease or pregnancy. This is not the moral core of God's view of sexuality; the dangers of sex are not the main reason God says no. But the dangers of sex are helpful reminders of the eternal validity of God's laws.

Turn "Accidents" into Choices

Human beings are not lower animals enslaved by their raging hormones. Neither are we psychologically programmed robots. Children need to be told that sexual acts do not just happen. The adolescent who protests, "I don't know what came over me," is denying responsibility for his or her actions.

Human beings make choices. Parents need to help their children understand, well before they go out on dates, that they have to have made up their minds about the kinds of things they will and will not do. The teenage boy who is open to the possibility of intercourse engages in wild petting in an empty apartment and happens to have a condom in his wallet; the teenage girl who is open to the possibility of intercourse drinks heavily with a boy with a reputation as a Don Juan.

We as parents must put the responsibility for choice squarely where it belongs — on our teenagers. We are not their bodyguards; we cannot make every decision for them. We must challenge them to face the enormity of their human responsibility. Except for rape, intercourse is not something that will "happen" to them; rather, they may choose as responsible persons to follow God's path, or they may choose to go their own way, to be their own gods. In the sexual area of their lives, they face just one of the many instances where they, like Adam and Eve, have to choose obedience or disobedience. They will either pursue the light or walk into darkness.

A Sample Monologue About Contraception

We return here to our opening case study; what should Anne tell her daughter Becca? We offer the following:

Becca, today I want to tell you a bit about contraception. What I have to say will not take long, but it is something I really don't want to talk about and that makes it hard. I don't want to talk about it because I pray that you won't need to know about this for yourself until you are married. Maybe you will be able to help someone else with what I have to say, but I say it for your benefit.

We have told you what we believe is God's view of sexuality and of sexual intercourse. Your female body, your ability to feel love and desire for a boy, your ability to have intercourse, to feel the pleasures of sex, and to carry and give birth to a child are all wonderful gifts from God. He wants you to use them well. Intercourse is made for marriage, as an act that will "glue" you to your husband, making the two of you one. Saving sex for marriage gives glory to God, builds your character, and lays the foundation for a better marriage than you might otherwise have.

Sadly, not all teenagers follow God's way in this matter. By the time you are a senior, probably more than half of the girls in your grade at school will have had sexual intercourse; some only once, some quite often. Some will have been pregnant and had abortions, some will even have had children. Some Christian friends will fall into sexual sin as well. I pray that will not be the story for you. Sex before marriage dishonors God and risks disease and pregnancy. You are gambling with your life and the lives of others when you have sex outside of the bounds God intends, outside of marriage.

In light of that, I have two things to tell you. First, sex never just happens—people decide to have sex. You must have the honesty and courage to be straight with yourself; are you living your life God's way or are you choosing to reject God's way for your own way? I pray you choose God's way, but either way is a choice. I know you can choose and live by the right way. I pray you will make that choice.

Second, if you do choose to sin, if you do choose to reject God's way and go the way that our society says is the way, I pray that you will choose to protect yourself and others against pregnancy and disease. It would be a sin that would break God's heart for you to reject His sexual rules. Imagine how much worse it would be not only to do that but also to get pregnant and thus hurt an innocent child, or to contract a disease that can haunt you for years, maybe even kill you. Using a condom and the pill do not make sex before marriage right, but they can prevent some horribly wrong things from happening.

Honey, I want you to know that you don't have to live a life of sexual sin. God wants more for you than that. He wants you pure. But if you choose not to be pure for God's sake and because it is right, then I pray that you will have the honesty to face your decision and the intelligence not to hurt yourself even more profoundly by not protecting yourself.

I want to tell you a little bit about contraception. No doubt you have heard plenty already, but I want to give you my perspective and make sure you have the big picture. I pray the only use you will make of this information before marriage will be to help a friend who is choosing the wrong path. I won't go into all the details of how to use the pill or a condom. A woman has to get the pill from a doctor who can tell her how to use it. It works only if she takes it every single day, and it takes time before it works. The pill prevents your getting pregnant by stopping your ovulation, but it does nothing to stop diseases.

Anyone can get condoms at any drugstore, but they have to be used right or they don't work. Using a condom the wrong way is the same as not using one at all. The condom slows down the transmission of most sexual diseases, but not all. Don't believe all the myths you may hear about how to keep from getting pregnant. Many kids who use the condom and the pill still wind up pregnant or with diseases.

I pray you will follow God's laws because they are good and right. If you decide to have sex anyway, tell me. I'll try to change your mind, but if I can't, I'll direct you to someone who can give you the information you need to lower your chances of getting pregnant or getting a disease. You can lower the chances, but sex outside marriage will never be safe. God didn't make it to be safe from pregnancy, not even in marriage. But in marriage, you experience it the way God intended, and you have a soul mate to share the challenges and the joys with.

CHAPTER 17

Conclusion

What Is True Purity?

Parenting is rather like all of the Christian life. It is a life of striving and of rest. We are to run the race (see 1 Corinthians 9:24), press on toward the goal (see Philippians 3:7-16), work out our salvation in fear and trembling (see Philippians 2:12), press on to maturity (see Hebrews 6:1), enter through the narrow gate (see Matthew 7:13), and bear our crosses and follow Christ (see Matthew 10:38). But the Christian life is also a life of rest. We are to trust in the Lord (see Proverbs 3:5-6), wait on Him (see Psalm 27:14), take up the easy yoke (see Matthew 11:29-30), abide in Christ (see John 15:4) and in His Word (see 8:31), and enter into His rest (see Hebrews 4:10-11).

Strive and rest. This is a deep paradox of the Christian life. Parenting embodies this paradox as well. This book has been almost completely pre-occupied with only one side of this paradox. We have urged you to strive with all your energy and creativity, to strive to shape your child's sexual character.

Some of us are in danger of not striving enough. Maybe we simply don't know where to start or what to do. Many of us have lost our vision of marriage and family as a vocation, as a life work that is well worth our investment of our whole selves.

But we would guess that if you have read this whole book you have done so because you are willing to work and searching for ways to do that work better. Some of us need to remember that life in Christ, and that includes parenting in Christ, is also a rest from striving. And so we close this book with an invitation to rest, to trust God. And perhaps nothing provides us more of an opportunity to rest than to reflect on the wonders of God's redemptive love and of the deepest meaning of true purity.

God's Redemptive Love

Bad things happen in good families. Good things happen in bad families. Kids may turn in the right direction despite our weaknesses and failings as parents, and kids may turn in the wrong direction despite our wonderful efforts to the contrary. Kids may become sexually active, even promiscuous; they may get pregnant or get someone pregnant; and they may get an abortion or abortions. How do we deal with the wrong choices of our children?

The heart of the gospel is the good news that, although we are alienated from God and cannot make ourselves right with Him, God Himself, through the forgiveness made possible by His Son, Jesus Christ, can make us right and can bring us into a relationship of love with Him. We want to offer this as our last key principle in shaping your child's sexual character:

Principle 12:
Our God can forgive, heal, and redeem anything.

No human actions are beyond the reach of God's redeeming intent and capability. Many beautiful passages in the Bible illustrate this truth. Here are two favorites from the Old Testament: Exodus 15:22-26 tells how the Israelites, only three days after their dramatic rescue by God from their enslavement to Pharaoh in Egypt, find a pool of bitter water in the desert. Thirsty, they begin to grumble about God's provision (what short memories!). The Lord shows Moses a tree, which Moses uproots and casts into the bitter pool. The water immediately becomes sweet, and the Lord declares, "I am the LORD, who heals you." The transforming tree seems to symbolize the cross of Christ, which when cast into the midst of the most bitter waters can make anything sweet.

The book of Joel prophesies God's judgment on His people for their sins. A plague of locusts that strips their fields and leaves them starving is God's symbol for His judgment. The people will be disciplined, chastised for their faithlessness and sinfulness. But if the people turn again from their sins to the Lord in confession and repentance, God promises to pour out His blessings on them. In Joel 2:25-27 He says,

"I will repay you for the years the locusts have eaten — . . .
You will have plenty to eat, until you are full,
     and you will praise the name of the LORD your God. . . .
Then you will know that I am in Israel,
     that I am the LORD your God,
     and that there is no other;
never again will my people be shamed."

Along with Romans 8:28 and many other passages in the Scriptures, these verses comfort us with the knowledge that God can heal and redeem anything if only we will turn to Him as our Healer and Redeemer.

Note that none of these passages says anything about God taking away the consequences of our acts or extricating us from our circumstances, or of God's discipline being comfortable and convenient. The life of a teenage daughter who bears and keeps a child to raise is changed forever, and so are the lives of her parents. The woman who gets an abortion will carry that act in her body and soul for the rest of her life. David was forgiven for his adultery (see 2 Samuel 11–12), but his life of faith, and especially the faith of his sons, was never the same. Moses' act of disobedience to God was forgiven, but he still was never allowed to enter the Promised Land because of that disobedience (see Numbers 20:6-12; Deuteronomy 34). So also we may be forgiven and even healed, but we may still have to bear for life the heavy consequences of our choices and of the things others do to us. As the psalmist wrote, "You were to Israel a forgiving God, though you punished their misdeeds" (Psalm 99:8).

God can heal a girl who is raped, but her life is forever different. Like Job, who was tested and sifted by Satan and changed forever but who experienced God's blessings and redemption in this life, or like the saints through the ages who endured horrible persecution and received God's strength to endure but had to wait until the next life to see the final redemption of their sufferings (for example, see Revelation 2:8-11), so too we have to trust that when horrible things happen to us, God is at work to redeem and heal, even when we must wait to receive the final fruits of that redemption until we pass from this life.

What Is True Purity?

The sexual behavior of your children matters to God, who loves them dearly. You hope with all your heart that they will live a chaste and pure life, and God shares this hope with you. But true purity, understood properly, is something that is done to all of us, both our children and us, and not something our efforts can accomplish, even guided and empowered by the Holy Spirit. This is because true purity is being washed in the blood of the Lamb. We urge you to meditate on biblical passages that state this truth clearly, such as Titus 2:14; Hebrews 9:14; 10:22; 1 John 1:7; and Revelation 7:14.

We are right to hope that our children will live sexually pure lives. Living such lives will bring glory to God and save them (and us) from much pain and distress. But like the righteousness of the Pharisees, right living may do more to instill a sense of arrogance and self-righteousness than to draw the person toward God. Often in the midst of brokenness we turn to God for healing and cleansing. That is how it was for the Christians in ancient Corinth. The apostle Paul exhorted them,

> Do you not know that the wicked will not inherit the kingdom of God? . . . Neither the sexually immoral nor idolaters nor adulterers nor male prostitutes nor homosexual offenders nor thieves nor the greedy nor drunkards nor slanderers nor swindlers will inherit the kingdom of God. And that is what some of you were. But you were washed, you were sanctified, you were justified in the name of the Lord Jesus Christ and by the Spirit of our God. (1 Corinthians 6:9-11)

"And that is what some of you were." God can redeem anyone from anything. God can transform anyone into His own child. We can take our best shots as parents at shaping our children's sexual characters and yet rest in trust in God because we realize that no matter what choices our kids make, God can always redeem them. No matter how pure and upright their lives may be, they will be in need of cleansing by the blood of the Lamb. No matter how awful and devastating their choices may be, they can be cleansed by the work of God and live in the true purity that only He can offer. Our ultimate hope for the true purity of our children does not lie in our efforts as parents, but in the work of Christ in their lives.

One of our heaviest responsibilities as parents is to live out these realities in our families. We have discussed parenting as the creation of a family environment in which our children will see the truths of God laid out in flesh before them. Parenting is a form of incarnation — God's work of incarnation did not stop with Christ, but continues as God inhabits His people, the church, through the work of the Holy Spirit. Incarnation continues as husbands and wives act out in their marriages the divine drama of the relationship of Christ and His church. And incarnation continues yet again as parents act out the divine drama of God's parenting of His children — a disciplining, teaching, pursuing, loving fathering of His children.

As we deal with the mistaken or wrong choices of our children, with their weaknesses and defects of character, and with the consequences that result, we must remember that we are to manifest God's very character in dealing with them. We have done our best to lay a groundwork for them to feel a loving, tenacious acceptance rooted in God's stubborn love. When they fall or are injured, then it is our time to live out that tenacious acceptance in their lives. We continue to discipline and instruct, but all discipline is rooted in a stubborn and unyielding love.

We are to forgive as God Himself forgives. Often our children's actions hurt God, them, *and us;* one dramatic example of this is the parent who unexpectedly becomes a grandparent out of season. Such an event can forever change the course of family life. We often also take our child's successes and failures as vindications or judgments of our worth as parents. These factors can make it difficult to forgive our kids, as we feel that their wrong choices have hurt us as well as them. But forgiveness is our responsibility and privilege as Christians.

We should also model godly repentance for our kids. We should have an entire life history of this as they come into adolescence, a pattern of confessing to our children when we have wronged them, of seeking their forgiveness, and of truly turning over a new leaf as true repentance demands. When our children fall, we should compose ourselves and devote time to prayer and reflection. We should ask God to give us insight into our roles in the situation, honestly ask Him to show us where we let our children down, where our weaknesses as parents might have affected them. At the same time, we should ask God to preserve us from taking blame that is not ours. God views our teenagers as responsible moral agents, and so should we. Pray that as we talk with our children about their behavior, we will evidence a spirit of love, grace, forgiveness, and strength.

There are no formulas for dealing with the family crises that come when children go astray. At those times, we must be guided by God Himself, by His Word in the Scriptures, by His body, the church, and by the love that only He can give.

So the foundation for dealing with all of the problems that can happen with our kids is the gospel itself — our confidence that our God can heal and redeem anything and that we as parents can find the strength in Him to embody His very character in dealing with them.

May God be with us in our parenting efforts. May the Creator God who made us all sexual beings give us wisdom as we teach our children of the magnitude of His good gift. May Jesus Christ, the Source of all that is pure, give us discernment and persuasiveness as we teach our children the Christian view of sexual ethics, and may He give us great effectiveness as we shape our children's characters to His greater glory. May the Holy Spirit fill us with the deepest and most vibrant love imaginable for our children, even the very love that the Father has for all His children.

Notes

CHAPTER 1: **The Big Picture**

1. D. Baumrind, "Parenting Styles and Adolescent Development," in *The Encyclopedia of Adolescence*, eds. Jeanne Brooks-Gunn, Richard M. Lerner, and Anne C. Petersen (New York: Garland Press, 1991).

2. This is similar to Kevin Huggins' concept of "incarnational parenting." See Kevin Huggins, *Parenting Adolescents* (Colorado Springs, CO: NavPress, 1989).

3. William D. Mosher, PhD, Anjani Chandra, PhD, and Jo Jones, PhD, National Center for Health Statistics of the Centers for Disease Control, "Sexual Behavior and Selected Health Measures: Men and Women 15–44 Years of Age, United States, 2002," *Advance Data from Vital and Health Statistics*, no. 362, September 15, 2005, http://www.cdc.gov/nchs/products/pubs/pubd/ad/361-370/ad362.htm.

4. Stephanie J. Ventura, MA et al., "Highlights of Trends in Pregnancies and Pregnancy Rates by Outcome: Estimates for the United States, 1976–96." *National Vital Statistics Reports* 47, no. 29 (December 15, 1999), www.cdc.gov/nchs/data/nvsr/nvsr47/nvs47_29.pdf; and Stephanie J. Ventura, MA et al., "Estimated Pregnancy Rates for the United States, 1990–2000: An Update," *National Vital Statistics Reports* 52, no. 23 (June 15, 2004), http://www.cdc.gov/nchs/data/nvsr/nvsr52/nvsr52_23.pdf.

5. Andrew M. Greeley, *Faithful Attraction: Discovering Intimacy, Love, and Fidelity in American Marriage* (New York: Tor Books, 1991),

63–64, 243–251. This book reports results from two major studies of marriage sponsored by the magazine *Psychology Today* and conducted by The Gallup Organization, along with findings from numerous other resources, including the results of the annual General Society Survey conducted by the National Opinion Research Center.

CHAPTER 2: **The Challenge**

1. William D. Mosher, PhD, Anjani Chandra, PhD, and Jo Jones, PhD, National Center for Health Statistics of the Centers for Disease Control, "Sexual Behavior and Selected Health Measures: Men and Women 15–44 Years of Age, United States, 2002," *Advance Data from Vital and Health Statistics*, no. 362, September 15, 2005, http://www.cdc.gov/nchs/products/pubs/pubd/ad/361-370/ad362.htm. The National Center for Health Statistics (NCHS) of the Centers for Disease Control (CDC) is the best source for current statistics about adolescent sexual activity and pregnancy (www.cdc.gov/nchs). Until otherwise noted, the following statistics are from this report.

2. Stephanie J. Ventura, MA et al., "Highlights of Trends in Pregnancies and Pregnancy Rates by Outcome: Estimates for the United States, 1976–96." *National Vital Statistics Reports* 47, no. 29 (December 15, 1999), www.cdc.gov/nchs/data/nvsr/nvsr47/nvs47_29.pdf; and Stephanie J. Ventura, MA et al., "Estimated Pregnancy Rates for the United States, 1990–2000: An Update," *National Vital Statistics Reports* 52, no. 23 (June 15, 2004), http://www.cdc.gov/nchs/data/nvsr/nvsr52/nvsr52_23.pdf.

3. Carrie Gordon Earll, "Abortion Statistics," *Focus on Social Issues*, December 12, 2005, http://www.family.org/cforum/fosi/bioethics/facts/a0027730.cfm.

4. Mosher, Chandra, and Jones, 5.

5. H. Weinstock, S. Berman, and W. Cates, "Sexually Transmitted Diseases Among American Youth: Incidence and Prevalence Estimates, 2000," *Perspectives on Sexual and Reproductive Health* 36, no. 1 (2004): 6–10.

6. While no cure for HPV exists, a vaccine against certain strains of HPV has been developed recently, with some medical profession-

als calling for wide-scale inoculation of female children before they reach the age at which they are likely to become sexually active. This suggestion has proven to be very controversial, with some arguing that this is a medically prudent prevention of a communicable disease, while others argue it is yet another example of promotion of strategies to make immoral sexual practice "safer" as part of a broader assault on traditional moral views.

7. "Cyber Sting Nets Sexual Predators: Perverted Justice Lures Pedophiles Lurking in Cyberspace," *CBSnews.com*, March 4, 2004, http://www.cbsnews.com/stories/2004/03/04/eveningnews/main604167.shtml.

8. L. Kirkendall and R. Libby, "Sex Education in the Future," *Journal of Sex Education and Therapy* 11, no. 1 (1985): 64–67.

9. We reviewed the most recent empirical research in S. Jones and J. Laskowski, "An Eclectic Theoretical Model to Guide Sex Education," *Marriage and Family: A Christian Journal* 4, no. 3 (2001): 213–226. Specific citations for research findings can be sought there.

10. Tim Stafford, "The Next Sexual Revolution," *Christianity Today*, March 9, 1992, 28–29.

CHAPTER 3: **Understanding Character Formation**

1. We are here using a collage of ideas from various personality theorists in this "working theory of character," including William Glasser's (Reality Therapy) understanding of basic human needs, modern object-relations theory's rich understanding of relatedness, Alfred Adler's and existential psychology's rich understandings of our human needs for purpose and meaning, cognitive therapy's focus on basic beliefs, the emphasis on cognitive and behavior skills and of understanding the impact of the social environment unique to the cognitive-behavioral psychologies, and Family Systems psychology's understanding of the impact of the family environment. For more, see Stanton L. Jones and Richard E. Butman, *Modern Psychotherapies: A Comprehensive Christian Appraisal* (Downers Grove, IL: InterVarsity, 1991).

2. "Determinants of Adolescent Sexual Behavior and Decision Making," in *Risking the Future: Adolescent Sexuality, Pregnancy,*

and Childbearing, ed. Cheryl D. Hayes (Washington, D.C.: National Academy Press, 1987), 100–101. We have summarized this research in S. Jones and J. Laskowski, "An Eclectic Theoretical Model to Guide Sex Education," *Marriage and Family: A Christian Journal* 4, no. 3 (2001): 213–226.

CHAPTER 4: **Biblical Foundations for Understanding Sexuality**

1. For example, a popular nonreligious book on sexuality defines a family as "two or more people who, regardless of gender, age (although one must be legally an adult), or marital status, elect to live together in commitment and trust in order to care for and about each other." Mary S. Calderone and Eric W. Johnson, *The Family Book About Sexuality*, rev. ed. (New York: Harper & Row, 1989), 123.

CHAPTER 8: **Gender Identification and Sexual Orientation**

1. See the discussion in Joseph Nicolosi, *Reparative Therapy of Male Homosexuality: A New Clinical Approach* (New York: Jason Aronson, 1991), 32–35.
2. See Stanton L. Jones and Mark A. Yarhouse, *Homosexuality: The Use of Scientific Research in the Church's Moral Debate* (Downers Grove, IL: InterVarsity, 2000). This book was updated in 2005 by the publication of S. Jones and A. Kwee, "Scientific Research, Homosexuality, and the Church's Moral Debate: An Update," *Journal of Psychology and Christianity* 24, no. 4 (2005): 304–316.
3. See Nicolosi.
4. Stan has written extensively about this; see, for example, Stanton L. Jones, *The Gay Debate* (Downers Grove, IL: InterVarsity, 1994) and a rebuttal written to a popular gay Christian activist: Stanton L. Jones, *A Study Guide and Response to Mel White's "What the Bible Says — and Doesn't Say — About Homosexuality,"* published at the Center for Applied Christian Ethics, http://www.wheaton.edu/CACE.
5. For other contemporary resources, visit the website of the major Christian ministry organization for homosexual persons, Exodus International (www.exodus.to) or the Focus on the Family bookstore (http://www.family.org/resources/section.cfm?sid=1151).
6. D. Ross Campbell's *How to Really Love Your Child* (Colorado

Springs, CO: Cook Communications, 2003) is still the classic discussion of concrete ways to communicate love to young children and to have a balanced approach to discipline, in our opinion.

7. R. Savin-Williams, "Who's Gay? Does It Matter?" *Current Directions in Psychological Science* 15, no. 1 (2006): 40–44; esp. 42.

CHAPTER 9: "What Is Sex? Why Is It Wrong Outside Marriage?"

1. Barbara Kantrowitz and Pat Wingert, "Sex Ed 101," *Newsweek*, February 15, 1993, 47.

2. Carolyn Nystrom, *Before I Was Born* (Colorado Springs, CO: NavPress, 2007), 27.

3. Lewis B. Smedes, *Sex for Christians* (Grand Rapids, MI: Eerdmans, 1976), 129 (emphasis added; a second edition of this book came out in 1994). For a more scholarly discussion of these issues, see Stanley J. Grenz, *Sexual Ethics: An Evangelical Perspective* (Dallas: Word, 1990).

CHAPTER 10: Inoculating Your Kids Against Destructive Moral Messages

1. Planned Parenthood Federation of America, *How to Talk with Your Child About Sexuality* (New York: Doubleday, 1986), 59.

2. Planned Parenthood, 98.

3. See the summary of David G. Myers in *Social Psychology*, 3rd ed. (New York: McGraw-Hill, 1990), 261–265.

4. Tim Stafford, *The Sexual Christian* (Wheaton, IL: Christianity Today/Victor, 1989), 17–19.

5. Planned Parenthood, 98–99.

6. Planned Parenthood, 104.

7. Planned Parenthood, 104.

8. Planned Parenthood, 104.

9. This last point is as yet being promoted only by several very liberal faculty members of seminaries in their books and is not likely to be heard in the pews, but it is an idea being discussed seriously in seminary circles. See Carter Heyward, *Touching Our Strength: The Erotic as Power and the Love of God* (San Francisco: Harper, 1989) and James B. Nelson, *Embodiment: An Approach to Sexuality and Christian Theology* (Minneapolis: Augsburg, 1978).

CHAPTER 11: **Preparing for Puberty and Adolescence**

1. We survey this research in S. Jones and J. Laskowski, "An Eclectic Theoretical Model to Guide Sex Education," *Marriage and Family: A Christian Journal* 4, no. 3 (2001): 213–226.

CHAPTER 12: **Preparing for Romance, Sexual Attraction, and Dating**

1. Some of the more popular books promoting this view are Joshua Harris's *Boy Meets Girl: Say Hello to Courtship* (Sisters, OR: Multnomah, 2005) and *I Kissed Dating Goodbye* (Sisters, OR: Multnomah, 1999), and John Piper and Justin Taylor, eds., *Sex and the Supremacy of Christ* (Wheaton, IL: Crossway, 2005).
2. C. S. Lewis, *Mere Christianity* (New York: Macmillan, 1943), 99.
3. "Determinants of Adolescent Sexual Behavior and Decision Making," in *Risking the Future: Adolescent Sexuality, Pregnancy, and Childbearing*, ed. Cheryl D. Hayes, (Washington, D.C.: National Academy Press, 1987), 103.
4. Dr. James Dobson, *Preparing for Adolescence: How to Survive the Coming Years of Change* (Ventura, CA: Regal, 1999), 87–95.
5. The following is based mostly on Josh McDowell and Dick Day, *Why Wait? What You Need to Know About the Teen Sexuality Crisis* (San Bernardino, CA: Here's Life, 1987).
6. P. Bearman and H. Bruckner, "Promising the Future: Virginity Pledges and the Transition to First Intercourse," *American Journal of Sociology* 106 (2001): 859–912.

CHAPTER 13: **Developing Moral Discernment About Masturbation and Petting**

1. We are aware of only one argument that attempts to draw directly from the Scriptures to establish a basis for the acceptance of masturbation, found in J. Johnson, "Toward a Biblical Approach to Masturbation," *Journal of Psychology and Theology* 10 (1982): 137–146. Johnson suggests that Leviticus 15:16-18 should set the tone for our dealing with masturbation. Verses 16 and 17 say that a man who has an emission of semen should wash and be ceremonially unclean until evening. Verse 18 goes on to say that if a man and woman have intercourse, the same cleanliness rules apply. By bringing up intercourse separately, the passage surely does imply that the emission of semen

in verses 16 and 17 occurred for the man individually. The passage may be referring to a nocturnal emission, or wet dream, rather than masturbation, but the passage is not specific. Johnson suggests that this Leviticus passage is significant for treating a solitary sexual experience, whether wet dream or masturbation, as a purely ceremonial cleanliness issue and not as a matter of morality. The passage also puts no more disapproval on the solitary experience than it does on intercourse. Because Christians today commonly view the Old Testament ceremonial law as no longer valid, this author suggests that masturbation is not in itself a moral concern from a biblical perspective and is no longer a ceremonial concern either. It is neutral in itself and can become immoral only if other elements, such as lust, are added to it.

2. Tim Stafford, "Great Sex: Reclaiming a Christian Sexual Ethic," *Christianity Today*, October 2, 1987, 33–34.

3. Lewis B. Smedes, *Sex for Christians*, 2nd ed. (Grand Rapids, MI: Eerdmans, 1994), 218–221.

4. Dr. James Dobson, *Preparing for Adolescence: How to Survive the Coming Years of Change* (Ventura, CA: Regal, 1999), 83–84.

CHAPTER 14: **Clear and Present Dangers: Pornography and Cybersex**

1. "Cyber Sting Nets Sexual Predators: Perverted Justice Lures Pedophiles Lurking in Cyberspace," *CBSnews.com*, March 4, 2004, http://www.cbsnews.com/stories/2004/03/04/eveningnews/main604167.shtml.

2. Mary S. Calderone and Eric W. Johnson, *The Family Book About Sexuality*, rev. ed. (New York: Harper & Row, 1989), 142.

3. E. Donnerstein, "Massive Exposure to Sexual Violence and Desensitization to Violence and Rape," unpublished paper summarized in William Masters, Virginia E. Johnson, and Robert C. Kolodny, *Human Sexuality*, 4th ed. (Glenview, IL: Scott, Foresman and Company, 1992), 352.

CHAPTER 15: **Supporting the Adolescent**

1. P. Bearman and H. Bruckner, "Promising the Future: Virginity Pledges and the Transition to First Intercourse," *American Journal of Sociology* 106 (2001): 859–912.

2. This was discussed in an excellent fashion in the book by Marion Howard, *How to Help Your Teenager Postpone Sexual Involvement* (New York: Continuum, 1989), 15–22.

3. These points are taken from Howard, 82–83.

CHAPTER 16: **Teaching About Contraception**

1. The Roman Catholic Church, due to its moral objections to all contraceptive and birth control methods except NFP, has the most well-developed and effective programs for NFP; the interested reader should check with a Catholic bookstore or visit the website of the Couple to Couple League (www.ccli.org) for kits that contain both detailed information about NFP and the requisite thermometer (which is much more sensitive than a fever thermometer).

2. For an introduction to the issues involved in this debate, an interested reader could seek out the two *Christianity Today* special issues that dealt with birth control a decade apart: November 12, 2001, and November 11, 1991.

3. D. Evans, "The Price of the Pill," *Christianity Today*, November 11, 1991, 39–40.

4. The reader interested in a historical background for this perspective might want to read the *Westminster Larger Catechism*, questions 150 and 151.

5. For the parent who wants specific information about effectiveness of contraceptive methods, here is the professional consensus: A couple who lives together and has sex all year without using any contraception method has an 85 percent chance of getting pregnant in that year. Estimating how well contraception methods work depends on whether you are supposing "perfect or ideal" use or "typical, real-world" use (in the real world, women forget their pills, and condoms break). By typical use, if that same couple used condoms or a diaphragm, their likelihood of getting pregnant would be 15 percent for the year, 8 percent if they use the contraceptive pill or patch, and less than 1 percent for surgical sterilization.

6. At the final stages of editing this book, a new study appeared on condoms and HPV transmission that received wide media attention. The study (Rachel Winer et al., "Condom Use and the Risk of

Genital Human Papillomavirus Infection in Young Women," *New England Journal of Medicine* 354, no. 25: 2645–2654) appears to provide strong evidence that condoms do slow down HPV transmission substantially. The study, but more the press releases surrounding it, directly attack moral conservatives who have been saying that condoms offer no protection against HPV. As an absolute claim, this appears wrong, as condoms appear to offer some protection. But we are concerned about the small sample size of the study, and we feel there are unanswered questions from the study about just how much protection condoms offer. This is an open issue.

About the Authors

STANTON L. JONES, PHD, is a professor of psychology at Wheaton College and also serves as the provost (academic vice president). He directed the development of the college's doctoral program in clinical psychology. He is the coauthor of *Modern Psychotherapies: A Comprehensive Christian Appraisal* and *Homosexuality: The Use of Scientific Research in the Church's Moral Debate* and has contributed many articles to professional journals and to such magazines as *Christianity Today*.

BRENNA B. JONES is a mother whose goals have focused on the nurture and formation of the character of her children. She served as a leader in a Bible study ministry with women for a number of years and now has an active ministry of discipleship and support for women. She has graduate training in biblical and theological studies.

Stan and Brenna are active in teaching about parenting and marriage in their church. They wrote the original versions of the GOD'S DESIGN FOR SEX series while their three children — Jennifer, Brandon, and Lindsay — were young; now they enjoy their three kids as adults, along with Brandon's wife, Emily, and son, Canon.

Be sure to check out the other books in the GOD'S DESIGN FOR SEX series.

The Story of Me
Book 1 (ages 3–5)   978-1-60006-013-7

A spiritual foundation for helping your children understand their sexuality. Identifies proper names for body parts and presents the family as God's intended framework for the nurture and love of children.

Before I Was Born
Book 2 (ages 5–8)   978-1-60006-014-4

Explains in age-appropriate language the basic nature of sexual intercourse between a husband and wife and discusses conception, fetal development, childbirth, and breastfeeding.

What's the Big Deal?
Book 3 (ages 8–11)   978-1-60006-016-8

Lays out the basic facts about sex, why God made adults so they want to have sex, what the Bible says about sex, and how to respond when faced with sexual pressure from peers, TV, movies, and magazines.

Facing the Facts
Book 4 (ages 11–14)   978-1-60006-015-1

Equips kids to deal with the changes of puberty. Also examines why God intends sex for marriage, discusses love and dating, and answers tough questions about sexuality.

To order copies, call NavPress at 1-800-366-7788,
or log on to www.navpress.com.

NAVPRESS

Discipleship Inside Out™